THIS IS YOUR **PASSBOOK**® FOR ...

HEALTH OCCUPATIONS APTITUDE EXAMINATION (HOAE)

NLC®

NATIONAL LEARNING CORPORATION®
passbooks.com

PASSBOOK® SERIES

THE *PASSBOOK® SERIES* has been created to prepare applicants and candidates for the ultimate academic battlefield – the examination room.

At some time in our lives, each and every one of us may be required to take an examination – for validation, matriculation, admission, qualification, registration, certification, or licensure.

Based on the assumption that every applicant or candidate has met the basic formal educational standards, has taken the required number of courses, and read the necessary texts, the *PASSBOOK® SERIES* furnishes the one special preparation which may assure passing with confidence, instead of failing with insecurity. Examination questions – together with answers – are furnished as the basic vehicle for study so that the mysteries of the examination and its compounding difficulties may be eliminated or diminished by a sure method.

This book is meant to help you pass your examination provided that you qualify and are serious in your objective.

The entire field is reviewed through the huge store of content information which is succinctly presented through a provocative and challenging approach – the question-and-answer method.

A climate of success is established by furnishing the correct answers at the end of each test.

You soon learn to recognize types of questions, forms of questions, and patterns of questioning. You may even begin to anticipate expected outcomes.

You perceive that many questions are repeated or adapted so that you can gain acute insights, which may enable you to score many sure points.

You learn how to confront new questions, or types of questions, and to attack them confidently and work out the correct answers.

You note objectives and emphases, and recognize pitfalls and dangers, so that you may make positive educational adjustments.

Moreover, you are kept fully informed in relation to new concepts, methods, practices, and directions in the field.

You discover that you arre actually taking the examination all the time: you are preparing for the examination by "taking" an examination, not by reading extraneous and/or supererogatory textbooks.

In short, this PASSBOOK®, used directedly, should be an important factor in helping you to pass your test.

HEALTH OCCUPATIONS APTITUDE EXAMINATION

Part I. Academic Aptitude
Academic aptitude as measured by the total (combined subtests), might be thought of as a type of ability to learn. The test content is specifically adapted for appraising the combination of innate and acquired abilities that are needed for work of an academic nature. The academic aptitude total emphasizes familiar experiences and concepts while requiring careful reasoning and the capacity to comprehend and draw conclusions.

Verbal: The Verbal aspect consists of 30 vocabulary-related test questions. Empirical evidence has shown this type of test item to be highly related to academic success.

Arithmetic: The numerical aspect consists of 30 items drawing largely from arithmetic. To some degree, it involves skill with arithmetical concepts along with computational speed. The content of the numerical items is that to which practically all eighth grade students have been exposed.

Nonverbal: The nonverbal aspect consists of 30 test items calling for a comprehension of form relationships. Measurement is in terms of the ability to manipulate "things" mentally, to reason out differences in pictured objects, and to deal with concrete materials through visualization. Recognition of relationships and of differences has been shown by research to be basic to learning aptitude.

Part II - Spelling
The spelling test measures skill with a tool essential to written expression or communication. . It also reflects educational achievement in basic tools of learning.

Part III- Reading Comprehension
This test measures ability to understand direct statements, interpret written content, see the authors intent, observe organization of ideas, and to extract information from written material with respect to ideas and purposes; thus to read and comprehend what is read.

Part IV- Information in the Natural Sciences
Measurement with this test concerns accumulation of information in the natural sciences, i.e., biology, chemistry, health, safety, etc., at a fundamental level. The relationship of knowledge in the area of the natural sciences to the course of study of the allied health educational program is an obvious one.

Part V- Vocational Adjustment Index
The person's characteristic life style is reflected in his or her distinctive educational and occupational adjustment. Feelings, attitudes, opinions, and other personality characteristics and behavioral traits, which may be quite acceptable in many situations, may not be those desirable for the prospective healthcare professional either as a student or as a practitioner.

———

SPECIMEN QUESTIONS FOR THE
PSB - Health Occupations Aptitude Examination - REVISED

ACADEMIC APTITUDE - Part I

DIRECTIONS: Part I measures how well you think and learn. The three sample exercises, demonstrating the three types of questions you will be expected to answer in this part of the Examination, are given below so that you may see how to do Part I of the Examination.

Sample 1. (A) Bad (B) Evil (C) Wicked (D) Good (E) Naughty

1. (A) (B) (C) (D) (E)

In the above "set" of words, which word is most different in meaning from that of the other words? GOOD is the correct answer. What is the letter in front of the word GOOD? The letter is D. The circle with the letter D in the center should be blackened in the answer row for sample question 1.

1. (A) (B) (C) ● (E)

REMEMBER that in the "sets" of words that follow in this part of the Examination, you are always to select the word that is most DIFFERENT in meaning.

Sample 2. You have $10 and give $3 to your mother. How much money do you have remaining?
(A) $1 (B) $2 (C) $4 (D) $5 (E) $7

2. (A) (B) (C) (D) (E)

Ten dollars minus three dollars is seven, so the circle with the letter E in the middle should be blackened in the answer row for sample question 2.

2. (A) (B) (C) (D) ●

Sample 3. ○ is to ○ as ☐ is to
(A) △ (B) ☐ (C) ▭ (D) ○ (E) ▯

3. (A) (B) (C) (D) (E)

The letter B, ☐ , is the correct answer

A large circle ○ is to a smaller circle ○

as a large square ☐ is to a smaller square ☐

You should blacken the circle with the letter B in the middle in the answer row for sample question 3.

3. (A) ● (C) (D) (E)

This is the way you mark all of your answers for the questions that follow.

---

1. (A) Vital (B) Wither (C) Fade (D) Vanish (E) Insipid

2. Five health professionals earned the following scores on an anatomy test: 65, 82, 77, 89, 72. What was the average score?
(A) 81 (B) 78 (C) 77 (D) 72 (E) 69

3. ○ is to (△) as ☐ is to - A (☐) B ○ C (◐) D (◑) E △

4. (A) Wane (B) Dwindle (C) Amplify (D) Ebb (E) Fade

5. A 72 inch roll of bandage at $1.08 per yard would cost?
(A) $1.08 (B) $1.96 (C) $2.16 (D) $2.96 (E) $3.24

6. △ is to ☐ as ◁ is to - A ◁ B ▭ C ⊔ D L E ⊥

7. (A) Hasty (B) Serene (C) Placid (D) Still (E) Calm

8. The first minute of a telephone call costs .24 and each additional minute .13. What is the cost of a 5 minute call?
(A) $1.20 (B) $1.12 (C) .96 (D) .76 (E) .63

9. ⌓ is to ⌂ as ⬠ is to - A ◇ B ◺ C ⬠ D ☐ E △

1 (A) (B) (C) (D) (E)
2 (A) (B) (C) (D) (E)
3 (A) (B) (C) (D) (E)
4 (A) (B) (C) (D) (E)
5 (A) (B) (C) (D) (E)
6 (A) (B) (C) (D) (E)
7 (A) (B) (C) (D) (E)
8 (A) (B) (C) (D) (E)
9 (A) (B) (C) (D) (E)

Go on to next page.

SPELLING - Part II

DIRECTIONS:

Part II measures how well you can spell and what you know about the various rules of grammar as they are reflected in the spelling of certain words. Each line below contains a word with three different spellings. Only one spelling is correct. Select the correctly spelled word from each line.

Sample 1. (A) acheive   (B) achieve   (C) achive

What is the letter in front of the word spelled correctly? The answer is the letter B. ACHIEVE. In the answer row to the right, the circle with the letter B in the center has been blackened. You will mark your answers in a similar fashion in the section headed, Spelling - Part II.

1. (A) emergancy   (B) emergancie   (C) emergency
2. (A) infectious   (B) enfecteous   (C) enfectious
3. (A) deoderizing   (B) deodorizing   (C) deodarizing
4. (A) densitty   (B) densitie   (C) density
5. (A) detergents   (B) detergants   (C) detergantes
6. (A) caffene   (B) caffine   (C) caffeine
7. (A) ageing   (B) aging   (C) agging
8. (A) erroneous   (B) eroneous   (C) eronious
9. (A) vitamine   (B) vitimine   (C) vitamin
10. (A) paralisis   (B) paralysis   (C) paralzsis

READING COMPREHENSION - Part III

DIRECTIONS:

Part III is a test of your ability to understand what you read. It is a measure of some of the skills and abilities you have been developing ever since you entered school. You will be asked to answer questions based on the material contained in written passages.

Begin by reading each passage carefully. Each of the questions if followed by four suggested answers. You are to decide which one of these answers you should choose based upon the material in the passage. You must mark all of your answers by blackening the circle having the same letter as the answer you have chosen.

Answer the questions about one passage before going on to the next. You may look back at the passage while you answer the questions. Work carefully but rapidly.

Sample: You will have 30 minutes to work on this test. There are 4 passages and 50 sets of questions.

   1. In the sample passage above it states that the number of sets of questions is
      (A) 50   (B) 30   (C) 25   (D) 20

The answer is 50 with a letter A in front of it. So the circle with A in the center should be blackened in the answer row for sample question 1.

Be sure to mark your answers in the section headed, Reading Comprehension - Part III.

A few years ago, although no one knew it, the gases in spray cans were harming the ozone layer. The ozone layer is a part of the atmosphere, a thick blanket of air that covers the world. The atmosphere is made up of many gases, especially nitrogen and oxygen. Close to the earth, the atmosphere is thick and heavy, but as it gets farther away from the earth, the atmosphere gets thin. There, the energy from the sun changes the way gases behave. For example, oxygen atoms usually travel in the air connected together in pairs, but high in the atmosphere, the sun's energy causes three oxygen atoms to connect together instead of two. These groups of three oxygen atoms are called ozone. The place high in the air where regular oxygen changes to ozone is called the ozone layer. The ozone layer is very important to life on earth. It soaks up dangerous rays from the sun that harm plants and animals. Even more important, the ozone layer helps keep the earth cool. Without it, the earth might become so hot that the icecaps would melt and flood much of the earth. Fortunately, safe gases are now used in spray cans, but some of the ozone layer has been destroyed.

Go on to next page.

HOW TO TAKE A TEST

You have studied long, hard and conscientiously.

With your official admission card in hand, and your heart pounding, you have been admitted to the examination room.

You note that there are several hundred other applicants in the examination room waiting to take the same test.

They all appear to be equally well prepared.

You know that nothing but your best effort will suffice. The "moment of truth" is at hand: you now have to demonstrate objectively, in writing, your knowledge of content and your understanding of subject matter.

You are fighting the most important battle of your life—to pass and/or score high on an examination which will determine your career and provide the economic basis for your livelihood.

What extra, special things should you know and should you do in taking the examination?

I. YOU MUST PASS AN EXAMINATION

A. *WHAT EVERY CANDIDATE SHOULD KNOW*
Examination applicants often ask us for help in preparing for the written test. What can I study in advance? What kinds of questions will be asked? How will the test be given? How will the papers be graded?

B. *HOW ARE EXAMS DEVELOPED?*
Examinations are carefully written by trained technicians who are specialists in the field known as "psychological measurement," in consultation with recognized authorities in the field of work that the test will cover. These experts recommend the subject matter areas or skills to be tested; only those knowledges or skills important to your success on the job are included. The most reliable books and source materials available are used as references. Together, the experts and technicians judge the difficulty level of the questions.

Test technicians know how to phrase questions so that the problem is clearly stated. Their ethics do not permit "trick" or "catch" questions. Questions may have been tried out on sample groups, or subjected to statistical analysis, to determine their usefulness.

Written tests are often used in combination with performance tests, ratings of training and experience, and oral interviews. All of these measures combine to form the best-known means of finding the right person for the right job.

II. HOW TO PASS THE WRITTEN TEST

A. BASIC STEPS

1) Study the announcement

How, then, can you know what subjects to study? Our best answer is: "Learn as much as possible about the class of positions for which you've applied." The exam will test the knowledge, skills and abilities needed to do the work.

Your most valuable source of information about the position you want is the official exam announcement. This announcement lists the training and experience qualifications. Check these standards and apply only if you come reasonably close to meeting them. Many jurisdictions preview the written test in the exam announcement by including a section called "Knowledge and Abilities Required," "Scope of the Examination," or some similar heading. Here you will find out specifically what fields will be tested.

2) Choose appropriate study materials

If the position for which you are applying is technical or advanced, you will read more advanced, specialized material. If you are already familiar with the basic principles of your field, elementary textbooks would waste your time. Concentrate on advanced textbooks and technical periodicals. Think through the concepts and review difficult problems in your field.

These are all general sources. You can get more ideas on your own initiative, following these leads. For example, training manuals and publications of the government agency which employs workers in your field can be useful, particularly for technical and professional positions. A letter or visit to the government department involved may result in more specific study suggestions, and certainly will provide you with a more definite idea of the exact nature of the position you are seeking.

3) Study this book!

III. KINDS OF TESTS

Tests are used for purposes other than measuring knowledge and ability to perform specified duties. For some positions, it is equally important to test ability to make adjustments to new situations or to profit from training. In others, basic mental abilities not dependent on information are essential. Questions which test these things may not appear as pertinent to the duties of the position as those which test for knowledge and information. Yet they are often highly important parts of a fair examination. For very general questions, it is almost impossible to help you direct your study efforts. What we can do is to point out some of the more common of these general abilities needed in public service positions and describe some typical questions.

1) General information

Broad, general information has been found useful for predicting job success in some kinds of work. This is tested in a variety of ways, from vocabulary lists to questions about current events. Basic background in some field of work, such as sociology or economics, may be sampled in a group of questions. Often these are principles which have become familiar to most persons through exposure rather than through formal training. It is difficult to advise you how to study for these questions; being alert to the world around you is our best suggestion.

2) Verbal ability

An example of an ability needed in many positions is verbal or language ability. Verbal ability is, in brief, the ability to use and understand words. Vocabulary and grammar tests are typical measures of this ability. Reading comprehension or paragraph interpretation questions are common in many kinds of civil service tests. You are given a paragraph of written material and asked to find its central meaning.

IV. KINDS OF QUESTIONS

1. Multiple-choice Questions

Most popular of the short-answer questions is the "multiple choice" or "best answer" question. It can be used, for example, to test for factual knowledge, ability to solve problems or judgment in meeting situations found at work.

A multiple-choice question is normally one of three types:
- It can begin with an incomplete statement followed by several possible endings. You are to find the one ending which *best* completes the statement, although some of the others may not be entirely wrong.
- It can also be a complete statement in the form of a question which is answered by choosing one of the statements listed.
- It can be in the form of a problem – again you select the best answer.

Here is an example of a multiple-choice question with a discussion which should give you some clues as to the method for choosing the right answer:

When an employee has a complaint about his assignment, the action which will *best* help him overcome his difficulty is to
  A. discuss his difficulty with his coworkers
  B. take the problem to the head of the organization
  C. take the problem to the person who gave him the assignment
  D. say nothing to anyone about his complaint

In answering this question, you should study each of the choices to find which is best. Consider choice "A" – Certainly an employee may discuss his complaint with fellow employees, but no change or improvement can result, and the complaint remains unresolved. Choice "B" is a poor choice since the head of the organization probably does not know what assignment you have been given, and taking your problem to him is known as "going over the head" of the supervisor. The supervisor, or person who made the assignment, is the person who can clarify it or correct any injustice. Choice "C" is, therefore, correct. To say nothing, as in choice "D," is unwise. Supervisors have and interest in knowing the problems employees are facing, and the employee is seeking a solution to his problem.

2. True/False

3. Matching Questions

Matching an answer from a column of choices within another column.

V. RECORDING YOUR ANSWERS

Computer terminals are used more and more today for many different kinds of exams.

For an examination with very few applicants, you may be told to record your answers in the test booklet itself. Separate answer sheets are much more common. If this separate answer sheet is to be scored by machine – and this is often the case – it is highly important that you mark your answers correctly in order to get credit.

VI. BEFORE THE TEST

YOUR PHYSICAL CONDITION IS IMPORTANT

If you are not well, you can't do your best work on tests. If you are half asleep, you can't do your best either. Here are some tips:

1) Get about the same amount of sleep you usually get. Don't stay up all night before the test, either partying or worrying—DON'T DO IT!
2) If you wear glasses, be sure to wear them when you go to take the test. This goes for hearing aids, too.
3) If you have any physical problems that may keep you from doing your best, be sure to tell the person giving the test. If you are sick or in poor health, you relay cannot do your best on any test. You can always come back and take the test some other time.

Common sense will help you find procedures to follow to get ready for an examination. Too many of us, however, overlook these sensible measures. Indeed, nervousness and fatigue have been found to be the most serious reasons why applicants fail to do their best on civil service tests. Here is a list of reminders:

- Begin your preparation early – Don't wait until the last minute to go scurrying around for books and materials or to find out what the position is all about.
- Prepare continuously – An hour a night for a week is better than an all-night cram session. This has been definitely established. What is more, a night a week for a month will return better dividends than crowding your study into a shorter period of time.
- Locate the place of the exam – You have been sent a notice telling you when and where to report for the examination. If the location is in a different town or otherwise unfamiliar to you, it would be well to inquire the best route and learn something about the building.
- Relax the night before the test – Allow your mind to rest. Do not study at all that night. Plan some mild recreation or diversion; then go to bed early and get a good night's sleep.
- Get up early enough to make a leisurely trip to the place for the test – This way unforeseen events, traffic snarls, unfamiliar buildings, etc. will not upset you.

- Dress comfortably – A written test is not a fashion show. You will be known by number and not by name, so wear something comfortable.
- Leave excess paraphernalia at home – Shopping bags and odd bundles will get in your way. You need bring only the items mentioned in the official notice you received; usually everything you need is provided. Do not bring reference books to the exam. They will only confuse those last minutes and be taken away from you when in the test room.
- Arrive somewhat ahead of time – If because of transportation schedules you must get there very early, bring a newspaper or magazine to take your mind off yourself while waiting.
- Locate the examination room – When you have found the proper room, you will be directed to the seat or part of the room where you will sit. Sometimes you are given a sheet of instructions to read while you are waiting. Do not fill out any forms until you are told to do so; just read them and be prepared.
- Relax and prepare to listen to the instructions
- If you have any physical problem that may keep you from doing your best, be sure to tell the test administrator. If you are sick or in poor health, you really cannot do your best on the exam. You can come back and take the test some other time.

VII. AT THE TEST

The day of the test is here and you have the test booklet in your hand. The temptation to get going is very strong. Caution! There is more to success than knowing the right answers. You must know how to identify your papers and understand variations in the type of short-answer question used in this particular examination. Follow these suggestions for maximum results from your efforts:

1) Cooperate with the monitor
The test administrator has a duty to create a situation in which you can be as much at ease as possible. He will give instructions, tell you when to begin, check to see that you are marking your answer sheet correctly, and so on. He is not there to guard you, although he will see that your competitors do not take unfair advantage. He wants to help you do your best.

2) Listen to all instructions
Don't jump the gun! Wait until you understand all directions. In most civil service tests you get more time than you need to answer the questions. So don't be in a hurry. Read each word of instructions until you clearly understand the meaning. Study the examples, listen to all announcements and follow directions. Ask questions if you do not understand what to do.

3) Identify your papers
Civil service exams are usually identified by number only. You will be assigned a number; you must not put your name on your test papers. Be sure to copy your number correctly. Since more than one exam may be given, copy your exact examination title.

4) Plan your time
Unless you are told that a test is a "speed" or "rate of work" test, speed itself is usually not important. Time enough to answer all the questions will be provided, but this

does not mean that you have all day. An overall time limit has been set. Divide the total time (in minutes) by the number of questions to determine the approximate time you have for each question.

5) Do not linger over difficult questions

If you come across a difficult question, mark it with a paper clip (useful to have along) and come back to it when you have been through the booklet. One caution if you do this – be sure to skip a number on your answer sheet as well. Check often to be sure that you have not lost your place and that you are marking in the row numbered the same as the question you are answering.

6) Read the questions

Be sure you know what the question asks! Many capable people are unsuccessful because they failed to *read* the questions correctly.

7) Answer all questions

Unless you have been instructed that a penalty will be deducted for incorrect answers, it is better to guess than to omit a question.

8) Speed tests

It is often better NOT to guess on speed tests. It has been found that on timed tests people are tempted to spend the last few seconds before time is called in marking answers at random – without even reading them – in the hope of picking up a few extra points. To discourage this practice, the instructions may warn you that your score will be "corrected" for guessing. That is, a penalty will be applied. The incorrect answers will be deducted from the correct ones, or some other penalty formula will be used.

9) Review your answers

If you finish before time is called, go back to the questions you guessed or omitted to give them further thought. Review other answers if you have time.

10) Return your test materials

If you are ready to leave before others have finished or time is called, take ALL your materials to the monitor and leave quietly. Never take any test material with you. The monitor can discover whose papers are not complete, and taking a test booklet may be grounds for disqualification.

VIII. EXAMINATION TECHNIQUES

1) Read the general instructions carefully. These are usually printed on the first page of the exam booklet. As a rule, these instructions refer to the timing of the examination; the fact that you should not start work until the signal and must stop work at a signal, etc. If there are any *special* instructions, such as a choice of questions to be answered, make sure that you note this instruction carefully.

2) When you are ready to start work on the examination, that is as soon as the signal has been given, read the instructions to each question booklet, underline any key words or phrases, such as *least, best, outline, describe*

and the like. In this way you will tend to answer as requested rather than discover on reviewing your paper that you *listed without describing*, that you selected the *worst* choice rather than the *best* choice, etc.

3) If the examination is of the objective or multiple-choice type – that is, each question will also give a series of possible answers: A, B, C or D, and you are called upon to select the best answer and write the letter next to that answer on your answer paper – it is advisable to start answering each question in turn. There may be anywhere from 50 to 100 such questions in the three or four hours allotted and you can see how much time would be taken if you read through all the questions before beginning to answer any. Furthermore, if you come across a question or group of questions which you know would be difficult to answer, it would undoubtedly affect your handling of all the other questions.

4) If the examination is of the essay type and contains but a few questions, it is a moot point as to whether you should read all the questions before starting to answer any one. Of course, if you are given a choice – say five out of seven and the like – then it is essential to read all the questions so you can eliminate the two that are most difficult. If, however, you are asked to answer all the questions, there may be danger in trying to answer the easiest one first because you may find that you will spend too much time on it. The best technique is to answer the first question, then proceed to the second, etc.

5) Time your answers. Before the exam begins, write down the time it started, then add the time allowed for the examination and write down the time it must be completed, then divide the time available somewhat as follows:
   - If 3-1/2 hours are allowed, that would be 210 minutes. If you have 80 objective-type questions, that would be an average of 2-1/2 minutes per question. Allow yourself no more than 2 minutes per question, or a total of 160 minutes, which will permit about 50 minutes to review.
   - If for the time allotment of 210 minutes there are 7 essay questions to answer, that would average about 30 minutes a question. Give yourself only 25 minutes per question so that you have about 35 minutes to review.

6) The most important instruction is to *read each question* and make sure you know what is wanted. The second most important instruction is to *time yourself properly* so that you answer every question. The third most important instruction is to *answer every question*. Guess if you have to but include something for each question. Remember that you will receive no credit for a blank and will probably receive some credit if you write something in answer to an essay question. If you guess a letter – say "B" for a multiple-choice question – you may have guessed right. If you leave a blank as an answer to a multiple-choice question, the examiners may respect your feelings but it will not add a point to your score. Some exams may penalize you for wrong answers, so in such cases *only*, you may not want to guess unless you have some basis for your answer.

7) Suggestions
   a. Objective-type questions
      1. Examine the question booklet for proper sequence of pages and questions
      2. Read all instructions carefully
      3. Skip any question which seems too difficult; return to it after all other questions have been answered
      4. Apportion your time properly; do not spend too much time on any single question or group of questions
      5. Note and underline key words – *all, most, fewest, least, best, worst, same, opposite,* etc.
      6. Pay particular attention to negatives
      7. Note unusual option, e.g., unduly long, short, complex, different or similar in content to the body of the question
      8. Observe the use of "hedging" words – *probably, may, most likely,* etc.
      9. Make sure that your answer is put next to the same number as the question
      10. Do not second-guess unless you have good reason to believe the second answer is definitely more correct
      11. Cross out original answer if you decide another answer is more accurate; do not erase until you are ready to hand your paper in
      12. Answer all questions; guess unless instructed otherwise
      13. Leave time for review

   b. Essay questions
      1. Read each question carefully
      2. Determine exactly what is wanted. Underline key words or phrases.
      3. Decide on outline or paragraph answer
      4. Include many different points and elements unless asked to develop any one or two points or elements
      5. Show impartiality by giving pros and cons unless directed to select one side only
      6. Make and write down any assumptions you find necessary to answer the questions
      7. Watch your English, grammar, punctuation and choice of words
      8. Time your answers; don't crowd material

8) Answering the essay question

Most essay questions can be answered by framing the specific response around several key words or ideas. Here are a few such key words or ideas:

M's: manpower, materials, methods, money, management
P's: purpose, program, policy, plan, procedure, practice, problems, pitfalls, personnel, public relations
   a. Six basic steps in handling problems:
      1. Preliminary plan and background development
      2. Collect information, data and facts
      3. Analyze and interpret information, data and facts
      4. Analyze and develop solutions as well as make recommendations

5. Prepare report and sell recommendations
6. Install recommendations and follow up effectiveness

b. Pitfalls to avoid
1. *Taking things for granted* – A statement of the situation does not necessarily imply that each of the elements is necessarily true; for example, a complaint may be invalid and biased so that all that can be taken for granted is that a complaint has been registered
2. *Considering only one side of a situation* – Wherever possible, indicate several alternatives and then point out the reasons you selected the best one
3. *Failing to indicate follow up* – Whenever your answer indicates action on your part, make certain that you will take proper follow-up action to see how successful your recommendations, procedures or actions turn out to be
4. *Taking too long in answering any single question* – Remember to time your answers properly

EXAMINATION SECTION

EXAMINATION SECTION
TEST 1

DIRECTIONS: Each question or incomplete statement is followed by several suggested answers or completions. Select the one that BEST answers the question or completes the statement. *PRINT THE CORRECT ANSWER IN THE SPACE AT THE RIGHT.*

1. Add: 37.10
           .006
         300.105
          16.02
        7341.
          72.50

1.____

2. Add: 25 7/8
          31 3/4
          72 1/8
          96 1/2
          89 3/8

2.____

3. Multiply: .18902
               .018

3.____

4. Divide: $.063\overline{)6048}$

4.____

5. To OSCILLATE means to

5.____

   A. quiver
   C. swing back and forth
   E. rebound
   B. freeze
   D. hate

6. *A New York broker who studied in Scotland during his younger years took a keen interest in the game of golf as it was played there. When he returned to the United States back in the seventies, he introduced the game over here by reproducing one of England's most famous courses.*
   According to the above paragraph, which one of the following statements is TRUE?

6.____

   A. Golf originated in the United States.
   B. The first golf course was built in England seventy years ago.
   C. Golf was introduced in the United States in the seventies.
   D. Golf was formerly played only by students.

7. CAT is to FELINE as COW is to

7.____

   A. quadruped   B. pedigreed   C. canine
   D. bovine   E. equine

8. BILL is to PAPER as COIN is to

8.____

   A. money   B. heavy   C. shiny   D. metal   E. round

9. WATER is to FLUID as IRON is to

9.____

   A. metal   B. rusty   C. solid   D. rails   E. mines

10. OVER is to UNDER as TRESTLE is to   10.____

    A. tunnel   B. bridge   C. trains
    D. skeleton   E. river

11. VAGUE means MOST NEARLY   11.____

    A. style   B. definite   C. not clear
    D. silly   E. tired

12. To AGGRAVATE is to   12.____

    A. indulge   B. counsel   C. inflate
    D. help   E. make worse

13. PRECISION means MOST NEARLY   13.____

    A. cutting   B. exactness   C. risky
    D. measurement   E. training

14. A TERSE statement is   14.____

    A. long   B. condensed   C. rude
    D. wild   E. exact

15. A car will go 3/8 of a given distance in one hour. What part will it cover in 5/8 of an hour?   15.____

16. An incubator was set with 120 eggs.   16.____
    If 18 eggs failed to hatch, what percent hatched?

17. At $2.00 a case, what fraction of a case can be bought for 7/8 of a dollar?   17.____

18. A earns $3.50 a day. B earns 1/4 more a day than A does. How many days will it take B   18.____
    to earn the same amount that A earns in 10 days?

19. What is the postage on a package weighing 12 lbs., if the rate is 8 cents for the first   19.____
    pound and 4 cents for each additional pound?

20. *Money orders may be cashed without gain or profit by any post office having surplus*   20.____
    money order funds.
    What one word in the above sentence is synonymous to *excess?*

21. The jury AKWITED the prisoner.   21.____
    The word in capitals is misspelled. Write it correctly at the right.

22. Dogs are SUGAYSHUS animals.   22.____
    The word in capitals is misspelled. Write it correctly at the right.

23. The parade caused a TRAFIK jam.   23.____
    The word in capitals is misspelled. Write it correctly at the right.

24. The soldiers were ready to drop with FATEEG.   24.____
    The word in capitals is misspelled. Write it correctly at the right.

25. To TOLERATE is to   25.____

    A. prohibit   B. spoil   C. endure
    D. liberate   E. rejoice

KEY (CORRECT ANSWERS)

1. 7766.731
2. 315 5/8
3. .00340236
4. 9.6
5. C

6. C
7. D
8. D
9. C
10. A

11. C
12. E
13. B
14. B
15. 15/64

16. 85%
17. 7/16
18. 8
19. 52¢
20. surplus

21. acquitted
22. sagacious
23. traffic
24. fatigue
25. C

TEST 2

DIRECTIONS: Each question or incomplete statement is followed by several suggested answers or completions. Select the one that BEST answers the question or completes the statement. *PRINT THE CORRECT ANSWER IN THE SPACE AT THE RIGHT.*

1. To CONCUR means to   1.____

    A. gather   B. repeat   C. assent
    D. cause   E. put together

2. *The world never knows its great men until it buries them* means MOST NEARLY   2.____

    A. worry kills more men than work
    B. when a thing is lost, its worth is known
    C. every shoe fits not every foot
    D. no man really lives who is buried in conceit

3. *The Congress of the United States provided for the cooperation of the federal govern-*   3.____
    ment with the states in the construction of rural roads all over the country and was a pow-
    erful force in the development of highways.
    Judging from the above paragraph, which one of the following statements is TRUE?

    A. Each state builds its highways and rural post roads unaided.
    B. Congress builds all highways in the United States.
    C. The states receive federal cooperation in the building of all roads.
    D. The federal government assists in the building of post roads.

4. LAKE is to LAND as ISLAND is to   4.____

    A. separated   B. land   C. lonely
    D. water   E. large

5. NOVELIST is to FICTION as HISTORIAN is to   5.____

    A. war   B. fact   C. books
    D. school   E. primitive

6. Four men agreed to dig a ditch in 20 days. After 10 days, only one-fourth of the ditch was   6.____
    completed.
    How many more men must be engaged to finish on time?

7. *Let a man be true to his intentions and his efforts to fulfill them, and the point is gained,*   7.____
    whether he succeed or not.
    The above statement states that

    A. a man cannot succeed unless he makes an effort to be true to his intentions
    B. he may be satisfied with himself if he makes an effort to be true to his intentions
    C. every point is gained whether a man succeeds or fails.
    D. no special effort is necessary for success
    E. a certain amount of accomplishment always attends conscientious effort

8. MASS is to the WHOLE as ATOM is to   8.____

    A. physics   B. weight   C. solids
    D. part   E. theory

9. DIME is to CENT as DOLLAR is to 9.____

    A. silver   B. dime   C. nickel   D. paper   E. coin

10. WISE is to FOOLISH as KNOWLEDGE is to 10.____

    A. simple   B. ignorance   C. books
    D. learned   E. intolerance

11. REPUBLIC is to PRESIDENT as MONARCHY is to 11.____

    A. communists   B. ruler   C. constitution
    D. elections   E. emperor

12. The distance from A to C is 423 miles. Tourists left A at 7 A.M. and traveled 225 miles at 45 miles an hour, then stopped 30 minutes for lunch. The remainder of the trip was made at 36 miles an hour.
At what time did they arrive at C? 12.____

13. The TRANSHENT population is quite large. 13.____
The word in capitals is misspelled. Write it correctly at the right.

14. The LYOOTENANT wore a new uniform. 14.____
The word in capitals is misspelled. Write it correctly at the right.

15. He stepped on the AKSELURAYTER. 15.____
The word in capitals is misspelled. Write it correctly at the right.

16. Paper is easily PUNGKTYOORD. 16.____
The word in capitals is misspelled. Write it correctly at the right.

17. Even in hot weather, the water supply is ADEKWAYT. 17.____
The word in capitals is misspelled. Write it correctly at the right.

18. PLAUSIBLE explanations are 18.____

    A. ample   B. untrue
    C. courageous   D. apparently right
    E. impossible

19. Which one of the following words may be applied to OPTION but not to PURCHASE or SALE? 19.____

    A. Legal   B. Document   C. Permanent
    D. Abstract   E. Temporary   F. Concession

20. ATTENTUATE means to 20.____

    A. wire   B. flatter   C. heed
    D. lessen   E. be present   F. extend

21. GIVING is to LENDING as TAKING is to 21.____

    A. alms   B. prison   C. thieves
    D. stealing   E. kindness   F. borrowing

22. A and B together earned $180.00 on piece work. B worked only 2/3 as fast as A, but he worked 6 days more and received $90.00.
How many days did A work?

22.____

23. CHEAP is to ABUNDANT as COSTLY is to

23.____

A. plenty	B. inexpensive	C. high priced
D. scarce	E. frugal	

24. *Two-thirds of all American fires are home fires, and the preponderant cause is careless-ness. This source of economic waste and human suffering can be checked only as we exercise greater care to eliminate such fire hazards as the accumulation of inflammable rubbish, careless smoking habits, overheated stoves, etc. Remember this, that even though you have no fire loss, you share in the loss of every fire in the country.*
According to the above paragraph, which one of the following statements is TRUE?

24.____

   A. There are fewer fires in homes than in industrial plants.
   B. Fires are no loss when they are covered by insurance.
   C. This economic waste can be overcome only as we exercise greater care.
   D. Waste is the preponderant cause of home fires.
   E. Carelessness in the accumulation of rubbish causes fires.

25. If a stock of 500 rugs is divided into two parts, one of which contains 2/3 as many as the other, how many rugs are there in the smaller part?

25.____

KEY (CORRECT ANSWERS)

1.	C		11.	E
2.	B		12.	6:00 P.M.
3.	D		13.	transient
4.	D		14.	lieutenant
5.	B		15.	accelerator
6.	8		16.	accumulated
7.	E		17.	adequate
8.	D		18.	D
9.	B		19.	E
10.	B		20.	D

21.	F
22.	12
23.	D
24.	C
25.	200

TEST 3

DIRECTIONS: Each question or incomplete statement is followed by several suggested answers or completions. Select the one that BEST answers the question or completes the statement. *PRINT THE CORRECT ANSWER IN THE SPACE AT THE RIGHT.*

1. John travels a mile in 1/3 of an hour. Ben travels a mile in 3/10 of an hour. How many minutes does Ben finish before John, each traveling 12 miles?

1.____

2. KITTEN is to CAT as COLT is to

2.____

    A. young   B. pasture   C. horse
    D. donkey   E. cattle

3. WOLF is to HOWL as DOG is to

3.____

    A. bite   B. pet   C. bark
    D. pedigree   E. whine

4. DYNAMYT is used for blasting.
The word in capitals is misspelled. Write it correctly at the right.

4.____

5. The champion's OPOHNENT won the boxing match.
The word in capitals is misspelled. Write it correctly at the right.

5.____

6. The hungry man's appetite was APEEZD.
The word in capitals is misspelled. Write it correctly at the right.

6.____

7. WHEN is to WHERE as TIME is to

7.____

    A. hour   B. place   C. clock   D. here   E. work

8. ATLANTIC is to OCEAN as BRAZIL is to

8.____

    A. South America   B. country   C. river
    D. large   E. small

9. REGIMENT is to ARMY as SHIP is to

9.____

    A. marines   B. wars   C. navy
    D. submarine   E. commerce

10. *Substitute or temporary clerks shall be paid at the rate of $9.75 an hour for each hour or part hour after 6:00 P.M.*
What one word in the above quotation is synonymous to *a fixed value?*

10.____

11. *The United States leads the world in the amount of sugar consumed per capita, more than a hundred pounds annually for every person in the nation. The rest of the world is just as fond of sugar but not so able to buy it.*
Judging from the above paragraph, which one of the following statements is TRUE?

11.____

    A. The United States leads in sugar production.
    B. Europeans pay more for sugar.
    C. Each person in the United States consumes a pound of sugar each week.
    D. The per capita consumption of sugar in the United States is the largest in the world.

E. Americans are not so able to buy sugar as the rest of the world.

F. More sugar is consumed in the United States than in the rest of the world.

12. HABITUAL means MOST NEARLY   12._____

    A. healthy   B. customary   C. clothing

    D. harness   E. deadly

13. A COMPETENT man is one who is   13._____

    A. capable   B. clever   C. idle

    D. ambitious   E. punctual

14. To ADHERE is to   14._____

    A. hate   B. tape   C. degrade

    D. cling to   E. listen

15. To CALCULATE is to   15._____

    A. number   B. compute   C. whitewash

    D. tell tales   E. think

16. Which one of the following terms may be applied to MOTORCYCLE and AIRPLANE but   16._____
not to BICYCLE?

    A. High speed   B. Padded seats   C. Metal

    D. Rubber tires   E. Two wheels

17. *He can who believes he can.*   17._____
The above quotation means MOST NEARLY

    A. to believe a thing impossible is the way to make it so

    B. we are able when we feel so

    C. the man who believes is the man who achieves

    D. we walk by faith, not by sight

    E. nothing is impossible to him who tries

18. *Have many acquaintances, but few friends.*   18._____
The above quotation means MOST NEARLY

    A. be courteous to all, but intimate with few

    B. a true friend is forever a friend

    C. friends in distress make trouble less

    D. the only way to have a friend is to be one

    E. make friends of all you meet

19. *A man of many trades begs his bread on Sunday.*   19._____
The above quotation means MOST NEARLY

    A. with too many irons in the fire some will burn

    B. doing everything is doing nothing

    C. one cannot do many things profitably at the same time

    D. an intense hour will do more than two dreamy years

    E. a man without a trade will beg his bread

20. *Caution is the parent of safety.*
    The above quotation means MOST NEARLY

    A. all things belong to the prudent
    B. better a mistake avoided than two corrected
    C. look before you leap
    D. better go around than jump and fall short

20.____

KEY (CORRECT ANSWERS)

1.	24 min.	11.	D
2.	C	12.	B
3.	C	13.	A
4.	dynamite	14.	D
5.	opponent	15.	B
6.	appeased	16.	A
7.	B	17.	C
8.	B	18.	A
9.	C	19.	C
10.	rate	20.	D

VERBAL ABILITIES TEST

DIRECTIONS AND SAMPLE QUESTIONS

Study the sample questions carefully. Each question has four suggested answers. Decide which one is the best answer. Find the question number on the Sample Answer Sheet. Show your answer to the question by darkening completely the space corresponding to the letter that is the same as the letter of your answer. Keep your mark within the space. If you have to erase a mark, be sure to erase it completely. Mark only one answer for each question. Do NOT mark space E for any question.

SAMPLE VERBAL QUESTIONS

I. *Previous* means most nearly

    A. abandoned   C. timely
    B. former   D. younger

II. *(Reading)* "Just as the procedure of a collection department must be clear cut and definite, the steps being taken with the sureness of a skilled chess player, so the various paragraphs of a collection letter must show clear organization, giving evidence of a mind that, from the beginning, has had a specific end in view."
The quotation best supports the statement that a collection letter should always

    A. show a spirit of sportsmanship
    B. be divided into several paragraphs
    C. be brief, but courteous
    D. be carefully planned

III. Decide which sentence is preferable with respect to grammar and usage suitable for a formal letter or report.

    A. They do not ordinarily present these kind of reports in detail like this.
    B. A report of this kind is not hardly ever given in such detail as this one.
    C. This report is more detailed than what such reports ordinarily are.
    D. A report of this kind is not ordinarily presented in as much detail as this one is.

IV. Find the correct spelling of the word and darken the proper answer space. If no suggested spelling is correct, darken space D.

    A. athalete   C. athlete
    B. athelete   D. none of these

V. SPEEDOMETER is related to POINTER as WATCH is related to

    A. case   C. dial
    B. hands   D. numerals

EXAMINATION SECTION
TEST 1

Read each question carefully. Select the best answer and darken the proper space on the answer sheet.

1. *Flexible* means most nearly

   A. breakable
   B. flammable
   C. pliable
   D. weak

2. *Option* means most nearly

   A. use
   B. choice
   C. value
   D. blame

3. To *verify* means most nearly to

   A. examine
   B. explain
   C. confirm
   D. guarantee

4. *Indolent* means most nearly

   A. moderate
   B. hopeless
   C. selfish
   D. lazy

5. *Respiration* means most nearly

   A. recovery
   B. breathing
   C. pulsation
   D. sweating

6. PLUMBER is related to WRENCH as PAINTER is related to

   A. brush
   B. pipe
   C. shop
   D. hammer

7. LETTER is related to MESSAGE as PACKAGE is related to

   A. sender
   B. merchandise
   C. insurance
   D. business

8. FOOD is related to HUNGER as SLEEP is related to

   A. night
   B. dream
   C. weariness
   D. rest

9. KEY is related to TYPEWRITER as DIAL is related to

   A. sun
   B. number
   C. circle
   D. telephone

Grammar

10. A. I think that they will promote whoever has the best record.
     B. The firm would have liked to have promoted all employees with good records.
     C. Such of them that have the best records have excellent prospects of promotion.
     D. I feel sure they will give the promotion to whomever has the best record.

11. A. The receptionist must answer courteously the questions of all them callers.
    B. The receptionist must answer courteously the questions what are asked by the callers.
    C. There would have been no trouble if the receptionist had have always answered courteously.
    D. The receptionist should answer courteously the questions of all callers.

Spelling

12. A. collapsible
    B. collapseble
    C. collapseble
    D. none of these

13. A. ambigeuous
    B. ambigeous
    C. ambiguous
    D. none of these

14. A. predesessor
    B. predecesar
    C. predecesser
    D. none of these

15. A. sanctioned
    B. sancktioned
    C. sanctionned
    D. none of these

Reading

16. "The secretarial profession is a very old one and has increased in importance with the passage of time. In modern times, the vast expansion of business and industry has greatly increased the need and opportunities for secretaries, and for the first time in history their number has become large."
    The quotation best supports the statement that the secretarial profession

    A. is older than business and industry
    B. did not exist in ancient times
    C. has greatly increased in size
    D. demands higher training than it did formerly

17. "Civilization started to move ahead more rapidly when man freed himself of the shackles that restricted his search for the truth."
    The quotation best supports the statement that the progress of civilization

    A. came as a result of man's dislike for obstacles
    B. did not begin until restrictions on learning were removed
    C. has been aided by man's efforts to find
    D. the truth is based on continually increasing efforts

18. *Vigilant* means most nearly

    A. sensible
    B. watchful
    C. suspicious
    D. restless

19. *Incidental* means most nearly

    A. independent
    B. needless
    C. infrequent
    D. casual

13

20. *Conciliatory* means most nearly

    A. pacific   C. obligatory
    B. contentious   D. offensive

21. *Altercation* means most nearly

    A. defeat   C. controversy
    B. concurrence   D. vexation

22. *Irresolute* means most nearly

    A. wavering   C. impudent
    B. insubordinate   D. unobservant

23. DARKNESS is related to SUNLIGHT as STILLNESS is related to

    A. quiet   C. sound
    B. moonlight   D. dark

24. DESIGNED is related to INTENTION as ACCIDENTAL is related to

    A. purpose   C. damage
    B. caution   D. chance

25. ERROR is related to PRACTICE as SOUND is related to

    A. deafness   C. muffler
    B. noise   D. horn

26. RESEARCH is related to FINDINGS as TRAINING is related to

    A. skill   C. supervision
    B. tests   D. teaching

27.   A   If properly addressed, the letter will reach my mother and I.
    B.   The letter had been addressed to myself and my mother,
    C.   I believe the letter was addressed to either my mother or I.
    D.   My mother's name, as well as mine, was on the letter.

28.   A.   The supervisor reprimanded the typist, whom she believed had made careless errors.
    B.   The typist would have corrected the errors had she of known that the supervisor would see the report.
    C.   The errors in the typed report were so numerous that they could hardly beoverlooked.
    D.   Many errors were found in the report which she typed and could not disregard them.

29.   A. minieture   C. mineature
    B. minneature   D. none of these

30.   A. extemporaneous   C. extemporaneous
    B. extempuraneus   D. none of these

31.   A. problemmatical   C. problematicle
    B. problematical   D. none of these

32.   A. descendant   C. desendant
      B. decendant   D. none of these

33.   "The likelihood of America's exhausting her natural resources seems to be growing less. All kinds of waste are being reworked and new uses are constantly being found for almost everything. We are getting more use out of our goods and are making many new byproducts out of what was formerly thrown away."
      The quotation best supports the statement that we seem to be in less danger of exhausting our resources because

      A. economy is found to lie in the use of substitutes
      B. more service is obtained from a given amount of material
      C. we are allowing time for nature to restore them
      D. supply and demand are better controlled

34.   "Memos should be clear, concise, and brief. Omit all unnecessary words. The parts of speech most often used in memos are nouns, verbs, adjectives, and adverbs. If possible, do without pronouns, prepositions, articles and copulative verbs. Use simple sentences, rather than complex or compound ones."
      The quotation best supports the statement that in writing memos one should always use

      A. common and simple words
      B. only nouns, verbs, adjectives, and adverbs
      C. incomplete sentences
      D. only the words essential to the meaning.

35.   To *counteract* means most nearly to

      A. undermine   C. preserve
      B. censure   D. neutralize

36.   *Deferred* means most nearly

      A. reversed   C. considered
      B. delayed   D. forbidden

37.   *Feasible* means most nearly

      A. capable   C. practicable
      B. justifiable   D. beneficial

38.   To *encounter* means most nearly to

      A. meet   C. overcome
      B. recall   D. retreat

39.   *Innate* means most nearly

      A. eternal   C. native
      B. well-developed   D. prospective

40.   STUDENT is related to TEACHER as DISCIPLE is related to

      A. follower   C. principal
      B. master   D. pupil

41. LECTURE is related to AUDITORIUM as EXPERIMENT is related to

    A. scientist
    B. chemistry
    C. laboratory
    D. discovery

42. BODY is related to FOOD as ENGINE is related to

    A. wheels
    B. fuel
    C. motion
    D. smoke

43. SCHOOL is related to EDUCATION as THEATER is related to

    A. management
    B. stage
    C. recreation
    D. preparation

44. A. Most all these statements have been supported by persons who are reliable and can be depended upon.
    B. The persons which have guaranteed these statements are reliable.
    C. Reliable persons guarantee the facts with regards to the truth of these statements.
    D. These statements can be depended on, for their truth has been guaranteed by reliable persons.

45. A. The success of the book pleased both his publisher and he.
    B. Both his publisher and he was pleased with the success of the book.
    C. Neither he or his publisher was disappointed with the success of the book.
    D. His publisher was as pleased as he with the success of the book

46. A. extercate
    B. extracate
    C. extricate
    D. none of these

47. A. hereditory
    B. hereditary
    C. hereditairy
    D. none of these

48. A. auspiceous
    B. auspiseous
    C. auspicious
    D. none of these

49. A. sequance
    B. sequence
    C. sequense
    D. none of these

50. "The prevention of accidents makes it necessary not only that safety devices be used to guard exposed machinery but also that mechanics be instructed in safety rules which they must follow for their own protection, and that the lighting in the plant be adequate."
    The quotation best supports the statement that industrial accidents

    A. may be due to ignorance
    B. are always avoidable
    C. usually result from inadequate machinery
    D. cannot be entirely overcome

51. "The English language is peculiarly rich in synonyms, and there is scarcely a language spoken among men that has not some representative in English speech. The spirit of the Anglo-Saxon race has subjugated these various elements to one idiom, making not a patchwork, but a composite language."
    The quotation best supports the statement that the English language

A. has few idiomatic expressions
B. is difficult to translate
C. is used universally
D. has absorbed words from other languages

52. To *acquiesce* means most nearly to

A. assent
B. acquire
C. complete
D. participate

53. *Unanimity* means most nearly

A. emphasis
B. namelessness
C. harmony
D. impartiality

54. *Precedent* means most nearly

A. example
B. theory
C. law
D. conformity

55. *Versatile* means most nearly

A. broad-minded
B. well-known
C. up-to-date
D. many-sided

56. *Authentic* means most nearly

A. detailed
B. reliable
C. valuable
D. practical

57. BIOGRAPHY is related to FACT as NOVEL is related to

A. fiction
B. literature
C. narration
D. book

58. COPY is related to CARBON PAPER as MOTION PICTURE is related to

A. theater
B. film
C. duplicate
D. television

59. EFFICIENCY is related to REWARD as CARELESSNESS is related to

A. improvement
B. disobedience
C. reprimand
D. repetition

60. ABUNDANT is related to CHEAP as SCARCE is related to

A. ample
B. costly
C. inexpensive
D. unobtainable

61. A Brown's & Company employees have recently received increases in salary.
B. Brown & Company recently increased the salaries of all its employees.
C. Recently, Brown & Company has increased their employees' salaries.
D. Brown & Company have recently increased the salaries of all its employees

62. A In reviewing the typists' work reports, the job analyst found records of unusual typing speeds.
    B. It says in the job analyst's report that some employees type with great speed.
    C. The job analyst found that, in reviewing the typists' work reports, that some unusual typing speeds had been made.
    D. In the reports of typists' speeds, the job analyst found some records that are kind of unusual.

63. A. obliterate   C. obbliterate
     B. oblitterat   D. none of these

64. A. diagnoesis   C. diagnosis
     B. diagnossis   D. none of these

65. A. contenance   C. knowledge
     B. countenance   D. none of these

66. A. conceivably   C. conceiveably
     B. concieveably   D. none of these

67. "Through advertising, manufacturers exercise a high degree of control over consumers' desires. However, the manufacturer assumes enormous risks in attempting to predict what consumers will want and in producing goods in quantity and distributing them in advance of final selection by the consumers."
     The quotation best supports the statement that manufacturers

     A. can eliminate the risk of overproduction by advertising
     B. distribute goods directly to the consumers
     C. must depend upon the final consumers for the success of their undertakings
     D. can predict with great accuracy the success of any product they put on the market

68. "In the relations of man to nature, the procuring of food and shelter is fundamental. With the migration of man to various climates, ever new adjustments to the food supply and to the climate became necessary."
     The quotation best supports the statement that the means by which man supplies his material needs are

     A. accidental
     B. varied
     C. limited
     D. inadequate

69. *Strident* means most nearly

     A. swaggering   C. angry
     B. domineering   D. harsh

70. To *confine* means most nearly to

     A. hide   C. eliminate
     B. restrict   D. punish

71. To *accentuate* means most nearly to

     A. modify   C. sustain
     B. hasten   D. intensify

72. *Banal* means most nearly

    A. commonplace   C. tranquil
    B. forceful   D. indifferent

73. *Incorrigible* means most nearly

    A. intolerable   C. irreformable
    B. retarded   D. brazen

74. POLICEMAN is related to ORDER as DOCTOR is related to

    A. physician   C. sickness
    B. hospital   D. health

75. ARTIST is related to EASEL as WEAVER is related to

    A. loom   C. threads
    B. cloth   D. spinner

76. CROWD is related to PERSONS as FLEET is related to

    A. expedition   C. navy
    B. officers   D. ships

77. CALENDAR is related to DATE as MAP is related to

    A. geography   C. mileage
    B. trip   D. vacation

78. A Since the report lacked the needed information, it was of no use to him.
    B. This report was useless to him because there were no needed information in it.
    C. Since the report did not contain the needed information, it was not real useful to him.
    D. Being that the report lacked the needed information, he could not use it.

79. A The company had hardly declared the dividend till the notices were prepared for mailing.
    B. They had no sooner declared the dividend when they sent the notices to the stockholders.
    C. No sooner had the dividend been declared than the notices were prepared for mailing.
    D. Scarcely had the dividend been declared than the notices were sent out.

80. A. compitition   C. competetion
    B. competition   D. none of these

81. A. occassion   C. ocassion
    B. occasion   D. none of these

82. A. knowlege   C. knowledge
    B. knolledge   D. none of these

83. A. deliborate   C. delibrate
    B. deliberate   D. none of these

84. "What constitutes skill in any line of work is not always easy to determine; economy of time must be carefully distinguished from economy of energy, as the quickest method may require the greatest expenditure of muscular effort, and may not be essential or at all desirable."
The quotation best supports the statement that

    A.   the most efficiently executed task is not always the one done in the shortest time
    B.   energy and time cannot both be conserved in performing a single task
    C.   a task is well done when it is performed in the shortest time
    D.   skill in performing a task should not be acquired at the expense of time

85. "It is difficult to distinguish between bookkeeping and accounting. In attempts to do so, bookkeeping is called the art, and accounting the science, of recording business transactions. Bookkeeping gives the history of the business in a systematic manner; and accounting classifies, analyzes, and interprets the facts thus recorded."
The quotation best supports the statement that

    A.   accounting is less systematic than bookkeeping
    B.   accounting and bookkeeping are closely related
    C.   bookkeeping and accounting cannot be distinguished from one another
    D.   bookkeeping has been superseded by accounting

———

KEY (CORRECT ANSWERS)

1. C	21. C	41. C	61. B	81. B
2. B	22. A	42. B	62. A	82. C
3. C	23. C	43. C	63. A	83. B
4. D	24. D	44. D	64. C	84. A
5. B	25. C	45. D	65. B	85. B
6. A	26. A	46. C	66. A	
7. B	27. D	47. B	67. C	
8. C	28. C	48. C	68. B	
9. D	29. D	49. B	69. D	
10. A	30. A	50. A	70. B	
11. D	31. B	51. D	71. D	
12. A	32. A	52. A	72. A	
13. C	33. B	53. C	73. C	
14. D	34. D	54. A	74. D	
15. A	35. D	55. D	75. A	
16. C	36. B	56. B	76. D	
17. C	37. C	57. A	77. C	
18. B	38. A	58. B	78. A	
19. D	39. C	59. C	79. C	
20. A	40. B	60. B	80. B	

TEST 2

Read each question carefully. Select the best answer and blacken the proper space on the answer sheet.

1. *Option* means most nearly

   A. use
   B. choice
   C. value
   D. blame
   E. mistake

2. *Irresolute* means most nearly

   A. wavering
   B. insubordinate
   C. impudent
   D. determined
   E. unobservant

3. *Flexible* means most nearly

   A. breakable
   B. inflammable
   C. pliable
   D. weak
   E. impervious

4. To *counteract* means most nearly to

   A. undermine
   B. censure
   C. preserve
   D. sustain
   E. neutralize

5. To *verify* means most nearly to

   A. justify
   B. explain
   C. confirm
   D. guarantee
   E. examine

6. *Indolent* means most nearly

   A. moderate
   B. relentless
   C. selfish
   D. lazy
   E. hopeless

7. To say that an action is *deferred* means most nearly that it is

   A. delayed
   B. reversed
   C. considered
   D. forbidden
   E. followed

8. To *encounter* means most nearly to

   A. meet
   B. recall
   C. overcome
   D. weaken
   E. retreat

9. *Feasible* means most nearly

   A. capable
   B. practicable
   C. justifiable
   D. beneficial
   E. reliable

10. *Respiration* means most nearly

    A. dehydration
    B. breathing
    C. pulsation
    D. sweating
    E. recovery

11. *Vigilant* means most nearly

    A. sensible
    B. ambitious
    C. watchful
    D. suspicious
    E. restless

12. To say that an action is taken *before the proper time* means most nearly that it is taken

    A. prematurely
    B. furtively
    C. temporarily
    D. punctually
    E. presently

13. *Innate* means most nearly

    A. eternal
    B. learned
    C. native
    D. prospective
    E. well-developed

14. *Precedent* means most nearly

    A. duplicate
    B. theory
    C. law
    D. conformity
    E. example

15. To say that the flow of work into an office is *incessant* means most nearly that it is

    A. more than can be handled
    B. uninterrupted
    C. scanty
    D. decreasing in volume
    E. orderly

16. *Unanimity* means most nearly

    A. emphasis
    B. namelessness
    C. disagreement
    D. harmony
    E. impartiality

17. *Incidental* means most nearly

    A. independent
    B. needless
    C. infrequent
    D. necessary
    E. casual

18. *Versatile* means most nearly

    A. broad-minded
    B. well-Known
    C. old-fashioned
    D. many-sided
    E. up-to-date

23

19. *Conciliatory* means most nearly

   A. pacific
   B. contentious
   C. disorderly
   D. obligatory
   E. offensive

20. *Altercation* means most nearly

   A. defeat
   B. concurrence
   C. controversy
   D. consensus
   E. vexation

21. *(Reading)* "The secretarial profession is a very old one and has increased in importance with the passage of time. In modern times, the vast expansion of business and industry has greatly increased the need and opportunities for secretaries, and for the first time in history their number has become large."

   The quotation best supports the statement that the secretarial profession

   A. is older than business and industry
   B. did not exist in ancient times
   C. has greatly increased in size
   D. demands higher training than it did formerly
   E. has always had many members

22. *(Reading)* "The modern system of production unites various kinds of workers into a well-organized body in which each has a definite place."
   The quotation best supports the statement that the modern system of production

   A. increases production
   B. trains workers
   C. simplifies tasks
   D. combines and places workers
   E. combines the various plants

23. *(Reading)* "The prevention of accidents makes it necessary not only that safety devices be used to guard exposed machinery but also that mechanics be instructed in safety rules which they must follow for their own protection, and that the lighting in the plant be adequate."

   The quotation best supports the statement that industrial accidents

   A. may be due to ignorance
   B. are always avoidable
   C. usually result from inadequate machinery
   D. cannot be entirely overcome
   E. result in damage to machinery

24. *(Reading)* "It is wise to choose a duplicating machine that will do the work required with the greatest efficiency and at the least cost. Users with a large volume of business need speedy machines that cost little to operate and are well made."

   The quotation best supports the statement that

24

A. most users of duplicating machines prefer low operating cost to efficiency
B. a well-built machine will outlast a cheap one
C. a duplicating machine is not efficient unless it is sturdy
D. a duplicating machine should be both efficient and economical
E. in duplicating machines speed is more usual than low operating cost

25. *(Reading)* "The likelihood of America's exhausting her natural resources seems to be growing less. All kinds of waste are being reworked and new uses are constantly being found for almost everything. We are getting more use out of our goods and are making many new byproducts out of what was formerly thrown away."

    The quotation best supports the statement that we seem to be in less danger of exhausting our resources because

    A. economy is found to lie in the use of substitutes
    B. more service is obtained from a given amount of material
    C. more raw materials are being produced
    D. supply and demand are better controlled
    E. we are allowing time for nature to restore them

26. *(Reading)* "Probably few people realize, as they drive on a concrete road, that steel is used to keep the surface flat and even, in spite of the weight of busses and trucks. Steel bars, deeply imbedded in the concrete, provide sinews to take the stresses so that they cannot crack the slab or make it wavy."

    The quotation best supports the statement that a concrete road

    A. is expensive to build
    B. usually cracks under heavy weights
    C. looks like any other road
    D. is used exclusively for heavy traffic
    E. is reinforced with other material

27. *(Reading)* "Through advertising, manufacturers exercise a high degree of control over consumers' desires. However, the manufac-turer assumes enormous risks in attempting to predict what consumers will want and in producing goods in quantity and distributing them in advance of final selection by the consumers."

    The quotation best supports the statement that manufacturers

    A. can eliminate the risk of overproduction by advertising
    B. completely control buyers' needs and desires
    C. must depend upon the final consumers for the success of their undertakings
    D. distribute goods directly to the consumers
    E. can predict with great accuracy the success of any product they put on the market

28. *(Reading)* "Success in shorthand, like success in any other study, depends upon the interest the student takes in it. In writing shorthand it is not sufficient to know how to write a word correctly; one must also be able to write it quickly."

    The quotation best supports the statement that

25

A. one must be able to read shorthand as well as to write it
B. shorthand requires much study
C. if a student can write correctly, he can also write quickly
D. proficiency in shorthand requires both speed and accuracy
E. interest in shorthand makes study unnecessary

29. *(Reading)* "The countries in the Western Hemisphere were settled by people who were ready each day for new adventure. The peoples of North and South America have retained, in addition to expectant and forwardlooking attitudes, the ability and the willingness that they have often shown in the past to adapt themselves to new conditions."

The quotation best supports the statement that the peoples in the Western Hemisphere

A. no longer have fresh adventures daily
B. are capable of making changes as new situations arise
C. are no more forward-looking than the peoples of other regions
D. tend to resist regulations
E. differ considerably among themselves

30. *(Reading)* "Civilization started to move ahead more rapidly when man freed himself of the shackles that restricted his search for the truth."
The quotation best supports the statement that the progress of civilization

A. came as a result of man's dislike for obstacles
B. did not begin until restrictions on learning were removed
C. has been aided by man's efforts to find the truth
D. is based on continually increasing efforts
E. continues at a constantly increasing rate

31. *(Reading)* "It is difficult to distinguish between bookkeeping and accounting. In attempts to do so, bookkeeping is called the art, and accounting the science, of recording business transactions. Bookkeeping gives the history of the business in a systematic manner, and accounting classifies, analyzes, and interprets the facts thus recorded."

The quotation best supports the statement that

A. accounting is less systematic than bookkeeping
B. accounting and bookkeeping are closely related
C. bookkeeping and accounting cannot be distinguished from one another
D. bookkeeping has been superseded by accounting
E. the facts recorded by bookkeeping may be interpreted in many ways

32. *(Reading)* "Some specialists are willing to give their services to the Government entirely free of charge; some feel that a nominal salary, such as will cover traveling expenses, is sufficient for a position that is recognized as being somewhat honorary in nature; many other specialists value their time so highly that they will not devote any of it to public service that does not repay them at a rate commensurate with the fees that they can obtain from a good private clientele."

The quotation best supports the statement that the use of specialists by the Government

A. is rare because of the high cost of securing such persons
B. may be influenced by the willingness of specialists to serve
C. enables them to secure higher salaries in private fields
D. has become increasingly common during the past few years
E. always conflicts with private demands for their services

33. *(Reading)* "The leader of an industrial enterprise has two principal functions. He must manufacture and distribute a product at a profit, and he must keep individuals and groups of individuals working effectively together."

The quotation best supports the statement that an industrial leader should be able to

A. increase the distribution of his plant's product
B. introduce large-scale production methods
C. coordinate the activities of his employees
D. profit by the experience of other leaders
E. expand the business rapidly

34. *(Reading)* "The coloration of textile fabrics composed of cotton and wool generally re-quires two processes, as the process used in dyeing wool is seldom capable of fixing the color upon cotton. The usual method is to immerse the fabric in the requisite baths to dye the wool and then to treat the partially dyed material in the manner found suitable for cot-ton."
The quotation best supports the statement that the dyeing of textile fabrics composed of cotton and wool

A. is less complicated than the dyeing of wool alone
B. is more successful when the material contains more cotton than wool
C. is not satisfactory when solid colors are desired
D. is restricted to two colors for any one fabric
E. is usually based upon the methods required for dyeing the different materials

35. *(Reading)* "The fact must not be overlooked that only about one-half of the international trade of the world crosses the oceans. The other half is merely exchanges of merchan-dise between countries lying alongside each other or at least within the same continent."

The quotation best supports the statement that

A. the most important part of any country's trade is transoceanic
B. domestic trade is insignificant when compared with foreign trade
C. the exchange of goods between neighboring countries is not considered interna-tional trade
D. foreign commerce is not necessarily carried on by water
E. about one-half of the trade of the world is international

36. *(Reading)* "In the relations of man to nature, the procuring of food and shelter is funda-mental. With the migration of man to various climates, ever new adjustments to the food supply and to the climate became necessary."

The quotation best supports the statement that the means by which man supplies his material needs are

A. accidental
B. varied
C. limited

D. uniform
E. inadequate

37. *(Reading)* "Every language has its peculiar word associations that have no basis in logic and cannot therefore be reasoned about. These idiomatic expressions are ordinarily acquired only by much reading and conversation although questions about such matters may sometimes be answered by the dictionary. Dictionaries large enough to include quota-tions from standard authors are especially serviceable in determining questions of idiom."

The quotation best supports the statement that idiomatic expressions

A. give rise to meaningless arguments because they have no logical basis
B. are widely used by recognized authors.
C. are explained in most dictionaries
D. are more common in some languages than in others
E. are best learned by observation of the language as actually used

38. *(Reading)* "Individual differences in mental traits assume importance in fitting workers to jobs because such personal characteristics are persistent and are relatively little influenced by training and experience."

The quotation best supports the statement that training and experience

A. are limited in their effectiveness in fitting workers to jobs
B. do not increase a worker's fitness for a job
C. have no effect upon a person's mental traits
D. have relatively little effect upon the individual's chances for success
E. should be based on the mental traits of an individual

39. *(Reading)* "The telegraph networks of the country now constitute wonderfully operated institutions, affording for ordinary use of modern, business an important means of communication. The transmission of messages by electricity has reached the goal for which the postal service has long been striving, namely, the elimination of distance as an effective barrier of communication."

The quotation best supports the statement that

A. a new standard of communication has been attained
B. in the telegraph service, messages seldom go astray
C. it is the distance between the parties which creates the need for communication
D. modern business relies more upon the telegraph than upon the mails
E. the telegraph is a form of postal service

40. *(Reading)* "The competition of buyers tends to keep prices up, the competition of sellers to send them down. Normally the pressure of competition among sellers is stronger than that among buyers since the seller has his article to sell and must get rid of it, whereas the buyer is not committed to anything."

The quotation best supports the statement that low prices are caused by

A. buyer competition
B. competition of buyers with sellers fluctuations in demand
C. greater competition among sellers than among buyers
D. more sellers than buyers

In each question from 41 through 60, find the CORRECT spelling of the word, and blacken the proper space on your answer sheet. Sometimes there is no correct spelling; if none of the suggested spellings is correct, blacken space D on your answer sheet.

41. A. compitition   C. competetion
     B. competition   D. none of these

42. A. diagnoesis   C. diagnosis
     B. diagnossis   D. none of these

43. A. contenance   C. countinance
     B. countenance   D. none of these

44. A. deliborate   C. delibrate
     B. deliberate   D. none of these

45. A. knowlege   C. knowledge
     B. knolledge   D. none of these

46. A. occassion   C. ocassion
     B. occasion   D. none of these

47. A. sanctioned   C. sanctionned
     B. sancktioned   D. none of these

48. A. predesessor   C. predecesser
     B. predecesar   D. none of these

49. A. problemmatical   C. problematicle
     B. problematical   D. none of these

50. A. descendant   C. desendant
     B. decendant   D. none of these

51. A. collapsible   C. collapseble
     B. collapseable   D. none of these

52. A. sequance   C. sequense
     B. sequence   D. none of these

53. A. oblitorate   C. obbliterate
     B. oblitterat   D. none of these

54. A. ambigeuous   C. ambiguous
     B. ambigeous   D. none of these

55. A. minieture   C. mineature
     B. minneature   D. none of these

56. A. extemporaneous   C. extemperaneous
     B. extempuraneus   D. none of these

57.   A. hereditory   C. hereditairy
       B. hereditary   D. none of these

58.   A. conceivably   C. conceiveably
       B. concieveably   D. none of these

59.   A. extercate   C. extricate
       B. extracate   D. none of these

60.   A. auspiceous   C. auspicious
       B. auspiseous   D. none of these

Select the sentence that is preferable with respect to grammar and usage such as would be suitable in a formal letter or report. Then blacken the proper space on the answer sheet.

61.   A   The receptionist must answer courteously the questions of all them callers.
       B.   The questions of all callers had ought to be answered courteously.
       C.   The receptionist must answer courteously the questions what are asked by the callers.
       D.   There would have been no trouble if the receptionist had have always answered courteously.
       E.   The receptionist should answer courteously the questions of all callers.

62.   A   I had to learn a great number of rules, causing me to dislike the course.
       B.   I disliked that study because it required the learning of numerous rules.
       C.   I disliked that course very much, caused by the numerous rules I had to memorize.
       D.   The cause of my dislike was on account of the numerous rules I had to learn in that course.
       E.   The reason I disliked this study was because there were numerous rules that had to be learned.

63.   A   If properly addressed, the letter will reach my mother and I.
       B.   The letter had been addressed to myself and mother.
       C.   I believe the letter was addressed to either my mother or I.
       D.   My mother's name, as well as mine, was on the letter.
       E.   If properly addressed, the letter it will reach either my mother or me.

64.   A   A knowledge of commercial subjects and a mastery of English are essential if one wishes to be a good secretary.
       B.   Two things necessary to a good secretary are that she should speak good English and to know commercial subjects.
       C.   One cannot be a good secretary without she knows commercial subjects and English grammar.
       D.   Having had good training in commercial subjects, the rules of English grammar should also be followed.
       E.   A secretary seldom or ever succeeds without training in English as well as in commercial subjects.

65. A   He suspicions that the service is not so satisfactory as it should be.
     B. He believes that we should try and find whether the service is satisfactory.
     C. He raises the objection that the way which the service is given is not satisfactory.
     D. He believes that the quality of our services are poor.
     E. He believes that the service that we are giving is unsatisfactory.

66. A   Most all these statements have been supported by persons who are reliable and can be depended upon.
     B. The persons which have guaranteed these statements are reliable.
     C. Reliable persons guarantee the facts with regards to the truth of these statements.
     D. These statements can be depended on, for their truth has been guaranteed by reliable persons.
     E. Persons as reliable as what these are can be depended upon to make accurate statements.

67. A   Brown's & Company's employees have all been given increases in salary.
     B. Brown & Company recently increased the salaries of all its employees.
     C. Recently Brown & Company has in-creased their employees' salaries.
     D. Brown's & Company employees have recently received increases in salary.
     E. Brown & Company have recently increased the salaries of all its employees.

68. A. The personnel office has charge of employment, dismissals, and employee's welfare.
     B. Employment, together with dismissals and employees' welfare, are handled by the personnel department.
     C. The personnel office takes charge of employment, dismissals, and etc.
     D. The personnel office hires and dismisses employees, and their welfare is also its responsibility.
     E. The personnel office is responsible for the employment, dismissal, and welfare of employees.

69. A. This kind of pen is some better than that kind.
     B. I prefer having these pens than any other.
     C. This kind of pen is the most satisfactory for my use.
     D. In comparison with that kind of pen, this kind is more preferable.
     E. If I were to select between them all, I should pick this pen.

70. A. He could not make use of the report, as it was lacking of the needed information.
     B. This report was useless to him because there were no needed information in it.
     C. Since the report lacked the needed information, it was of no use to him.
     D. Being that the report lacked the needed information, he could not use it.
     E. Since the report did not contain the needed information, it was not real useful to him.

71. A. The paper we use for this purpose must be light, glossy, and stand hard usage as well.
     B. Only a light and a glossy, but durable, paper must be used for this purpose.
     C. For this purpose, we want a paper that is light, glossy, but that will stand hard wear.
     D. For this purpose, paper that is light, glossy, and durable is essential.
     E. Light and glossy paper, as well as standing hard usage, is necessary for this purpose.

72. A The company had hardly declared the dividend till the notices were prepared for mailing.
    B. They had no sooner declared the dividend when they sent the notices to the stockholders.
    C. No sooner had the dividend been declared than the notices were prepared for mailing.
    D. Scarcely had the dividend been declared than the notices were sent out.
    E. The dividend had not scarcely been declared when the notices were ready for mailing.

73. A Of all the employees, he spends the most time at the office.
    B. He spends more time at the office than that of his employees.
    C. His working hours are longer or at least equal to those of the other employees.
    D. He devotes as much, if not more, time to his work than the rest of the employees.
    E. He works the longest of any other employee in the office.

74. A In the reports of typists' speeds, the job analyst found some records that are kind of unusual.
    B. It says in the job analyst's report that some employees type with great speed.
    C. The job analyst found that, in reviewing the typists' work Reports, that some unusual typing speeds had been made.
    D. Work reports showing typing speeds include some typists who are unusual.
    E. In reviewing the typists' work reports, the job analyst found records of unusual typing speeds.

75. A It is quite possible that we shall reemploy anyone whose training fits them to do the work.
    B. It is probable that we shall reemploy those who have been trained to do the work.
    C. Such of our personnel that have been trained to do the work will be again employed.
    D. We expect to reemploy the ones who have had training enough that they can do the work.
    E. Some of these people have been trained

76. A He as well as his publisher were pleased with the success of the book.
    B. The success of the book pleased both his publisher and he.
    C. Both his publisher and he was pleased with the success of the book.
    D. Neither he or his publisher was disappointed with the success of the book.
    E. His publisher was as pleased as he with the success of the book.

77. A You have got to get rid of some of these people if you expect to have the quality of the work improve.
    B. The quality of the work would improve if they would leave fewer people do it.
    C. I believe it would be desirable to have fewer persons doing this work.
    D. If you had planned on employing fewer people than this to do the work, this situation would not have arose.
    E. Seeing how you have all those people on that work, it is not surprising that you have a great deal of confusion.

78.   A   She made lots of errors in her typed report, and which caused her to be repri-
            manded.
       B.   The supervisor reprimanded the typist, whom she believed had made careless
            errors.
       C.   Many errors were found in the report which she typed and could not disregard
            them.
       D.   The typist would have corrected the errors, had she of known that the super-
            visor would see the report.
       E.   The errors in the typed report were so numerous that they could hardly be over-
            looked.

79.   A.   This kind of a worker achieves success through patience.
       B.   Success does not often come to men of this type except they who are patient.
       C.   Because they are patient, these sort of workers usually achieve success.
       D.   This worker has more patience than any man in his office.
       E.   This kind of worker achieves success through patience.

80.   A.   I think that they will promote whoever has the best record.
       B.   The firm would have liked to have promoted all employees with good records.
       C.   Such of them that have the best records have excellent prospects of promotion.
       D.   I feel sure they will give the promotion to whomever has the best record.
       E.   Whoever they find to have the best record will, I think, be promoted.

———

KEY (CORRECT ANSWERS)

1. B	21. C	41. B	61. E
2. A	22. D	42. C	62. B
3. C	23. A	43. B	63. D
4. E	24. D	44. B	64. A
5. C	25. B	45. C	65. E
6. D	26. E	46. B	66. D
7. A	27. C	47. A	67. B
8. A	28. D	48. D	68. E
9. B	29. B	49. B	69. C
10. B	30. C	50. A	70. C
11. C	31. B	51. A	71. D
12. A	32. B	52. B	72. C
13. C	33. C	53. D	73. A
14. E	34. E	54. C	74. E
15. B	35. D	55. D	75. B
16. D	36. B	56. A	76. E
17. E	37. E	57. B	77. C
18. D	38. A	58. A	78. E
19. A	39. A	59. C	79. E
20. C	40. D	60. C	80. A

SPELLING

COMMENTARY

Spelling forms an integral part of tests of academic aptitude and achievement and of general and mental ability. Moreover, the spelling question is a staple of verbal and clerical tests in civil service entrance and promotional examinations.

Perhaps, the most rewarding way to learn to spell successfully is the direct, functional approach of learning to spell correctly, both orally and in writing, all words as they appear, both singly and in context.

In accordance with this positive method, the spelling question is presented here in "test" form, as it might appear on an actual examination.

The spelling question may appear on examinations in the following format:

> Four words are listed in each question. These are lettered A, B, C, and D. A fifth option, E, is also given, which always reads "none misspelled." The examinee is to select one of the five (lettered) choices: either A, B, C, or D if one of the words is misspelled, or item E, none misspelled, if all four words have been correctly spelled in the question.

SAMPLE QUESTIONS

The directions for this part are approximately as follows:

DIRECTIONS: Mark the space corresponding to the one MISSPELLED word in each of the following groups of words. If NO word is misspelled, mark the last space on the answer sheet.

SAMPLE O
- A. walk
- B. talk
- C. play
- D. dance
- E. *none misspelled*

Since none of the words is misspelled, E would be marked on the answer sheet.

SAMPLE OO
- A. seize
- B. yield
- C. define
- D. reccless
- E. *none misspelled*

Since "reccless" (correct spelling, reckless) has been misspelled, D would be marked on the answer. sheet

SPELLING
EXAMINATION SECTION
TEST 1

DIRECTIONS: Each question or incomplete statement is followed by several suggested answers or completions. Select the one that BEST answers the question or completes the statement. *PRINT THE LETTER OF THE CORRECT ANSWER IN THE SPACE AT THE RIGHT.*

Questions 1-5.

DIRECTIONS: Questions 1 through 5 consist of four words. Indicate the letter of the word that is CORRECTLY spelled.

1. A. harassment   B. harrasment   1._____
     C. harasment   D. harrassment

2. A. maintainance   B. maintenence   2._____
     C. maintainence   D. maintenance

3. A. comparable   B. comprable   3._____
     C. comparible   D. commparable

4. A. suficient   B. sufficiant   4._____
     C. sufficient   D. suficiant

5. A. fairly   B. fairley   C. farely   D. fairlie   5._____

Questions 6-10.

DIRECTIONS: Questions 6 through 10 consist of four words. Indicate the letter of the word that is INCORRECTLY spelled.

6. A. pallor   B. ballid   C. ballet   D. pallid   6._____

7. A. urbane   B. surburbane
     C. interurban   D. urban

8. A. facial   B. physical   C. fiscle   D. muscle   8._____

9. A. interceed   B. benefited
     C. analogous   D. altogether

10. A. seizure   B. irrelevant
     C. inordinate   D. dissapproved

KEY (CORRECT ANSWERS)

1.	A	6.	B
2.	D	7.	B
3.	A	8.	C
4.	C	9.	A
5.	A	10.	D

TEST 2

DIRECTIONS: Each of Questions 1 through 15 consists of two words preceded by the letters A and B. In each question, one of the words may be spelled INCORRECTLY or both words may be spelled CORRECTLY. If one of the words in a question is spelled INCORRECTLY, print in the space at the right the capital letter preceding the INCORRECTLY spelled word. If both words are spelled CORRECTLY, print the letter C.

1. A. easely   B. readily   1._____
2. A. pursue   B. decend   2._____
3. A. measure   B. laboratory   3._____
4. A. exausted   B. traffic   4._____
5. A. discussion   B. unpleasant   5._____
6. A. campaign   B. murmer   6._____
7. A. guarantee   B. sanatary   7._____
8. A. communication   B. safty   8._____
9. A. numerus   B. celebration   9._____
10. A. nourish   B. begining   10._____
11. A. courious   B. witness   11._____
12. A. undoubtedly   B. thoroughly   12._____
13. A. accessible   B. artifical   13._____
14. A. feild   B. arranged   14._____
15. A. admittence   B. hastily   15._____

KEY (CORRECT ANSWERS)

1.	A	6.	B	11.	A
2.	B	7.	B	12.	C
3.	C	8.	B	13.	B
4.	A	9.	A	14.	A
5.	C	10.	B	15.	A

TEST 3

DIRECTIONS: In each of the following sentences, one word is misspelled. Following each sentence is a list of four words taken from the sentence. Indicate the letter of the word which is MISSPELLED in the sentence. *PRINT THE LETTER OF THE CORRECT ANSWER IN THE SPACE AT THE RIGHT.*

1. The placing of any inflammable substance in any building, or the placing of any device or contrivence capable of producing fire, for the purpose of causing a fire is an attempt to burn.

   A. inflammable
   C. device
   B. substance
   D. contrivence

   1._____

2. The word *break* also means obtaining an entrance into a building by any artifice used for that purpose, or by colussion with any person therein.

   A. obtaining
   C. artifice
   B. entrance
   D. colussion

   2._____

3. Any person who with intent to provoke a breech of the peace causes a disturbance or is offensive to others may be deemed to have committed disorderly conduct.

   A. breech
   C. offensive
   B. disturbance
   D. committed

   3._____

4. When the offender inflicts a grevious harm upon the person from whose possession, or in whose presence, property is taken, he is guilty of robbery.

   A. offender
   C. possession
   B. grevious
   D. presence

   4._____

5. A person who wilfuly encourages or advises another person in attempting to take the latter's life is guilty of a felony.

   A. wilfuly
   C. advises
   B. encourages
   D. attempting

   5._____

6. He maliciously demurred to an ajournment of the proceedings.

   A. maliciously
   C. ajournment
   B. demurred
   D. proceedings

   6._____

7. His innocence at that time is irrelevant in view of his more recent villianous demeanor.

   A. innocence
   C. villianous
   B. irrelevant
   D. demeanor

   7._____

8. The mischievous boys aggrevated the annoyance of their neighbor.

   A. mischievous
   C. annoyance
   B. aggrevated
   D. neighbor

   8._____

9. While his perseverence was commendable, his judgment was debatable.

   A. perseverence
   C. judgment
   B. commendable
   D. debatable

   9._____

10. He was hoping the appeal would facilitate his aquittal.   10.____

    A. hoping   B. appeal
    C. facilitate   D. aquittal

11. It would be preferable for them to persue separate courses.   11.____

    A. preferable   B. persue
    C. separate   D. courses

12. The litigant was complimented on his persistance and achievement.   12.____

    A. litigant   B. complimented
    C. persistance   D. achievement

13. Ocassionally there are discrepancies in the descriptions of miscellaneous items. 13.____

    A. ocassionally   B. discrepancies
    C. descriptions   D. miscellaneous

14. The councilmanic seargent-at-arms enforced the prohibition.   14.____

    A. councilmanic   B. seargent-at-arms
    C. enforced   D. prohibition

15. The teacher had an ingenious device for maintaning attendance.   15.____

    A. ingenious   B. device
    C. maintaning   D. attendance

16. A worrysome situation has developed as a result of the assessment that absenteeism is   16.____
increasing despite our conscientious efforts.

    A. worrysome   B. assessment
    C. absenteeism   D. conscientious

17. I concurred with the credit manager that it was practicable to charge purchases on a   17.____
biennial basis, and the company agreed to adhear to this policy.

    A. concurred   B. practicable
    C. biennial   D. adhear

18. The pastor was chagrined and embarassed by the irreverent conduct of one of his   18.____
parishioners.

    A. chagrined   B. embarassed
    C. irreverent   D. parishioners

19. His inate seriousness was belied by his flippant demeanor.   19.____

    A. inate   B. belied
    C. flippant   D. demeanor

20. It was exceedingly regrettable that the excessive number   20.____
of challanges in the court delayed the start of the trial.

    A. exceedingly   B. regrettable
    C. excessive   D. challanges

KEY (CORRECT ANSWERS)

1.	D	11.	B
2.	D	12.	C
3.	A	13.	A
4.	B	14.	B
5.	A	15.	C
6.	C	16.	A
7.	C	17.	D
8.	B	18.	B
9.	A	19.	A
10.	D	20.	D

———

TEST 4

Questions 1-11.

DIRECTIONS: Each question consists of three words. In each question, one of the words may be spelled incorrectly or all three may be spelled correctly. For each question. if one of the words is spelled INCORRECTLY, write the letter of the incorrect word in the space at the right. If all three words are spelled CORRECTLY, write the letter D in the space at the right.

SAMPLE I: (A) guide (B) department (C) stranger
SAMPLE II: (A) comply (B) valuable (C) window
In Sample I, departmint is incorrect. It should be spelled department. Therefore, B is the answer.
In Sample II, all three words are spelled correctly. Therefore, D is the answer.

1.	A.	argument	B.	reciept	C.	complain	1.	___
2.	A.	sufficient	B.	postpone	C.	visible	2.	___
3.	A.	expirience	B.	dissatisfy	C.	alternate	3.	___
4.	A.	occurred	B.	noticable	C.	appendix	4.	___
5.	A.	anxious	B.	guarantee	C.	calender	5.	___
6.	A.	sincerely	B.	affectionately	C.	truly	6.	___
7.	A.	excellant	B.	verify	C.	important	7.	___
8.	A.	error	B.	quality	C.	enviroment	8.	___
9.	A.	exercise	B.	advance	C.	pressure	9.	___
10.	A.	citizen	B.	expence	C.	memory	10.	___
11.	A.	flexable	B.	focus	C.	forward	11.	___

Questions 12-15.

DIRECTIONS: Each of Questions 12 through 15 consists of a group of four words. Examine each group carefully; then in the space at the right, indicate
A - if only one word in the group is spelled correctly
B - if two words in the group are spelled correctly
C - if three words in the group are spelled correctly
D - if all four words in the group are spelled correctly

12. Wendsday, particular, similar, hunderd   12. ___

13. realize, judgment, opportunities, consistent   13. ___

14. equel, principle, assistense, commitee   14. ___

15. simultaneous, privilege, advise, ocassionaly   15. ___

KEY (CORRECT ANSWERS)

1.	B	6.	D	11.	A
2.	D	7.	A	12.	B
3.	A	8.	C	13.	D
4.	B	9.	D	14.	A
5.	C	10.	B	15.	C

———

TEST 5

DIRECTIONS: Each of Questions 1 through 15 consists of two words preceded by the letters A and B. In each item, one of the words may be spelled INCORRECTLY or both words may be spelled CORRECTLY. If one of the words in a question is spelled INCORRECTLY, print in the space at the right the letter preceding the INCORRECTLY spelled word. If both words are spelled CORRECTLY, print the letter C.

1.	A. justified	B. offering		1.____
2.	A. predjudice	B. license		2.____
3.	A. label	B. pamphlet		3.____
4.	A. bulletin	B. physical		4.____
5.	A. assure	B. exceed		5.____
6.	A. advantagous	B. evident		6.____
7.	A. benefit	B. occured		7.____
8.	A. acquire	B. graditude		8.____
9.	A. amenable	B. boundry		9.____
10.	A. deceive	B. voluntary		10.____
11.	A. imunity	B. conciliate		11.____
12.	A. acknoledge	B. presume		12.____
13.	A. substitute	B. prespiration		13.____
14.	A. reputible	B. announce		14.____
15.	A. luncheon	B. wretched		15.____

KEY (CORRECT ANSWERS)

1.	C	6.	A	11.	A
2.	A	7.	B	12.	A
3.	C	8.	B	13.	B
4.	C	9.	B	14.	A
5.	C	10.	C	15.	C

TEST 6

DIRECTIONS: Questions 1 through 15 contain lists of words, one of which is misspelled. Indicate the MISSPELLED word in each group. *PRINT THE LETTER OF THE CORRECT ANSWER IN THE SPACE AT THE RIGHT.*

1. A. felony   B. lacerate
    C. cancellation   D. seperate

2. A. batallion   B. beneficial
    C. miscellaneous   D. secretary

3. A. camouflage   B. changeable   C. embarass   D. inoculate   3.____

4. A. beneficial   B. disasterous
    C. incredible   D. miniature

5. A. auxilliary   B. hypocrisy   C. phlegm   D. vengeance   5.____

6. A. aisle   B. cemetary
    C. courtesy   D. extraordinary

7. A. crystallize   B. innoculate
    C. eminent   D. symmetrical

8. A. judgment   B. maintainance
    C. bouillon   D. eery

9. A. isosceles   B. ukulele   C. mayonaise   D. iridescent   9.____

10. A. remembrance   B. occurence
    C. correspondence   D. countenance

11. A. corpuscles   B. mischievous
    C. batchelor   D. bulletin

12. A. terrace   B. banister   C. concrete   D. masonery   12.____

13. A. balluster   B. gutter   C. latch   D. bridging   13.____

14. A. personnell   B. navel   C. therefor   D. emigrant   14.____

15. A. committee   B. submiting   15.____
    C. amendment   D. electorate

KEY (CORRECT ANSWERS)

1.	D	6.	B	11.	C
2.	A	7.	B	12.	D
3.	C	8.	B	13.	A
4.	B	9.	C	14.	A
5.	A	10.	B	15.	B

TEST 7

Questions 1-5.

DIRECTIONS: Questions 1 through 5 consist of groups of four words. Select answer:
A if only ONE word is spelled correctly in a group
B if TWO words are spelled correctly in a group
C if THREE words are spelled correctly in a group
D if all FOUR words are spelled correctly in a group

1.   counterfeit,   embarass,   panicky,   supercede   1.___

2.   benefited,   personnel,   questionnaire,   unparalelled   2.___

3.   bankruptcy   describable,   proceed,   vacuum   3.___

4.   handicapped,   mispell,   offerred,   pilgrimmage   4.___

5.   corduroy,   interfere,   privilege,   separator   5.___

Questions 6-10.

DIRECTIONS: Questions 6 through 10 consist of four pairs of words each. Some of the words are spelled correctly; others are spelled incorrectly. For each question, indicate in the space at the right the letter preceding that pair of words in which BOTH words are spelled CORRECTLY.

6.   A.   hygienic, inviegle   B.   omniscience, pittance   6.___
     C.   plagarize, nullify   D.   seargent, perilous

7.   A.   auxilary, existence   B.   pronounciation, accordance   7.___
     C.   ignominy, indegence   D.   suable, baccalaureate

8.   A.   discreet, inaudible   B.   hypocrisy, currupt   8.___
     C.   liquidate, maintainance   D.   transparancy, onerous

9.   A.   facility, stimulent   B.   frugel, sanitary   9.___
     C.   monetary, prefatory   D.   punctileous, credentials

10.   A.   bankruptsy, perceptible   B.   disuade, resilient   10.___
      C.   exhilerate, expectancy   D.   panegyric, disparate

Questions 11-15

DIRECTIONS: Each question or incomplete statement is followed by several suggested answers or completions. Select the one that BEST answers the question or completes the statement. PRINT THE LETTER OF THE CORRECT ANSWER IN THE SPACE AT THE RIGHT.

11.   The silent e must be retained when the suffix -able is added to the word   11.___

   A.   argue   B.   love   C.   move   D.   notice

12.   The CORRECTLY spelled word in the choices below is   12.___

   A.   kindergarden   B.   zylophone
   C.   hemorrhage   D.   mayonaise

13. Of the following words, the one spelled CORRECTLY is   13.____

    A. begger   B. cemetary
    C. embarassed   D. coyote

14. Of the following words, the one spelled CORRECTLY is   14.____

    A. dandilion   B. wiry   C. sieze   D. rythmic

15. Of the following words, the one spelled CORRECTLY is   15.____

    A. beligerent   B. anihilation
    C. facetious   D. adversery

KEY (CORRECT ANSWERS)

1.	B	6.	B	11.	D
2.	C	7.	D	12.	C
3.	D	8.	A	13.	D
4.	A	9.	C	14.	B
5.	D	10.	D	15.	C

TEST 8

DIRECTIONS: In each of the following sentences, one word is misspelled. Following each sentence is a list of four words taken from the sentence. Indicate the letter of the word which is MISSPELLED. *PRINT THE LETTER OF THE CORRECT ANSWER IN THE SPACE AT THE RIGHT.*

1. If the administrator attempts to withold information, there is a good likelihood that there will be serious repercussions.

   A. administrator
   C. likelihood

   B. withold
   D. repercussions

   1._____

2. He condescended to apologize, but we felt that a beligerent person should not occupy an influential position.

   A. condescended
   C. beligerent

   B. apologize
   D. influential

   2._____

3. Despite the sporadic delinquent payments of his indebtedness, Mr. Johnson has been an exemplery customer.

   A. sporadic
   C. indebtedness

   B. delinquent
   D. exemplery

   3._____

4. He was appreciative of the support he consistantly acquired, but he felt that he had waited an inordinate length of time for it.

   A. appreciative
   C. acquired

   B. consistantly
   D. inordinate

   4._____

5. Undeniably they benefited from the establishment of a receivership, but the question of statutary limitations remained unresolved.

   A. undeniably
   C. receivership

   B. benefited
   D. statutary

   5._____

6. Mr. Smith profered his hand as an indication that he considered it a viable contract, but Mr. Nelson alluded to the fact that his colleagues had not been consulted.

   A. profered
   C. alluded

   B. viable
   D. colleagues

   6._____

7. The treatments were beneficial according to the optometrists, and the consensus was that minimal improvement could be expected.

   A. beneficial
   C. consensus

   B. optomotrists
   D. minimal

   7._____

8. Her frivalous manner was unbecoming because the air of solemnity at the cemetery was pervasive.

   A. frivalous
   C. cemetery

   B. solemnity
   D. pervasive

   8._____

9. The clandestine meetings were designed to make the two adversaries more amicable, but they served only to intensify their emnity.

   A. clandestine
   C. amicable

   B. adversaries
   D. emnity

   9._____

10. Do you think that his innovative ideas and financial acumen will help stabalize the fluctu-   10.____
ations of the stock market?

    A. innovative   B. acumen
    C. stabalize   D. fluctuations

11. In order to keep a perpetual inventory, you will have to keep an uninterrupted surveil-   11.____
lance of all the miscellanious stock.

    A. perpetual   B. uninterrupted
    C. surveillance   D. miscellanious

12. She used the art of pursuasion on the children because she found that caustic remarks   12.____
had no perceptible effect on their behavior.

    A. pursuasion   B. caustic
    C. perceptible   D. effect

13. His sacreligious outbursts offended his constituents, and he was summarily removed   13.____
from office by the City Council.

    A. sacreligious   B. constituents
    C. summarily   D. Council

14. They exhorted the contestants to greater efforts, but the exhorbitant costs in terms of   14.____
energy expended resulted in a feeling of lethargy.

    A. exhorted   B. contestants
    C. exhorbitant   D. lethargy

15. Since he was knowledgable about illicit drugs, he was served with a subpoena to appear   15.____
for the prosecution.

    A. knowledgable   B. illicit
    C. subpoena   D. prosecution

16. In spite of his lucid statements, they denigrated his report and decided it should be suc-   16.____
cintly paraphrased.

    A. lucid   B. denigrated
    C. succintly   D. paraphrased

17. The discussion was not germane to the contraversy, but the indicted man's insistence on   17.____
further talk was allowed.

    A. germane   B. contraversy
    C. indicted   D. insistence

18. The legislators were enervated by the distances they had traveled during the election   18.____
year to fullfil their speaking engagements.

    A. legislators   B. enervated
    C. traveled   D. fullfil

19. The plaintiffs' attornies charged the defendant in the case with felonious assault.   19.____

    A. plaintiffs'   B. attornies
    C. defendant   D. felonious

20. It is symptomatic of the times that we try to placate all, but a proposal for new forms of   20.____
disciplinery action was promulgated by the staff.

    A. symptomatic   B. placate
    C. disciplinery   D. promulgated

KEY (CORRECT ANSWERS)

1. B	6. A	11. D	16. C
2. C	7. B	12. A	17. B
3. D	8. A	13. A	18. D
4. B	9. D	14. C	19. B
5. D	10. C	15. A	20. C

TEST 9

DIRECTIONS: Each of Questions 1 through 15 consists of a single word which is spelled either correctly or incorrectly. If the word is spelled CORRECTLY, you are to print the letter C (Correct) in the space at the right. If the word is spelled INCORRECTLY, you are to print the letter W (Wrong).

1. pospone   1._____

2. diffrent   2._____

3. height   3._____

4. carefully   4._____

5. ability   5._____

6. temper   6._____

7. deslike   7._____

8. seldem   8._____

9. alcohol   9._____

10. expense   10._____

11. vegatable   11._____

12. dispensary   12._____

13. specemin   13._____

14. allowance   14._____

15. exersise   15._____

KEY (CORRECT ANSWERS)

1.	W	6.	C	11.	W
2.	W	7.	W	12.	C
3.	C	8.	W	13.	W
4.	C	9.	C	14.	C
5.	C	10.	C	15.	W

TEST 10

DIRECTIONS: Each of Questions 1 through 10 consists of four words, one of which may be spelled incorrectly or all four words may be spelled correctly. If one of the words in a question is spelled incorrectly, print in the space at the right the capital letter preceding the word which is spelled INCORRECTLY. If all four words are spelled CORRECTLY, print the letter E.

1.	A.	dismissal	B.	collateral	C.	leisure	D.	proffession	1.___
2.	A.	subsidary	B.	outrageous	C.	liaison	D.	assessed	2.___
3.	A.	already	B.	changeable	C.	mischevous	D.	cylinder	3.___
4.	A.	supersede	B.	deceit	C.	dissension	D.	imminent	4.___
5.	A.	arguing	B.	contagious	C.	comparitive	D.	accessible	5.___
6.	A.	indelible	B.	existance	C.	presumptuous	D.	mileage	6.___
7.	A.	extention	B.	aggregate	C.	sustenance	D.	gratuitous	7.___
8.	A.	interrogate	B.	exaggeration	C.	vacillate	D.	moreover	8.___
9.	A.	parallel	B.	derogatory	C.	admissable	D.	appellate	9.___
10.	A.	safety	B.	cumalative	C.	disappear	D.	usable	10.___

KEY (CORRECT ANSWERS)

1.	D		6.	B
2.	A		7.	A
3.	C		8.	E
4.	E		9.	C
5.	C		10.	B

TEST 11

DIRECTIONS: Each of Questions 1 through 10 consists of four words, one of which may be spelled incorrectly or all four words may be spelled correctly. If one of the words in a question is spelled INCORRECTLY, print in the space at the right the capital letter preceding the word which is spelled incorrectly. If all four words are spelled CORRECTLY, print the letter E.

1.	A.	vehicular	B.	gesticulate		1.____	
	C.	manageable	D.	fullfil			
2.	A.	inovation	B.	onerous		2.____	
	C.	chastise	D.	irresistible			
3.	A.	familiarize	B.	dissolution		3.____	
	C.	oscillate	D.	superflous			
4.	A.	census	B.	defender		4.____	
	C.	adherence	D.	inconceivable			
5.	A.	voluminous	B.	liberalize		5.____	
	C.	bankrupcy	D.	conversion			
6.	A.	justifiable	B.	executor		6.____	
	C.	perpatrate	D.	dispelled			
7.	A.	boycott	B.	abeyence		7.____	
	C.	enterprise	D.	circular			
8.	A.	spontaineous	B.	dubious		8.____	
	C.	analyze	D.	premonition			
9.	A.	intelligible	B.	apparently		9.____	
	C.	genuine	D.	crucial			
10.	A.	plentiful	B.	ascertain		10.____	
	C.	carreer	D.	preliminary			

KEY (CORRECT ANSWERS)

1.	D	6.	C
2.	A	7.	B
3.	D	8.	A
4.	E	9.	E
5.	C	10.	C

TEST 12

DIRECTIONS: Questions 1 through 25 consist of four words each, of which one of the words may be spelled incorrectly or all four words may be spelled correctly. If one of the words in a question is spelled INCORRECTLY, print in the space at the right the capital letter preceding the word which is spelled incorrectly. If all four words are spelled CORRECTLY, print the letter E.

1. A. temporary   B. existance   1.___
    C. complimentary   D. altogether

2. A. privilege   B. changeable   2.___
    C. jeopardize   D. commitment

3. A. grievous   B. alloted   3.___
    C. outrageous   D. mortgage

4. A. tempermental   B. accommodating   4.___
    C. bookkeeping   D. panicky

5. A. auxiliary   B. indispensable   5.___
    C. ecstasy   D. fiery

6. A. dissappear   B. buoyant   6.___
    C. imminent   D. parallel

7. A. loosly   B. medicine   7.___
    C. schedule   D. defendant

8. A. endeavor   B. persuade   8.___
    C. retroactive   D. desparate

9. A. usage   B. servicable   9.___
    C. disadvantageous D. remittance

10. A. beneficary   B. receipt   10.___
    C. excitable   D. implement

11. A. accompanying   B. intangible   11.___
    C. offerred   D. movable

12. A. controlling   B. seize   12.___
    C. repetitious   D. miscellaneous

13. A. installation   B. accommodation   13.___
    C. consistant   D. illuminate

14. A. incidentaly   B. privilege   14.___
    C. apparent   D. chargeable

15. A. prevalent   B. serial   15.___
    C. briefly   D. disatisfied

54

16.	A. reciprocal C. persistence	B. concurrence D. withold	16.____
17.	A. deferred C. fulfilled	B. suing D. pursuant	17.____
18.	A. questionnable C. acknowledgment	B. omission D. insistent	18.____
19.	A. guarantee C. mitigate	B. committment D. publicly	19.____
20.	A. prerogative C. extrordinary	B. apprise D. continual	20.____
21.	A. arrogant C. judicious	B. handicapped D. perennial	21.____
22.	A. permissable C. innumerable	B. deceive D. retrieve	22.____
23.	A. notable C. reimburse	B. allegiance D. illegal	23.____
24.	A. wholly C. hindrance	B. disbursement D. conciliatory	24.____
25.	A. guidance C. publically	B. condemn D. coercion	25.____

KEY (CORRECT ANSWERS)

1.	B	11.	C
2.	E	12.	E
3.	B	13.	C
4.	A	14.	A
5.	E	15.	D
6.	A	16.	D
7.	A	17.	E
8.	D	18.	A
9.	B	19.	B
10.	A	20.	C

21.	E
22.	A
23.	E
24.	E
25.	C

SPELLING
EXAMINATION SECTION
TEST 1

DIRECTIONS: In each of the following tests in this part, select the letter of the one MIS-SPELLED word in each of the following groups of words. *PRINT THE LETTER OF THE CORRECT ANSWER IN THE SPACE AT THE RIGHT.*

1. A. grateful   B. fundimental   1.____
    C. census   D. analysis

2. A. installment   B. retrieve   2.____
    C. concede   D. dissapear

3. A. accidentaly   B. dismissal   3.____
    C. conscientious   D. indelible

4. A. perceive   B. carreer   C. anticipate   D. acquire   4.____

5. A. facillity   B. reimburse   C. assortment   D. guidance   5.____

6. A. plentiful   B. across   6.____
    C. advantagous   D. similar

7. A. omission   B. pamphlet   C. guarrantee   D. repel   7.____

8. A. maintenance   B. always   8.____
    C. liable   D. anouncement

9. A. exaggerate   B. sieze   C. condemn   D. commit   9.____

10. A. pospone   B. altogether   C. grievance   D. excessive   10.____

11. A. banana   B. trafic   C. spectacle   D. boundary   11.____

12. A. commentator   B. abbreviation   12.____
    C. battaries   D. monastery

13. A. practically   B. advise   13.____
    C. pursuade   D. laboratory

14. A. fatigueing   B. invincible   14.____
    C. strenuous   D. ceiling

15. A. propeller   B. reverence   C. piecemeal   D. underneth   15.____

16. A. annonymous   B. envelope   C. transit   D. variable   16.____

17. A. petroleum   B. bigoted   C. meager   D. resistence   17.____

18. A. permissible   B. indictment   18.____
    C. fundemental   D. nowadays

19. A. thief   B. bargin   C. nuisance   D. vacant   19.____

20. A. technique   B. vengeance   C. aquatic   D. heighth   20.____

KEY (CORRECT ANSWERS)

1. B. fundamental
2. D. disappear
3. A. accidentally
4. B. career
5. A. facility

6. C. advantageous
7. C. guarantee
8. D. announcement
9. B. seize
10. A. postpone

11. B. traffic
12. C. batteries
13. C. persuade
14. A. fatiguing
15. D. underneath

16. A. anonymous
17. D. resistance
18. C. fundamental
19. B. bargain
20. D. height

———

TEST 2

DIRECTIONS: In each of the following tests in this part, select the letter of the one MIS-
SPELLED word in each of the following groups of words. *PRINT THE LETTER
OF THE CORRECT ANSWER IN THE SPACE AT THE RIGHT.*

1. A. apparent   B. superintendent   1._____
    C. releive   D. calendar

2. A. foreign   B. negotiate   C. typical   D. disipline   2._____

3. A. posponed   B. argument   3._____
    C. susceptible   D. deficit

4. A. preferred   B. column   C. peculiar   D. equiped   4._____

5. A. exaggerate   B. disatisfied   5._____
    C. repetition   D. already

6. A. livelihood   B. physician   C. obsticle   D. strategy   6._____

7. A. courageous   B. ommission   C. ridiculous   D. awkward   7._____

8. A. sincerely   B. abundance   C. negligable   D. elementary   8._____

9. A. obsolete   B. mischievous   9._____
    C. enumerate   D. atheletic

10. A. fiscel   B. beneficiary   10._____
    C. concede   D. translate

11. A. segregate   B. excessivly   C. territory   D. obstacle   11._____

12. A. unnecessary   B. monopolys   12._____
    C. harmonious   D. privilege

13. A. sinthetic   B. intellectual   13._____
    C. gracious   D. archaic

14. A. beneficial B. fulfill   C. sarcastic   D. disolve   14._____

15. A. umbrella   B. sentimental   15._____
    C. ineffecent   D. psychiatrist

16. A. noticable   B. knapsack   C. librarian   D. meant   16._____

17. A. conference B. upheaval   C. vulger   D. odor   17._____

18. A. surmount   B. pentagon   C. calorie   D. inumerable   18._____

19. A. classifiable   B. moisturize   19._____
    C. monitor   D. assesment

20. A. thermastat B. corrupting   C. approach   D. thinness   20._____

_____

KEY (CORRECT ANSWERS)

1. C. relieve
2. D. discipline
3. A. postponed
4. D. equipped
5. B. dissatisfied

6. C. obstacle
7. B. omission
8. C. negligible
9. D. athletic
10. A. fiscal

11. B. excessively
12. B. monopolies
13. A. synthetic
14. D. dissolve
15. C. inefficient

16. A. noticeable
17. C. vulgar
18. D. innumerable
19. D. assessment
20. A. thermostat

———

TEST 3

DIRECTIONS: In each of the following tests in this part, select the letter of the one MIS-SPELLED word in each of the following groups of words. *PRINT THE LETTER OF THE CORRECT ANSWER IN THE SPACE AT THE RIGHT.*

1.   A. typical   B. descend   C. summarize   D. continuel   1._____

2.   A. courageous   B. recomend   C. omission   D. eliminate   2._____

3.   A. compliment   B. illuminate   3._____
     C. auxilary   D. installation

4.   A. preliminary   B. aquainted   4._____
     C. syllable   D. analysis

5.   A. accustomed   B. negligible   C. interupted   D. bulletin   5._____

6.   A. summoned   B. managment   C. mechanism   D. sequence   6._____

7.   A. commitee   B. surprise   C. noticeable   D. emphasize   7._____

8.   A. occurrance   B. likely   C. accumulate   D. grievance   8._____

9.   A. obstacle   B. particuliar   9._____
     C. baggage   D. fascinating

10.   A. innumerable   B. seize   10._____
     C. applicant   D. dictionery

11.   A. monkeys   B. rigid   C. unnatural   D. roomate   11._____

12.   A. surveying   B. figurative   C. famous   D. curiosety   12._____

13.   A. rodeo   B. inconcievable   13._____
     C. calendar   D. magnificence

14.   A. handicaped   B. glacier   C. defiance   D. emperor   14._____

15.   A. schedule   B. scrawl   C. seclusion   D. sissors   15._____

16.   A. tissues   B. tomatos   C. tyrants   D. tragedies   16._____

17.   A. casette   B. graceful   C. penicillin   D. probably   17._____

18.   A. gnawed   B. microphone   C. clinicle   D. batch   18._____

19.   A. amateur   B. altitude   C. laborer   D. expence   19._____

20.   A. mandate   B. flexable   C. despise   D. verify   20._____

KEY (CORRECT ANSWERS)

1. D. continual
2. B. recommend
3. C. auxiliary
4. B. acquainted
5. C. interrupted

6. B. management
7. A. committee
8. A. occurrence
9. B. particular
10. D. dictionary

11. D. roommate
12. D. curiosity
13. B. inconceivable
14. A. handicapped
15. D. scissors

16. B. tomatoes
17. A. cassette
18. C. clinical
19. D. expense
20. B. flexible

TEST 4

DIRECTIONS: In each of the following tests in this part, select the letter of the one MIS-SPELLED word in each of the following groups of words. *PRINT THE LETTER OF THE CORRECT ANSWER IN THE SPACE AT THE RIGHT.*

1. A. primery   B. mechanic   C. referred   D. admissible   1.____

2. A. cessation   B. beleif   C. aggressive   D. allowance   2.____

3. A. leisure   B. authentic   3.____
   C. familiar   D. contemptable

4. A. volume   B. forty   C. dilemma   D. seldum   4.____

5. A. discrepancy   B. aquisition   5.____
   C. exorbitant   D. lenient

6. A. simultanous   B. penetrate   6.____
   C. revision   D. conspicuous

7. A. ilegible   B. gracious   C. profitable   D. obedience   7.____

8. A. manufacturer   B. authorize   8.____
   C. compelling   D. pecular

9. A. anxious   B. rehearsal   C. handicaped   D. tendency   9.____

10. A. meticulous   B. accompaning   10.____
    C. initiative   D. shelves

11. A. hammaring   B. insecticide   11.____
    C. capacity   D. illogical

12. A. budget   B. luminous   C. aviation   D. lunchon   12.____

13. A. moniter   B. bachelor   13.____
    C. pleasurable   D. omitted

14. A. monstrous   B. transistor   C. narrative   D. anziety   14.____

15. A. engagement B. judical   C. pasteurize   D. tried   15.____

16. A. fundimental   B. innovation   16.____
    C. perpendicular   D. extravagant

17. A. bookkeeper B. brutality   C. gymnaseum   D. cemetery   17.____

18. A. sturdily   B. pretentious   18.____
    C. gourmet   D. enterance

19. A. resturant   B. tyranny   19.____
    C. kindergarten   D. ancestry

20. A. benefit   B. possess   C. speciman   D. noticing   20.____

KEY (CORRECT ANSWERS)

1. A. primary
2. B. belief
3. D. contemptible
4. D. seldom
5. B. acquisition

6. A. simultaneous
7. A. illegible
8. D. peculiar
9. C. handicapped
10. B. accompanying

11. A. hammering
12. D. luncheon
13. A. monitor
14. D. anxiety
15. B. judicial

16. A. fundamental
17. C. gymnasium
18. D. entrance
19. A. restaurant
20. C. specimen

TEST 5

DIRECTIONS: In each of the following tests in this part, select the letter of the one MIS-SPELLED word in each of the following groups of words. *PRINT THE LETTER OF THE CORRECT ANSWER IN THE SPACE AT THE RIGHT.*

1. A. arguing   B. correspondance   1._____
    C. forfeit   D. dissension

2. A. occasion   B. description   2._____
    C. prejudice   D. elegible

3. A. accomodate   B. initiative   C. changeable   D. enroll   3._____

4. A. temporary   B. insistent   C. benificial   D. separate   4._____

5. A. achieve   B. dissappoint   5._____
    C. unanimous   D. judgment

6. A. procede   B. publicly   C. sincerity   D. successful   6._____

7. A. deceive   B. goverment   C. preferable   D. repetitive   7._____

8. A. emphasis   B. skillful   C. advisible   D. optimistic   8._____

9. A. tendency   B. rescind   C. crucial   D. noticable   9._____

10. A. privelege   B. abbreviate   C. simplify   D. divisible   10._____

11. A. irresistible   B. varius   11._____
    C. mutual   D. refrigerator

12. A. amateur   B. distinguish   12._____
    C. rehearsal   D. poision

13. A. biased   B. ommission   C. precious   D. coordinate   13._____

14. A. calculated   B. enthusiasm   C. sincerely   D. parashute   14._____

15. A. sentry   B. materials   C. incredable   D. budget   15._____

16. A. chocolate   B. instrument   C. volcanoe   D. shoulder   16._____

17. A. ancestry   B. obscure   C. intention   D. ninty   17._____

18. A. artical   B. bracelet   C. beggar   D. hopeful   18._____

19. A. tournament   B. sponsor   19._____
    C. perpendiclar   D. dissolve

20. A. yeild   B. physician   C. greasiest   D. admitting   20._____

—————

KEY (CORRECT ANSWERS)

1. B. correspondence
2. D. eligible
3. A. accommodate
4. C. beneficial
5. B. disappoint

6. A. proceed
7. B. government
8. C. advisable
9. D. noticeable
10. A. privilege

11. B. various
12. D. poison
13. B. omission
14. D. parachute
15. C. incredible

16. C. volcano
17. D. ninety
18. A. article
19. C. perpendicular
20. A. yield

TEST 6

DIRECTIONS: In each of the following tests in this part, select the letter of the one MIS-
SPELLED word in each of the following groups of words. *PRINT THE LETTER
OF THE CORRECT ANSWER IN THE SPACE AT THE RIGHT.*

1.   A.   achievment   B.   maintenance   1.____
     C.   questionnaire   D.   all are correct

2.   A.   prevelant   B.   pronunciation   2.____
     C.   separate   D.   all are correct

3.   A.   permissible   B.   relevant   3.____
     C.   seize   D.   all are correct

4.   A.   corroborate   B.   desparate   4.____
     C.   eighth   D.   all are correct

5.   A.   exceed   B.   feasibility   5.____
     C.   psycological   D.   all are correct

6.   A.   parallel   B.   aluminum   C.   calendar   D.   eigty   6.____

7.   A.   microbe   B.   ancient   C.   autograph   D.   existance   7.____

8.   A.   plentiful   B.   skillful   C.   amoung   D.   capsule   8.____

9.   A.   erupt   B.   quanity   C.   opinion   D.   competent   9.____

10. A.   excitement   B.   discipline   C.   luncheon   D.   regreting   10.____

11. A.   magazine   B.   expository   C.   imitation   D.   permenent   11.____

12. A.   ferosious   B.   machinery   12.____
     C.   precise   D.   magnificent

13. A.   conceive   B.   narritive   C.   separation   D.   management   13.____

14. A.   muscular   B.   witholding   C.   pickle   D.   glacier   14.____

15. A.   vehicel   B.   mismanage   15.____
     C.   correspondence   D.   dissatisfy

16. A.   sentince   B.   bulletin   C.   notice   D.   definition   16.____

17. A.   appointment   B.   exactly   17.____
     C.   typest   D.   light

18. A.   penalty   B.   suparvise   C.   consider   D.   division   18.____

19. A.   schedule   B.   accurate   C.   corect   D.   simple   19.____

20. A.   suggestion   B.   installed   C.   proper   D.   agincy   20.____

KEY (CORRECT ANSWERS)

1. A. achievement
2. A. prevalent
3. D all are correct
4. B. desperate
5. C. psychological

6. D. eighty
7. D. existence
8. C. among
9. B. quantity
10. D. regretting

11. D. permanent
12. A. ferocious
13. B. narrative
14. B. withholding
15. A. vehicle

16. A. sentence
17. C. typist
18. B. supervise
19. C. correct
20. D. agency

_____

TEST 7

DIRECTIONS: In each of the following tests in this part, select the letter of the one MIS-SPELLED word in each of the following groups of words. *PRINT THE LETTER OF THE CORRECT ANSWER IN THE SPACE AT THE RIGHT.*

1.   A. symtom   B. serum   C. antiseptic   D. aromatic   1.____

2.   A. register   B. registrar   C. purser   D. burser   2.____

3.   A. athletic   B. tragedy   C. batallion   D. sophomore   3.____

4.   A. latent   B. godess   C. aisle   D. whose   4.____

5.   A. rhyme   B. rhythm   C. thime   D. thine   5.____

6.   A. eighth   B. exaggerate   C. electorial   D. villain   6.____

7.   A. statute   B. superintendent   7.____
      C. iresistible   D. colleague

8.   A. sieze   B. therefor   C. auxiliary   D. changeable   8.____

9.   A. siege   B. knowledge   C. lieutenent   D. weird   9.____

10.   A. acquitted   B. polititian   C. professor   D. conqueror   10.____

11.   A. changeable   B. chargeable   C. salable   D. useable   11.____

12.   A. promissory   B. prisoner   C. excellent   D. tyrrany   12.____

13.   A. conspicuous   B. essance   13.____
      C. comparative   D. brilliant

14.   A. notefying   B. accentuate   C. adhesive   D. primarily   14.____

15.   A. exercise   B. sublime   C. stuborn   D. shameful   15.____

16.   A. presume   B. transcript   C. strech   D. wizard   16.____

17.   A. specify   B. regional   17.____
      C. arbitrary   D. segragation

18.   A. requirement   B. happiness   18.____
      C. achievement   D. gentlely

19.   A. endurance   B. fusion   C. balloon   D. enormus   19.____

20.   A. luckily   B. schedule   C. simplicity   D. sanwich   20.____

KEY (CORRECT ANSWERS)

1. A. symptom
2. D. bursar
3. C. battalion
4. B. goddess
5. C. thyme

6. C. electoral
7. C. irresistible
8. A. seize
9. C. lieutenant
10. B. politician

11. D. usable
12. D. tyranny
13. B. essence
14. A. notifying
15. C. stubborn

16. C. stretch
17. D. segregation
18. D. gently
19. D. enormous
20. D. sandwich

TEST 8

DIRECTIONS: In each of the following tests in this part, select the letter of the one MIS-SPELLED word in each of the following groups of words. *PRINT THE LETTER OF THE CORRECT ANSWER IN THE SPACE AT THE RIGHT.*

1. A. maintain   B. maintainance   1._____
    C. sustain   D. sustenance

2. A. portend   B. portentious   2._____
    C. pretend   D. pretentious

3. A. prophesize   B. prophesies   3._____
    C. farinaceous   D. spaceous

4. A. choose   B. chose   C. choosen   D. chasten   4._____

5. A. censure   B. censorious   5._____
    C. pleasure   D. pleasurible

6. A. cover   B. coverage   C. adder   D. adege   6._____

7. A. balloon   B. diregible   C. direct   D. descent   7._____

8. A. whemsy   B. crazy   C. flimsy   D. lazy   8._____

9. A. derision B. pretention C. sustention D. contention   9._____

10. A. question   B. questionaire   10._____
    C. legion   D. legionary

11. A. chattle   B. cattle   C. dismantle D. kindle   11._____

12. A. canal   B. cannel   C. chanel   D. colonel 12._____

13. A. hemorrage B. storage   C. manage   D. foliage 13._____

14. A. surgeon   B. sturgeon   C. luncheon   D. stancheon 14._____

15. A. diploma   B. commission C. dependent D. luminious 15._____

16. A. likelihood B. blizzard   C. machanical D. suppress 16._____

17. A. commercial B. releif   C. disposal   D. endeavor 17._____

18. A. operate   B. bronco   C. excaping   D. grammar 18._____

19. A. orchard   B. collar   C. embarass   D. distant 19._____

20. A. sincerly B. possessive C. weighed   D. waist   20._____

KEY (CORRECT ANSWERS)

1. B. maintenance
2. B. portentous
3. D. spacious
4. C. chosen
5. D. pleasurable

6. D. adage
7. B. dirigible
8. A. whimsy
9. B. pretension
10. B. questionnaire

11. A. chattel
12. C. channel
13. A. hemorrhage
14. D. stanchion
15. D. luminous

16. C. mechanical
17. B. relief
18. C. escaping
19. C. embarrass
20. A. sincerely

TEST 9

DIRECTIONS: In each of the following tests in this part, select the letter of the one MIS-SPELLED word in each of the following groups of words. *PRINT THE LETTER OF THE CORRECT ANSWER IN THE SPACE AT THE RIGHT.*

1.   A.   statute   B.   stationary   1.____
     C.   staturesque   D.   stature

2.   A.   practicible   B.   practical   2.____
     C.   particle   D.   reticule

3.   A.   plague   B.   plaque   C.   ague   D.   aigrete   3.____

4.   A.   theology   B.   idealogy   C.   psychology   D.   philology   4.____

5.   A.   dilema   B.   stamina   C.   feminine   D.   strychnine 5.____

6.   A.   deceit   B.   benefit   C.   grieve   D.   hienous   6.____

7.   A.   commensurable   B.   measurable   7.____
     C.   duteable   D.   salable

8.   A.   homogeneous   B.   heterogeneous   8.____
     C.   advantageous   D.   religeous

9.   A.   criticize   B.   dramatise   C.   exorcise   D.   exercise   9.____

10. A.   ridiculous   B.   comparable C.   merciful   D.   cotten   10.____

11. A.   antebiotic   B.   stitches   C.   pitiful   D.   sneaky   11.____

12. A.   amendment   B.   candadate   12.____
     C.   accountable   D.   recommendation

13. A.   avocado   B.   recruit   C.   tripping   D.   probally   13.____

14. A.   calendar   B.   desirable   C.   familar   D.   vacuum   14.____

15. A.   deteriorate   B.   elligible   15.____
     C.   liable   D.   missile

16. A.   amateur   B.   competent   16.____
     C.   mischeivous   D.   occasion

17. A.   friendliness   B.   saleries   17.____
     C.   cruelty   D.   ammunition

18. A.   wholesome   B.   cieling   C.   stupidity   D.   eligible   18.____

19. A.   comptroller   B.   traveled   19.____
     C.   accede   D.   procede

20. A.   Britain   B.   Brittainica   20.____
     C.   conductor   D.   vendor

KEY (CORRECT ANSWERS)

1. C. statuesque
2. A. practicable
3. D. aigrette
4. B. ideology
5. A. dilemma

6. D. heinous
7. C. dutiable
8. D. religious
9. B. dramatize
10. D. cotton

11. A. antibiotic
12. B. candidate
13. D. probably
14. C. familiar
15. B. eligible

16. C. mischievous
17. B. salaries
18. B. ceiling
19. D. proceed
20. B. Brittanica

TEST 10

DIRECTIONS: In each of the following tests in this part, select the letter of the one MIS-SPELLED word in each of the following groups of words. *PRINT THE LETTER OF THE CORRECT ANSWER IN THE SPACE AT THE RIGHT.*

1. A. lengthen   B. region   C. gases   D. inspecter   1.____

2. A. imediately   B. forbidden
    C. complimentary   D. aeronautics   2.____

3. A. continuous   B. paralel   C. opposite   D. definite   3.____

4. A. Antarctic   B. Wednesday   C. Febuary   D. Hungary   4.____

5. A. transmission   B. exposure
    C. pistol   D. customery   5.____

6. A. juvinile   B. martyr
    C. deceive   D. collaborate   6.____

7. A. unnecessary   B. repetitive
    C. cancellation   D. airey   7.____

8. A. transit   B. availible   C. objection   D. galaxy   8.____

9. A. ineffective   B. believeable
    C. arrangement   D. aggravate   9.____

10. A. possession   B. progress   C. reception   D. predjudice   10.____

11. A. congradulate   B. percolate
    C. major   D. leisure   11.____

12. A. convenience   B. privilige
    C. emerge   D. immerse   12.____

13. A. erasable   B. inflammable
    C. audable   D. laudable   13.____

14. A. final   B. fines   C. finis   D. Finish   14.____

15. A. emitted   B. representative
    C. discipline   D. insistance   15.____

16. A. diphthong   B. rarified   C. library   D. recommend   16.____

17. A. compel   B. belligerent
    C. successful   D. sargeant   17.____

18. A. dispatch   B. dispise   C. dispose   D. dispute   18.____

19. A. administrator   B. adviser
    C. diner   D. celluler   19.____

20. A. ignite   B. ignision   C. igneous   D. ignited   20.____

KEY (CORRECT ANSWERS)

1. D. inspector
2. A. immediately
3. B. parallel
4. C. February
5. D. customary

6. A. juvenile
7. D. airy
8. B. available
9. B. believable
10. D. prejudice

11. A. congratulate
12. B. privilege
13. C. audible
14. D. Finnish
15. D. insistence

16. B. rarefied
17. D. sergeant
18. B. despise
19. D. cellular
20. B. ignition

_____

TEST 11

DIRECTIONS: In each of the following tests in this part, select the letter of the one MIS-
SPELLED word in each of the following groups of words. *PRINT THE LETTER
OF THE CORRECT ANSWER IN THE SPACE AT THE RIGHT.*

1. A. repellent   B. secession   C. sebaceous   D. saxaphone   1.____

2. A. navel   B. counteresolution   2.____
    C. marginalia   D. perceptible

3. A. Hammerskjold   B. Nehru   3.____
    C. U Thamt   D. Khrushchev

4. A. perculate   B. periwinkle   4.____
    C. perigee   D. retrogression

5. A. buccaneer   B. tobacco   C. buffalo   D. oscilate   5.____

6. A. siege   B. wierd   C. seize   D. cemetery   6.____

7. A. equaled   B. bigoted   7.____
    C. benefited   D. kaleideoscope

8. A. blamable   B. bullrush   8.____
    C. questionnaire   D. irascible

9. A. tobagganed   B. acquiline   9.____
    C. capillary   D. cretonne

10. A. daguerrotype   B. elegiacal   10.____
    C. iridescent   D. inchoate

11. A. bayonet   B. braggadocio   11.____
    C. corollary   D. connoiseur

12. A. equinoctial   B. fusillade   12.____
    C. fricassee   D. potpouri

13. A. octameter   B. impressario   13.____
    C. hyetology   D. hieroglyphics

14. A. innanity   B. idyllic   C. fylfot   D. inimical   14.____

15. A. liquefy   B. rarefy   C. putrify   D. sapphire   15.____

16. A. canonical   B. stupified   16.____
    C. millennium   D. memorabilia

17. A. paraphenalia   B. odyssey   17.____
    C. onomatopoeia   D. osseous

18. A. peregrinate   B. pecadillo   18.____
    C. reptilian   D. uxorious

19. A. pharisaical   B. vicissitude   19.____
    C. puissance   D. wainright

20. A. holocaust   B. tesselate   C. scintilla   D. staccato   20.____

KEY (CORRECT ANSWERS)

1. D. saxophone
2. B. counterresolution
3. C. U Thant
4. A. percolate
5. D. oscillate

6. B. weird
7. D. kaleidoscope
8. B. bulrush
9. B. aquiline
10. A. daguerreotype

11. D. connoisseur
12. D. potpourri
13. B. impresario
14. A. inanity
15. C. putrefy

16. B. stupefied
17. A. paraphernalia
18. B. peccadillo
19. D. wainwright
20. B. tessellate

TEST 12

DIRECTIONS: In each of the following tests in this part, select the letter of the one MIS-SPELLED word in each of the following groups of words. *PRINT THE LETTER OF THE CORRECT ANSWER IN THE SPACE AT THE RIGHT.*

1. A. questionnaire   B. gondoleer   C. chandelier   D. acquiescence   1._____

2. A. surveillance   B. surfeit   C. vaccinate   D. belligerent   2._____

3. A. occassionally   B. recurrence   C. silhouette   D. incessant   3._____

4. A. transferral   B. benefical   C. descendant   D. dependent   4._____

5. A. separately   B. flouresence   C. deterrent   D. parallel   5._____

6. A. acquittal   B. enforceable   C. counterfeit   D. indispensible   6._____

7. A. susceptible   B. accelarate   C. exhilarate   D. accommodation   7._____

8. A. impedimenta   B. collateral   C. liason   D. epistolary   8._____

9. A. inveigle   B. panegyric   C. reservoir   D. manuver   9._____

10. A. synopsis   B. paraphernalia   C. affidavit   D. subpoena   10._____

11. A. grosgrain   B. vermilion   C. abbatoir   D. connoiseur   11._____

12. A. gabardine   B. camoflage   C. hemorrhage   D. contraband   12._____

13. A. opprobrious   B. defalcate   13._____
     C. fiduciery   D. recommendations

14. A. nebulous   B. necessitate   C. impricate   D. discrepancy   14._____

15. A. discrete   B. condesension   C. condign   D. condiment   15._____

16. A. cavalier   B. effigy   C. legitimatly   D. misalliance   16._____

17. A. rheumatism   B. vaporous   C. cannister   D. hallucinations   17._____

18. A. paleonthology   B. octogenarian   C. gradient   D. impingement   18._____

19. A. fusilade   B. fusilage   C. ensilage   D. desiccate   19._____

20. A. rationale   B. raspberry   C. reprobate   D. varigated   20._____

KEY (CORRECT ANSWERS)

1. B. gondolier
2. A. surveillance
3. A. occasionally
4. B. beneficial
5. B. fluorescence

6. D. indispensable
7. B. accelerate
8. C. liaison
9. D. maneuver
10. B. paraphernalia

11. D. connoisseur
12. B. camouflage
13. C. fiduciary
14. C. imprecate
15. B. condescension

16. C. legitimately
17. C. canister
18. A. paleontology
19. A. fusillade
20. D. variegated

WORD MEANING

EXAMINATION SECTION
TEST 1

DIRECTIONS: For the following questions, select the word or group of words lettered A, B, C, D, or E that means MOST NEARLY the same as the word in capital letters. *PRINT THE LETTER OF THE CORRECT ANSWER IN THE SPACE AT THE RIGHT.*

1. To IMPLY means *most nearly* to   1.____

    A. agree to   B. hint at   C. laugh at   D. mimic   E. reduce

2. APPRAISAL means *most nearly*   2.____

    A. allowance   B. composition
    C. prohibition   D. quantity
    E. valuation

3. To DISBURSE means *most nearly* to   3.____

    A. approve   B. expend   C. prevent   D. relay   E. restrict

4. POSTERITY means *most nearly*   4.____

    A. back payment   B. current procedure   C. final effort
    D. future generations   E. rare specimen

5. PUNCTUAL means *most nearly*   5.____

    A. clear   B. honest   C. polite   D. prompt   E. prudent

6. PRECARIOUS means *most nearly*   6.____

    A. abundant   B. alarmed   C. cautious   D. insecure   E. placid

7. To FOSTER means *most nearly* to   7.____

    A. delegate   B. demote   C. encourage   D. plead   E. surround

8. PINNACLE means *most nearly*   8.____

    A. center   B. crisis
    C. outcome   D. peak
    E. personification

9. COMPONENT means *most nearly*   9.____

    A. flattery   B. opposite   C. trend   D. revision   E. element

10. To SOLICIT means *most nearly* to   10.____

    A. ask   B. prohibit   C. promise   D. revoke   E. surprise

11. LIAISON means *most nearly*   11.____

    A. asset   B. coordination
    C. difference   D. policy
    E. procedure

12. To ALLEGE means *most nearly* to   12.____

    A. assert   B. break   C. irritate   D. reduce   E. wait

13. INFILTRATION means *most nearly*   13.____

    A. consumption   B. disposal
    C. enforcement   D. penetration
    E. seizure

14. To SALVAGE means *most nearly* to   14.____

    A. announce   B. combine   C. prolong   D. try   E. save

15. MOTIVE means *most nearly*   15.____

    A. attack   B. favor   C. incentive   D. patience   E. tribute

16. To PROVOKE means *most nearly* to   16.____

    A. adjust   B. incite   C. leave   D. obtain   E. practice

17. To SURGE means *most nearly* to   17.____

    A. branch   B. contract   C. revenge   D. rush   E. want

18. To MAGNIFY means *most nearly* to   18.____

    A. attract   B. demand   C. generate   D. increase   E. puzzle

19. PREPONDERANCE means *most nearly*   19.____

    A. decision   B. judgment   C. superiority   D. submission   E. warning

20. To ABATE means *most nearly* to   20.____

    A. assist   B. coerce   C. diminish   D. indulge   E. trade

---

KEY (CORRECT ANSWERS)

1. B	6. D	11. B	16. B
2. E	7. C	12. A	17. D
3. B	8. D	13. D	18. D
4. D	9. E	14. E	19. C
5. D	10. A	15. C	20. C

TEST 2

DIRECTIONS: For the following questions, select the word or group of words lettered A, B, C, D, or E that means MOST NEARLY the same as the word in capital letters. *PRINT THE LETTER OF THE CORRECT ANSWER IN THE SPACE AT THE RIGHT.*

1. AVARICE means *most nearly*
   A. flight   B. greed   C. pride   D. thrift   E. average

   1.____

2. PREDATORY means *most nearly*
   A. offensive   B. plundering   C. previous   D. timeless   E. perilous

   2.____

3. To VINDICATE means *most nearly* to
   A. clear   B. conquer   C. correct   D. illustrate   E. alleviate

   3.____

4. INVETERATE means *most nearly*
   A. backward   B. erect   C. habitual   D. lucky   E. gradual

   4.____

5. To DISCERN means most nearly to
   A. describe   B. fabricate   C. recognize   D. seek   E. dilute

   5.____

6. COMPLACENT means *most nearly*
   7. indulgent   8. listless   9. overjoyed   10. satisfied   11. pliant

   6.____

7. ILLICIT means *most nearly*
   A. insecure   B. unclear   C. eligible   D. unlimited   E. unlawful

   7.____

8. To PROCRASTINATE means *most nearly* to
   A. declare   B. multiply   C. postpone   D. steal   E. proclaim

   8.____

9. IMPASSIVE means *most nearly*
   A. calm   B. frustrated   C. thoughtful   D. unhappy   E. perturbed

   9.____

10. AMICABLE means *most nearly*
    A. cheerful   B. flexible   C. friendly   D. poised   E. amorous

    10.____

11. FEASIBLE means *most nearly*
    A. breakable   B. easy   C. likeable   D. practicable   E. fearful

    11.____

12. INNOCUOUS means *most nearly*
    A. harmless   B. insecure   C. insincere   D. unfavorable   E. innate

    12.____

13. OSTENSIBLE means most nearly
    A. apparent   B. hesitant   C. reluctant   D. showy   E. concealed

    13.____

14. INDOMITABLE means *most nearly*   14.____

    A. excessive   B. unconquerable   C. unreasonable
    D. unthinkable   E. indubitable

15. CRAVEN means *most nearly*   15.____

    A. carefree   B. hidden   C. miserly   D. needed   E. cowardly

16. To ALLAY means *most nearly* to   16.____

    A. discuss   B. quiet   C. refine   D. remove   E. arrange

17. To ALLUDE means *most nearly* to   17.____

    A. denounce   B. refer   C. state   D. support   E. align

18. NEGLIGENCE means most nearly   18.____

    A. carelessness   B. denial
    C. objection   D. refusal
    E. eagerness

19. To AMEND means *most nearly* to   19.____

    A. correct   B. destroy   C. end   D. list   E. dissent

20. RELEVANT means most nearly   20.____

    A. conclusive   B. careful
    C. obvious   D. related
    E. incompetent

KEY (CORRECT ANSWERS)

1. B	6. D	11. D	16. B
2. B	7. E	12. A	17. B
3. A	8. C	13. A	18. A
4. C	9. A	14. B	19. A
5. C	10. C	15. E	20. D

TEST 3

DIRECTIONS: For the following questions, select the word or group of words lettered A, B, C, D, or E that means MOST NEARLY the same as the word in capital letters. *PRINT THE LETTER OF THE CORRECT ANSWER IN THE SPACE AT THE RIGHT.*

1. CONFIRM means *most nearly*   1.____

   A. belong   B. limit   C. think over   D. verify   E. refine

2. PERILOUS means *most nearly*   2.____

   A. dangerous   B. mysterious   C. tiring   D. undesirable   E. fickle

3. PROFICIENT means *most nearly*   3.____

   A. likable   B. obedient   C. profitable   D. profound   E. skilled

4. IMPLICATE means *most nearly*   4.____

   A. arrest   B. confess   C. involve   D. question   E. imply

5. ASSERT means *most nearly*   5.____

   A. confide   B. help   C. state   D. wish   E. confirm

6. TEDIOUS means *most nearly*   6.____

   A. boring   B. easy   C. educational   D. difficult   E. timorous

7. CONSEQUENCE means *most nearly*   7.____

   A. punishment   B. reason   C. result   D. tragedy   E. basis

8. REPUTABLE means *most nearly*   8.____

   A. durable   B. effective   C. powerful   D. honorable   E. tangible

9. REPROACH means *most nearly*   9.____

   A. anger   B. blame   C. pardon   D. trap   E. repel

10. DIVERSE means *most nearly*   10.____

   A. confused   B. indistinct
   C. unacceptable   D. destructive
   E. unlike

11. EVENTUAL means *most nearly*   11.____

   A. complete   B. exciting   C. final   D. important   E. enticing

12. ACCESSORY means *most nearly*   12.____

   A. accomplice   B. dishonest   C. fugitive   D. planner   E. perpetrator

13. ALLEVIATE means *most nearly*   13.____

   A. enrage   B. increase   C. lessen   D. omit   E. lift up

14. RETICENT means *most nearly*   14.____

    A. doubtful   B. humorous   C. intelligent   D. reserved   E. reliant

15. DILEMMA means *most nearly*   15.____

    A. caution   B. decision
    C. hope   D. direction
    E. predicament

16. FLAUNT means *most nearly*   16.____

    A. compliment B. display   C. punish   D. warn   E. reserve

17. CONCUR means *most nearly*   17.____

    A. agree   B. capture   C. rescue   D. trust   E. disagree

18. REPUDIATE means *most nearly*   18.____

    A. plot   B. reject   C. revise   D. strike   E. attest

19. FRANTIC means *most nearly*   19.____

    A. criminal B. desperate C. jealous   D. indirect   E. sanguine

20. PREMONITION means *most nearly*   20.____

    A. certainty   B. forewarning
    C. puzzle   D. thinking
    E. promise

KEY (CORRECT ANSWERS)

1.	D	6.	A	11.	C	16.	B
2.	A	7.	C	12.	A	17.	A
3.	E	8.	D	13.	C	18.	B
4.	C	9.	B	14.	D	19.	B
5.	C	10.	E	15.	E	20.	B

TEST 4

DIRECTIONS: For the following questions, select the word or group of words lettered A, B, C, D, or E that means MOST NEARLY the same as the word in capital letters. *PRINT THE LETTER OF THE CORRECT ANSWER IN THE SPACE AT THE RIGHT.*

1.   To CONTEND means *most nearly* to   1.____

   A.   claim   B.   defeat   C.   refuse   D.   penalize   E.   contest

2.   EXPEDIENT means *most nearly*   2.____

   A.   fearless   B.   suitable   C.   dishonest   D.   convincing   E.   famous

3.   PROPONENT means *most nearly*   3.____

   A.   basic truth   B.   witness   C.   driver
   D.   supporter   E.   antongist

4.   DUBIOUS means *most nearly*   4.____

   A.   uneventful   B.   silly   C.   uncertain   D.   untrue   E.   firm

5.   CONTRITE means *most nearly*   5.____

   A.   painful   B.   sorry   C.   guilty   D.   hopeful   E.   joyful

6.   To CONCEDE means *most nearly* to   6.____

   A.   suggest   B.   decide   C.   admit   D.   trust   E.   consign

7.   EQUITABLE means *most nearly*   7.____

   A.   peaceful   B.   insurable   C.   lenient   D.   just   E.   equine

8.   To ALIGN means *most nearly* to   8.____

   A.   cheat   B.   slander   C.   misinform   D.   criticize   E.   malinger

9.   To REPRIMAND means *most nearly* to   9.____

   A.   shout   B.   scold
   C.   complain   D.   punish
   E.   recommend

10.   INFLEXIBLE means *most nearly*   10.____

   A.   powerful   B.   impartial   C.   unpopular   D.   unbending   E.   lax

11.   INTACT means *most nearly*   11.____

   A.   considerate   B.   inside   C.   whole   D.   lasting   E.   incomplete

12.   To DETER means *most nearly* to   12.____

   A.   strike   B.   prevent   C.   disagree   D.   loosen   E.   detract

87

13. PRUDENT means *most nearly*   13.____

    A. prudish   B. strict   C. stingy   D. shy   E. cautious

14. REMISS MEANS *most nearly*   14.____

    A. neglectful   B. dishonest   C. prevented   D. evil   E. deceived

15. APPREHENSIVE means *most nearly*   15.____

    A. dangerous   B. harmful   C. sad   D. fearful   E. approved

16. CONTRABAND means *most nearly*   16.____

    A. dissolved   B. illegal   C. fake   D. unknown   E. grouped

17. To DISSEMINATE means *most nearly* to   17.____

    A. spread   B. mislead   C. undermine   D. disagree   E. divert

18. CONTEMPT means *most nearly*   18.____

    A. pity   B. hatred   C. scorn   D. brutality   E. opinion

19. To HARASS means *most nearly* to   19.____

    A. retreat   B. whip   C. control   D. torment   E. harangue

20. OPAQUE means *most nearly*   20.____

    A. thick   B. invisible   C. lucid
    D. light colored   E. not transparent

KEY (CORRECT ANSWERS)

1.	A	6.	C	11.	C	16.	B
2.	B	7.	D	12.	B	17.	A
3.	D	8.	B	13.	E	18.	C
4.	C	9.	B	14.	A	19.	D
5.	B	10.	D	15.	D	20.	E

WORD MEANING
EXAMINATION SECTION
TEST 1

DIRECTIONS: Each question or incomplete statement is followed by several suggested answers or completions. Select the one that BEST answers the question or completes the statement. *PRINT THE LETTER OF THE CORRECT ANSWER IN THE SPACE AT THE RIGHT.*

1. He implied that he would work overtime if necessary.
   In this sentence, the word *implied* means
   1._____

   A. denied
   C. guaranteed
   B. explained
   D. hinted

2. The bag of the vacuum cleaner was inflated.
   In this sentence, the word *inflated* means
   2._____

   A. blown up with air
   C. loose
   B. filled with dirt
   D. torn

3. Burning material during certain hours is prohibited.
   In this sentence, the word *prohibited* means
   3._____

   A. allowed   B. forbidden   C. legal   D. required

4. He was rejected when he applied for the job. In this sentence, the word *rejected* means
   4._____

   A. discouraged
   C. tested
   B. put to work
   D. turned down

5. The foreman was able to substantiate his need for extra supplies.
   In this sentence, the word *substantiate* means
   5._____

   A. estimate   B. meet   C. prove   D. reduce

6. The new instructions supersede the old ones.
   In this sentence, the word *supersede* means
   6._____

   A. explain   B. improve   C. include   D. replace

7. Shake the broom free of surplus water and hang it up to dry.
   In this sentence, the word *surplus* means
   7._____

   A. dirty   B. extra   C. rinse   D. soapy

8. When a crack is filled, the asphalt must be tamped.
   In this sentence, the word *tamped* means
   8._____

   A. cured
   C. packed down
   B. heated
   D. wet down

9. The apartment was left vacant.
   In this sentence, the word *vacant* means
   9._____

   A. clean   B. empty   C. furnished   D. locked

10. The caretaker spent the whole day doing various repairs.
    In this sentence, the word *various* means

    A. different   B. necessary   C. small   D. special

10.____

11. He came back to assist his partner.
    In this sentence, the word *assist* means

    A. call   B. help   C. stop   D. question

11.____

12. A person who is biased cannot be a good foreman.
    In this sentence, the word *biased* means

    A. easy-going   B. prejudiced
    C. strict   D. uneducated

12.____

13. The lecture for the new employees was brief.
    In this sentence, the word *brief* means

    A. educational   B. free
    C. interesting   D. short

13.____

14. He was asked to clarify the order.
    In this sentence, the word *clarify* means

    A. follow out   B. make clear
    C. take back   D. write out

14.____

15. The employee was commended by his foreman.
    In this sentence, the word *commended* means

    A. assigned   B. blamed   C. picked   D. praised

15.____

16. Before the winter, the lawnmower engine was dismantled.
    In this sentence, the word *dismantled* means

    A. oiled   B. repaired
    C. stored away   D. taken apart

16.____

17. They excavated a big hole on the project lawn.
    In this sentence, the word *excavated* means

    A. cleaned out   B. discovered
    C. dug out   D. filled in

17.____

18. The new man was told to sweep the exterior area.
    In this sentence, the word *exterior* means

    A. asphalt   B. nearby   C. outside   D. whole

18.____

19. The officer refuted the statement of the driver.
    As used in this sentence, the word *refuted* means MOST NEARLY

    A. disproved   B. elaborated upon
    C. related   D. supported

19.____

20. The mechanism of the parking meter is not intricate.   20.____
   As used in this sentence, the word *intricate* means MOST NEARLY

   A. cheap   B. complicated
   C. foolproof   D. strong

21. The weight of each box fluctuates.   21.____
   As used in this sentence, the word *fluctuates* means MOST NEARLY

   A. always changes   B. decreases
   C. increases gradually   D. is similar

22. The person chosen to investigate the new procedure should be impartial.   22.____
   As used in this sentence, the word *impartial* means MOST NEARLY

   A. experienced   B. fair
   C. forward looking   D. important

23. Carelessness in the safekeeping of keys will not be tolerated.   23.____
   As used in this sentence, the word *tolerated* means MOST NEARLY

   A. forgotten   B. permitted
   C. punished lightly   D. understood

24. The traffic was easily diverted.   24.____
   As used in this sentence, the word *diverted* means MOST NEARLY

   A. controlled   B. speeded up
   C. stopped   D. turned aside

25. A transcript of the report was prepared in the office.   25.____
   As used in this sentence, the word *transcript* means MOST NEARLY

   A. brief   B. copy
   C. record   D. translation

26. The change was authorized by the supervisor.   26.____
   As used in this sentence, the word *authorized* means MOST NEARLY

   A. completed   B. corrected   C. ordered   D. permitted

27. The supervisor read the excerpt of the collector's report.   27.____
   According to this sentence, the supervisor read _____ the report.

   A. a passage from   B. a summary of
   C. the original of   D. the whole of

28. During the probation period, the worker proved to be inept.   28.____
   The word *inept* means MOST NEARLY

   A. incompetent   B. insubordinate
   C. satisfactory   D. uncooperative

29. The putative father was not living with the family.   29.____
   The word *putative* means MOST NEARLY

   A. reputed   B. unemployed
   C. concerned   D. indifferent

30. The adopted child researched various documents of vital statistics in an effort to discover the names of his natural parents.
The words *vital statistics* mean MOST NEARLY statistics relating to

   A. human life
   C. important facts
   B. hospitals
   D. health and welfare

30.____

31. Despite many requests for them, there was a scant supply of new blotters.
The word *scant* means MOST NEARLY

   A. adequate
   C. insufficient
   B. abundant
   D. expensive

31.____

32. Did they replenish the supply of forms in the cabinet?
The word *replenish* means MOST NEARLY

   A. straighten up
   C. sort out
   B. refill
   D. use

32.____

33. Employees may become bored if they are assigned diverse duties.
The word *diverse* means MOST NEARLY

   A. interesting
   C. challenging
   B. different
   D. enjoyable

33.____

Questions 34-37.

DIRECTIONS: Each of Questions 34 through 37 consists of a capitalized word followed by four suggested meanings of the word. Select the word or phrase which means MOST NEARLY the same as the capitalized word.

34. PROFICIENCY

   A. vocation
   C. repugnancy
   B. competency
   D. prominence

34.____

35. BIBLIOGRAPHY

   A. description
   C. photograph
   B. stenography
   D. compilation of books

35.____

36. FIDELITY

   A. belief
   C. strength
   B. treachery
   D. loyalty

36.____

37. ACCELERATE

   A. adjust   B. press   C. quicken   D. strip

37.____

38. One of the machinists in your shop enjoys the reputation of being a great equivocator.
This means MOST NEARLY that he

   A. takes pride and is happy in his work
   B. generally hedges and often gives misleading answers
   C. is a strong union man with great interest in his fellow workers' welfare
   D. is good at resolving disputes

38.____

39. When a person has the reputation of persistently making foolish or silly remarks, it may be said that he is

    A. inane
    B. meticulous
    C. a procrastinator
    D. a prevaricator

39.____

40. When two mechanics, called A and B, make measurements of the same workpiece and find significant discrepancies in their measurements, it is MOST NEARLY correct to state that

    A. mechanic B made an erroneous reading
    B. mechanic A was careless in making his measurements
    C. both mechanics made their measurements correctly
    D. there was considerable difference in the two sets of measurements

40.____

41. A foreman who *expedites* a job,

    A. abolishes it
    B. makes it bigger
    C. slows it down
    D. speeds it up

41.____

42. If a man is working at a *uniform* speed, it means he is working at a speed which is

    A. changing   B. fast   C. slow   D. steady

42.____

43. To say that a caretaker is *obstinate* means that he is

    A. cooperative
    B. patient
    C. stubborn
    D. willing

43.____

44. To say that a caretaker is *negligent* means that he is

    A. careless   B. neat   C. nervous   D. late

44.____

45. To say that something is *absurd* means that it is

    A. definite
    B. not clear
    C. ridiculous
    D. unfair

45.____

46. To say that a foreman is *impartial* means that he is

    A. fair   B. improving   C. in a hurry   D. watchful

46.____

47. A man who is *lenient* is one who is

    A. careless
    B. harsh
    C. inexperienced
    D. mild

47.____

48. A man who is *punctual* is one who is

    A. able   B. polite   C. prompt   D. sincere

48.____

49. If you think one of your men is too *awkward* to do a job, it means you think he is too

    A. clumsy   B. lazy   C. old   D. weak

49.____

50. A person who is *seldom* late, is late

    A. always   B. never   C. often   D. rarely

50.____

—————

KEY (CORRECT ANSWERS)

1.	D	11.	B	21.	A	31.	C	41.	D
2.	A	12.	B	22.	B	32.	B	42.	D
3.	B	13.	D	23.	B	33.	B	43.	C
4.	D	14.	B	24.	D	34.	B	44.	A
5.	C	15.	D	25.	B	35.	D	45.	C
6.	D	16.	D	26.	D	36.	D	46.	A
7.	B	17.	C	27.	A	37.	C	47.	D
8.	C	18.	C	28.	A	38.	B	48.	C
9.	B	19.	A	29.	A	39.	B	49.	A
10.	A	20.	B	30.	A	40.	D	50.	D

———

TEST 2

DIRECTIONS: Each question or incomplete statement is followed by several suggested answers or completions. Select the one that BEST answers the question or completes the statement. *PRINT THE LETTER OF THE CORRECT ANSWER IN THE SPACE AT THE RIGHT.*

1. The Department of Health can certify that conditions in a housing accommodation are detrimental to life or health.
   As used in the above sentence, the word *detrimental* means MOST NEARLY

   1._____

   A. injurious
   C. satisfactory
   B. serious
   D. necessary

2. The Administrator shall have the power to revoke any adjustment in rents granted either the landlord or the tenant.
   As used in the above sentence, the word *revoke* means MOST NEARLY

   2._____

   A. increase   B. decrease   C. rescind   D. restore

Questions 3-5.

DIRECTIONS: Each of Questions 3 through 5 consists of a capitalized word followed by four suggested meanings of the word. Select the word which means MOST NEARLY the same as the capitalized word.

3. DOGMATISM

   3._____

   A. dramatism
   C. doubtful
   B. positiveness
   D. tentativeness

4. ELECTRODE

   4._____

   A. officer
   C. terminal
   B. electrolyte
   D. positive

5. EMIT

   5._____

   A. return   B. enter   C. omit   D. discharge

6. The word *inflammable* means MOST NEARLY

   6._____

   A. burnable   B. acid   C. poisonous   D. explosive

7. The word *disinfect* means MOST NEARLY

   7._____

   A. deodorize   B. sterilize   C. bleach   D. dissolve

8. He wanted to ascertain the facts before arriving at a conclusion.
   The word *ascertain* means MOST NEARLY

   8._____

   A. disprove   B. determine   C. convert   D. provide

9. Did the supervisor assent to her request for annual leave?
   The word *assent* means MOST NEARLY

   9._____

   A. allude   B. protest   C. agree   D. refer

10. The new worker was fearful that the others would rebuff her.
    The word *rebuff* means MOST NEARLY

    A. ignore   B. forget   C. copy   D. snub

10.____

11. The supervisor of that office does not condone lateness.
    The word *condone* means MOST NEARLY

    A. mind   B. excuse   C. punish   D. remember

11.____

12. Each employee was instructed to be as concise as possible when preparing a report.
    The word *concise* means MOST NEARLY

    A. exact   B. sincere   C. flexible   D. brief

12.____

13. The shovelers should not distribute the asphalt faster than it can be properly handled by the rakers.
    As used above, *distribute* means MOST NEARLY

    A. dump   B. pick-up   C. spread   D. heat

13.____

14. Any defective places should be cut out.
    As used above, *defective* means MOST NEARLY

    A. low   B. hard   C. soft   D. faulty

14.____

15. *Sphere of authority* is called

    A. constituency   B. dictatorial
    C. jurisdiction   D. vassal

15.____

16. Rollers are made in several sizes.
    As used above, *several* means MOST NEARLY

    A. large   B. heavy   C. standard   D. different

16.____

17. Sometimes a roller is run over an old surface to detect weak spots.
    As used above, *detect* means MOST NEARLY

    A. compact   B. remove   C. find   D. strengthen

17.____

18. Reconstruction of the old base is sometimes required as a preliminary operation.
    As used above, *preliminary* means MOST NEARLY

    A. first   B. necessary   C. important   D. local

18.____

19. If a man makes an *absurd* remark, he makes one which is MOST NEARLY

    A. misleading   B. ridiculous
    C. unfair   D. wicked

19.____

20. A worker who is *adept* at his job is one who is MOST NEARLY

    A. cooperative   B. developed
    C. diligent   D. skilled

20.____

21. If a man states a condition is *general,* he means it is MOST NEARLY

    A. artificial   B. prevalent
    C. timely   D. transient

21.____

Questions 22-50.

DIRECTIONS: Each of Questions 22 through 50 consists of a sentence in which a word is italicized. Of the four words following each sentence, select the word whose
meaning is MOST NEARLY the same as the meaning of the italicized word.

22.   The agent's first *assignment* was to patrol on Hicks Avenue.   22._____

   A.   test   B.   sign   C.   job   D.   deadline

23.   Agents get many *inquiries* from the public.   23._____

   A.   complaints   B.   suggestions
   C.   compliments   D.   questions

24.   The names of all fifty states were written in *abbreviated* form.   24._____

   A.   shortened   B.   corrected
   C.   eliminated   D.   illegible

25.   The meter was examined and found to be *defective.*   25._____

   A.   small   B.   operating   C.   destroyed   D.   faulty

26.   Agent Roger's reports are *legible,* but Agent Baldwin's are not.   26._____

   A.   similar   B.   readable   C.   incorrect   D.   late

27.   The time allowed, as shown by the meter, had *expired.*   27._____

   A.   started   B.   broken   C.   ended   D.   violated

28.   The busy *commercial* area is quiet in the evenings.   28._____

   A.   deserted   B.   growing   C.   business   D.   local

29.   The district office *authorized* the giving of summonses to illegally parked trucks.   29._____

   A.   suggested   B.   approved
   C.   prohibited   D.   recorded

30.   Department property must be used *exclusively* for official business.   30._____

   A.   occasionally   B.   frequently
   C.   only   D.   properly

31.   The District Commander *banned* driving in the area.   31._____

   A.   detoured   B.   permitted
   C.   encouraged   D.   prohibited

32.   Two copies of the summons are *retained* by the Enforcement Agent.   32._____

   A.   kept   B.   distributed
   C.   submitted   D.   signed

33.   The Agent *detected* a parking violation.   33._____

   A.   cancelled   B.   discovered
   C.   investigated   D.   reported

34. *Pedestrians* may be given summonses for violating traffic regulations.   34.____

    A. Bicycle riders   B. Horsemen
    C. Motorcyclists   D. Walkers

35. Parked cars are not allowed to *obstruct* traffic.   35.____

    A. direct   B. lead   C. block   D. speed

36. It was *obvious* to the Agent that the traffic light was broken.   36.____

    A. uncertain   B. surprising
    C. possible   D. clear

37. The signs stated that parking in the area was *restricted* to vehicles of foreign diplomats.   37.____

    A. allowed   B. increased   C. desired   D. limited

38. Each violation carries an *appropriate* fine.   38.____

    A. suitable   B. extra   C. light   D. heavy

39. Strict enforcement of parking regulations helps to *alleviate* traffic congestion.   39.____

    A. extend   B. build   C. relieve   D. increase

40. The Bureau has a rule which states that an Agent shall speak and act *courteously* in any   40.____
relationship with the public.

    A. respectfully   B. timidly
    C. strangely   D. intelligently

41. City traffic regulations prohibit parking at *jammed* meters.   41.____

    A. stuck   B. timed   C. open   D. installed

42. A *significant* error was made by the collector.   42.____

    A. doubtful   B. foolish   C. important   D. strange

43. It is better to *disperse* a crowd.   43.____

    A. hold back   B. quiet   C. scatter   D. talk to

44. Business groups wish to *expand* the program.   44.____

    A. advertise   B. defeat   C. enlarge   D. expose

45. The procedure was *altered* to assist the storekeepers.   45.____

    A. abolished   B. changed
    C. improved   D. made simpler

46. The collector was instructed to *survey* the damage to the parking meter.   46.____

    A. examine   B. give the reason for
    C. repair   D. report

47. It is *imperative* that a collector's report be turned in after each collection.   47.____

    A. desired   B. recommended
    C. requested   D. urgent

48. The collector was not able to *extricate* the key.   48.____

   A. find   B. free
   C. have a copy made of   D. turn

49. Parking meters have *alleviated* one of our major traffic problems.   49.____

   A. created   B. lightened
   C. removed   D. solved

50. Formerly drivers with learners' permits could drive only on *designated* streets. 50.____

   A. dead-end   B. not busy   C. one way   D. specified

KEY (CORRECT ANSWERS)

1.	A	11.	B	21.	B	31.	D	41.	A
2.	C	12.	D	22.	C	32.	A	42.	C
3.	B	13.	C	23.	D	33.	B	43.	C
4.	C	14.	D	24.	A	34.	D	44.	C
5.	D	15.	C	25.	D	35.	C	45.	B
6.	A	16.	D	26.	B	36.	D	46.	A
7.	B	17.	C	27.	C	37.	D	47.	D
8.	B	18.	A	28.	C	38.	A	48.	B
9.	C	19.	B	29.	B	39.	C	49.	B
10.	D	20.	D	30.	C	40.	A	50.	D

TEST 3

DIRECTIONS: Each question or incomplete statement is followed by several suggested answers or completions. Select the one that BEST answers the question or completes the statement. *PRINT THE LETTER OF THE CORRECT ANSWER IN THE SPACE AT THE RIGHT.*

1. Sprinkler systems in buildings can retard the spread of fires.
    As used in this sentence, the word *retard* means MOST NEARLY

    A. quench   B. slow   C. reveal   D. aggravate

1.____

2. Although there was widespread criticism, the director refused to curtail the program.
    As used in this sentence, the word *curtail* means MOST NEARLY

    A. change   B. discuss   C. shorten   D. expand

2.____

3. Argon is an inert gas.
    As used in this sentence, the word *inert* means MOST NEARLY

    A. unstable   B. uncommon   C. volatile   D. inactive

3.____

4. The firemen turned their hoses on the shed and the main building simultaneously.
    As used in this sentence, the word *simultaneously* means MOST NEARLY

    A. in turn   B. without hesitation
    C. with great haste   D. at the same time

4.____

5. The officer was rebuked for his failure to act promptly. As used in this sentence, the word *rebuked* means MOST NEARLY

    A. demoted   B. reprimanded
    C. discharged   D. reassigned

5.____

6. Parkways in the city may be used to facilitate responses to fire alarms.
    As used in this sentence, the word *facilitate* means MOST NEARLY

    A. reduce   B. alter   C. complete   D. ease

6.____

7. Fire extinguishers are most effective when the fire is incipient.
    As used in this sentence, the word *incipient* means MOST NEARLY

    A. accessible   B. beginning
    C. red hot   D. confined

7.____

8. It is important to convey to new members the fundamentals of the procedure.
    As used in this sentence, the words *convey to* means MOST NEARLY

    A. prove for   B. confirm for
    C. suggest to   D. impart to

8.____

9. The explosion was a graphic illustration of the effects of neglect and carelessness.
    As used in this sentence, the word *graphic* means MOST NEARLY

    A. terrible   B. typical   C. unique   D. vivid

9.____

10. The worker was assiduous in all things relating to his duties.
    As used in this sentence, the word *assiduous* means MOST NEARLY

    A. aggressive   B. careless   C. persistent   D. cautious

10.____

11. A worker must be adept to be successful at his work.
    As used in this sentence, the word *adept* means MOST NEARLY

    A. ambitious   B. strong   C. agile   D. skillful

11._____

12. The extinguisher must be inverted before it will operate. As used in this sentence, the word *inverted* means MOST NEARLY

    A. turned over   B. completely filled
    C. lightly shaken   D. unhooked

12._____

13. Assume that the bridge operator may at times be assigned to the task of coordinating the bridge crew for the various routine jobs.
    As used in this sentence, the word *coordinating* means MOST NEARLY

    A. ordering   B. testing
    C. scheduling   D. instructing

13._____

14. The worker made an insignificant error.
    As used in this sentence, the word *insignificant* means MOST NEARLY

    A. latent   B. serious
    C. accidental   D. minor

14._____

15. An Assistant Supervisor should be attentive.
    As used in this sentence, the word *attentive* means MOST NEARLY

    A. watchful   B. prompt   C. negligent   D. willing

15._____

16. The Assistant Supervisor reported a cavity in the roadway.
    As used in this sentence, the word *cavity* means MOST NEARLY

    A. lump   B. wreck   C. hollow   D. oil-slick

16._____

17. Anyone working in traffic must be cautious.
    As used in this sentence, the word *cautious* means MOST NEARLY

    A. brave   B. careful   C. expert   D. fast

17._____

Questions 18-20.

DIRECTIONS: Each of Questions 18 through 20 consists of a capitalized word followed by four suggested meanings of the word. Select the word or phrase which means MOST NEARLY the same as the capitalized word.

18. OSMOSIS

    A. combining   B. diffusion
    C. ossification   D. incantation

18._____

19. COLLOIDAL

    A. mucinous   B. powdered   C. hairy   D. beautiful

19._____

20. PRETEXT

    A. ritual   B. fictitious reason
    C. sermon   D. truthful motive

20._____

21. *Easily broken or snapped* defines the word

    A. brittle   B. pliable   C. cohesive   D. volatile

21._____

22. *At right angles to a given line or surface* defines the word

    A. horizontal   B. oblique
    C. perpendicular   D. adjacent

22._____

23. *Tools with cutting edges for enlarging or shaping holes* are

    A. screwdrivers   B. pliers
    C. reamers   D. nippers

23._____

24. *An instrument used for measuring very small distances* is called a

    A. gage   B. compass
    C. slide ruler   D. micrometer

24._____

25. When the phrase *acrid smoke* is used, it refers to smoke that is

    A. irritating   B. dense
    C. black   D. very hot

25._____

26. The officer gave explicit directions on how the work was to be done.
As used in this sentence, the word *explicit* means MOST NEARLY

    A. implied   B. clear   C. vague   D. brief

26._____

27. After the fire had been extinguished, the debris was taken outside and soaked.
As used in this sentence, the word *debris* means MOST NEARLY

    A. wood   B. rubbish   C. couch   D. paper

27._____

28. The trapped man blanched when he saw the life net below him.
As used in this sentence, the word *blanched* means MOST NEARLY

    A. turned pale   B. sprang forward
    C. flushed   D. fainted

28._____

29. The worker and his supervisor discussed the problem candidly.
As used in this sentence, the word *candidly* means MOST NEARLY

    A. angrily   B. frankly
    C. tolerantly   D. understandingly

29._____

30. The truck came careening down the street.
As used in this sentence, the word *careening* means MOST NEARLY

    A. with sirens screaming
    B. at a slow speed
    C. swaying from side to side
    D. out of control

30._____

31. The population of the province is fairly homogeneous.
    As used in this sentence, the word *homogeneous* means MOST NEARLY
    31.____

    A. devoted to agricultural pursuits
    B. conservative in outlook
    C. essentially alike
    D. sophisticated

32. The reports of injuries during the past month are being tabulated.
    As used in this sentence, the word *tabulated* means MOST NEARLY
    32.____

    A. analyzed
    B. placed in a file
    C. put in the form of a table
    D. verified

33. The terms offered were tantamount to surrender.
    As used in this sentence, the word *tantamount* means MOST NEARLY
    33.____

    A. equivalent   B. opposite
    C. preferable   D. preliminary

34. The man's injuries were superficial.
    As used in this sentence, the word *superficial* means MOST NEARLY
    34.____

    A. on the surface   B. not fatal
    C. free from infection D. not painful

35. This experience warped his outlook on life.
    As used in this sentence, the word *warped* means MOST NEARLY
    35.____

    A. changed   B. improved
    C. strengthened   D. twisted

36. Hotel guests usually are transients.
    As used in this sentence, the word *transients* means MOST NEARLY
    36.____

    A. persons of considerable wealth
    B. staying for a short time
    C. visitors from other areas
    D. untrustworthy persons

37. The pupil's work specimen was considered unsatisfactory because of his failure to
    observe established tolerances. As used in this sentence, the word *tolerances* means
    MOST NEARLY
    37.____

    A. safety precautions
    B. regard for the rights of others
    C. allowable variations in dimensions
    D. amount of waste produced in an operation

38. Punishment was severe because the act was considered willful.
    As used in this sentence, the word *willful* means MOST NEARLY
    38.____

    A. brutal   B. criminal
    C. harmful   D. intentional

39. The malfunctioning of the system was traced to a defective thermostat.
As used in this sentence, the word *thermostat* means MOST NEARLY a device that reacts to changes in

    A. amperage
    C. temperature
    B. water pressure
    D. atmospheric pressure

39.____

40. His garden contained a profusion of flowers, shrubs, and bushes.
As used in this sentence, the word *profusion* means MOST NEARLY

    A. abundance
    C. representation
    B. display
    D. scarcity

40.____

41. The inspector would not approve the work because it was out of plumb.
As used in this sentence, the words *out of plumb* means MOST NEARLY not

    A. properly seasoned
    C. vertical
    B. of the required strength
    D. fireproof

41.____

42. The judge admonished the witness for his answer.
As used in this sentence, the word *admonished* means MOST NEARLY

    A. complimented
    C. questioned
    B. punished
    D. warned

42.____

43. A millimeter is a measure of length.
The length represented by *one millimeter* is

    A. one-thousandth of a meter
    B. one thousand meters
    C. one-millionth of a meter
    D. one million meters

43.____

44. It is not possible to misconstrue his letter.
As used in this sentence, the word *misconstrue* means MOST NEARLY

    A. decipher
    C. ignore
    B. forget
    D. misinterpret

44.____

45. The wire connecting the two terminals must be kept taut.
As used in this sentence, the word *taut* means MOST NEARLY without

    A. defects
    C. electrical charge
    B. slack
    D. pressure

45.____

46. Reaching the summit appeared beyond the capacity of the hikers.
As used in this sentence, the word *summit* means MOST NEARLY

    A. canyon   B. peak   C. plateau   D. ravine

46.____

47. The plot was thwarted by the quick action of the police. As used in this sentence, the word *thwarted* means MOST NEARLY

    A. blocked
    C. punished
    B. discovered
    D. solved

47.____

48. An abrasive was required by the machinist to complete his task.   48._____
    As used in this sentence, the word *abrasive* means a substance used for

    A. coating   B. lubricating
    C. measuring   D. polishing

49. The facades of the building were dirty and grimy.   49._____
    As used in this sentence, the word *facades* means MOST NEARLY

    A. cellars   B. fronts
    C. residents   D. surroundings

50. Several firemen were injured by the detonation.   50._____
    As used in this sentence, the word *detonation* means MOST NEARLY

    A. accident   B. collapse   C. collision   D. explosion

KEY (CORRECT ANSWERS)

1. B	11. D	21. A	31. C	41. C
2. C	12. A	22. C	32. C	42. D
3. D	13. C	23. C	33. A	43. A
4. D	14. D	24. D	34. A	44. D
5. B	15. A	25. A	35. D	45. B
6. D	16. C	26. B	36. B	46. B
7. B	17. B	27. B	37. C	47. A
8. D	18. B	28. A	38. D	48. D
9. D	19. A	29. B	39. C	49. B
10. C	20. B	30. C	40. A	50. D

VERBAL ANALOGIES

EXAMINATION SECTION
TEST 1

DIRECTIONS: In Questions 1 to 10, the first two *italicized* words have a relationship to each other. Determine that relationship, and then match the third *italicized* word with the one of the lettered choices with which it has the same relationship as the words of the first pair have to each other. *PRINT THE LETTER OF THE CORRECT ANSWER IN THE SPACE AT THE RIGHT.*

In order to help you understand the procedure, a sample question is given:

SAMPLE: *dog* is to *bark* as *cat* is to
      A. animal   B. small   C. meow
      D. pet   E. snarl

The relationship between *dog* and *bark* is that the sound which a dog normally emits is a bark. In the same way, the sound which a cat emits is a meow. Thus, C is the CORRECT answer.

1. *Fine* is to *speeding* as *jail* is to   1._____

    A. bars   B. prisoner   C. warden
    D. confinement   E. steal

2. *Orchid* is to *rose* as *gold* is to   2._____

    A. watch   B. copper   C. mine   D. coin   E. mint

3. *Pistol* is to *machine gun* as *button* is to   3._____

    A. coat   B. bullet   C. zipper
    D. tailor   E. needle and thread

4. *Spontaneous* is to *unrehearsed* as *planned* is to   4._____

    A. completed   B. organized   C. restricted
    D. understood   E. informal

5. *Friendly* is to *hostile* as *loyalty* is to   5._____

    A. fealty   B. evil   C. devotion
    D. warlike   E. treachery

6. *Fear* is to *flight* as *bravery* is to   6._____

    A. courage   B. danger   C. resistance
    D. injury   E. unyielding

7. *Economical* is to *stingy* as *sufficient* is to   7._____

    A. abundant   B. adequate   C. expensive
    D. needy   E. greedy

8. *Astronomer* is to *observation* as *senator* is to   8.____

    A. caucus   B. election   C. convention
    D. legislation   E. patronage

9. *Hunger* is to *food* as *exhaustion* is to   9.____

    A. labor   B. play   C. illness
    D. debility   E. rest

10. *Entertainment* is to *boredom* as *efficiency* is to   10.____

    A. ignorance   B. government   C. waste
    D. expert   E. time and motion stud-
                    ies

KEY (CORRECT ANSWERS)

1.	E		6.	C
2.	B		7.	A
3.	C		8.	D
4.	B		9.	E
5.	E		10.	C

TEST 2

DIRECTIONS: In Questions 1 to 10, the first two *italicized* words have a relationship to each other. Determine that relationship, and then match the third *italicized* word with the one of the lettered choices with which it has the same relationship as the words of the first pair have to each other. *PRINT THE LETTER OF THE CORRECT ANSWER IN THE SPACE AT THE RIGHT.*

1. *Diamond* is to *glass* as *platinum* is to   1.____

    A. jewelry   B. metal   C. aluminum
    D. mine   E. white

2. *Water* is to *aqueduct* as *electricity* is to   2.____

    A. meter   B. battery   C. fuse   D. wire   E. solenoid

3. *Oratory* is to *filibuster* as *reign* is to   3.____

    A. tyrant   B. terror   C. government
    D. bluster   E. confusion

4. *Gravity* is to *gaiety* as *taunt* is to   4.____

    A. ridicule   B. console   C. avoid
    D. amuse   E. condone

5. *Electron* is to *atom* as *earth* is to   5.____

    A. sun   B. solar system   C. moon
    D. planet   E. center

6. *Flattery* is to *adulation* as *cruelty* is to   6.____

    A. pain   B. barbarity   C. censorious
    D. compassion   E. duality

7. *Rowboat* is to *oar* as *automobile* is to   7.____

    A. land   B. engine   C. driver
    D. passenger   E. piston

8. *Friction* is to *oil* as *war* is to   8.____

    A. conference   B. peace   C. munitions
    D. satellite   E. retaliation

9. *Disease* is to *infection* as *reaction* is to   9.____

    A. control   B. injury   C. relapse
    D. stipulation   E. sensation

10. *Persecution* is to *martyr* as *swindle* is to   10.____

    A. embezzler   B. refuge   C. confidence man
    D. bank   E. dupe

KEY (CORRECT ANSWERS)

1.	C		6.	B
2.	D		7.	B
3.	E		8.	A
4.	B		9.	E
5.	B		10.	E

TEST 3

DIRECTIONS: In Questions 1 to 10, the first two *italicized* words have a relationship to each other. Determine that relationship, and then match the third *italicized* word with the one of the lettered choices with which it has the same relationship as the words of the first pair have to each other. *PRINT THE LETTER OF THE CORRECT ANSWER IN THE SPACE AT THE RIGHT.*

1. *Woman* is to *man* as *Mary* is to   1._____

    A. woman   B. child   C. female   D. John   E. male

2. *Land* is to *ocean* as *soldier* is to   2._____

    A. river   B. sailor   C. shore   D. uniform   E. sailing

3. *Sugar* is to *candy* as *flour* is to   3._____

    A. eat   B. cook   C. candy   D. bread   E. sweet

4. *Sorrow* is to *joy* as *laugh* is to   4._____

    A. amuse   B. tears   C. fun   D. weep   E. cry

5. *Heat* is to *fire* as *pain* is to   5._____

    A. injury   B. wind   C. weather   D. cool   E. summer

6. *Grass* is to *cattle* as *milk* is to   6._____

    A. growing   B. lawn   C. baby   D. green   E. sun

7. *Winter* is to *spring* as *autumn* is to   7._____

    A. summer   B. winter   C. warm   D. cold   E. flower

8. *Rising* is to *falling* as *smile* is to   8._____

    A. climbing   B. baking   C. scolding
    D. frown   E. laughing

9. *Day* is to *night* as *succeed* is to   9._____

    A. fail   B. sunshine   C. evening
    D. afternoon   E. morning

10. *Apple* is to *fruit* as *corn* is to   10._____

    A. orange   B. eat   C. grain   D. cereal   E. food

KEY (CORRECT ANSWERS)

1.	D	6.	C
2.	B	7.	B
3.	D	8.	D
4.	E	9.	A
5.	A	10.	C

TEST 4

DIRECTIONS: In Questions 1 to 10, the first two *italicized* words have a relationship to each other. Determine that relationship, and then match the third *italicized* word with the one of the lettered choices with which it has the same relationship as the words of the first pair have to each other. *PRINT THE LETTER OF THE COR-RECT ANSWER IN THE SPACE AT THE RIGHT.*

1. *Robin* is to *feathers* as *cat* is to   1.____

    A. sing   B. fur   C. eat   D. bird   E. fly

2. *Late* is to *end* as *early* is to   2.____

    A. prompt   B. enter   C. begin   D. start   E. end

3. *Beginning* is to *end* as *horse* is to   3.____

    A. cart   B. automobile   C. wagon
    D. travel   E. ride

4. *Kitten* is to *cat* as *baby* is to   4.____

    A. rabbit   B. mother   C. dog   D. cow   E. lamb

5. *Little* is to *weak* as *big* is to   5.____

    A. boy   B. man   C. tall   D. baby   E. strong

6. *Arm* is to *hand* as *leg* is to   6.____

    A. knee   B. toe   C. elbow   D. foot   E. finger

7. *Alive* is to *dead* as *well* is to   7.____

    A. grow   B. sick   C. decay   D. sleep   E. play

8. *In* is to *out* as *bad* is to   8.____

    A. up   B. open   C. good   D. shut   E. on

9. *Dust* is to *dry* as *mud* is to   9.____

    A. wet   B. blow   C. splash   D. fly   E. settle

10. *Width* is to *wide* as *height* is to   10.____

    A. high   B. low   C. tall   D. brief   E. short

KEY (CORRECT ANSWERS)

1.	B	6.	D
2.	C	7.	B
3.	A	8.	C
4.	B	9.	A
5.	E	10.	C

———

TEST 5

DIRECTIONS: In Questions 1 to 10, the first two *italicized* words have a relationship to each other. Determine that relationship, and then match the third *italicized* word with the one of the lettered choices with which it has the same relationship as the words of the first pair have to each other. *PRINT THE LETTER OF THE CORRECT ANSWER IN THE SPACE AT THE RIGHT.*

1. *Above* is to *below* as *before* is to   1.____

   A. beyond   B. behind   C. beside   D. between   E. after

2. *Start* is to *stop* as *begin* is to   2.____

   A. go   B. run   C. wait   D. finish   E. work

3. *Everything* is to *nothing* as *always* is to   3.____

   A. forever   B. usually   C. never
   D. sometimes   E. something

4. *Search* is to *find* as *question* is to   4.____

   A. answer   B. reply   C. study
   D. problem   E. explain

5. *Top* is to *spin* as *spear* is to   5.____

   A. bottom   B. roll   C. throw   D. sharp   E. pin

6. *Scale* is to *weight* as *thermometer* is to   6.____

   A. weather   B. temperature   C. pounds
   D. spring   E. chronometer

7. *Congress* is to *senator* as *convention* is to   7.____

   A. election   B. chairman   C. delegate
   D. nominee   E. representative

8. *Dividend* is to *investor* as *wage* is to   8.____

   A. employee   B. salary   C. consumer
   D. price   E. employer

9. *Terminate* is to *commence* as *adjourn* is to   9.____

   A. enact   B. convene   C. conclude
   D. veto   E. prorogue

10. *Administrator* is to *policy* as *clerk* is to   10.____

   A. subornation   B. organization   C. coordination
   D. direction   E. application

———

KEY (CORRECT ANSWERS)

1.	E		6.	B
2.	D		7.	C
3.	C		8.	A
4.	A		9.	B
5.	C		10.	E

———

VERBAL ANALOGIES
EXAMINATION SECTION

DIRECTIONS: Each question or incomplete statement is followed by several suggested answers or completions. Select the one that BEST answers the question or completes the statement. *PRINT THE LETTER OF THE CORRECT ANSWER IN THE SPACE AT THE RIGHT.*

Questions 1-10.

DIRECTIONS: In each of Questions 1 through 10, a pair of related words written in capital letters is followed by four other pairs of words. For each question, select the pair of words which MOST closely expresses a relationship similar to that of the pair in capital letters.

SAMPLE QUESTION:

BOAT - DOCK
    A. airplane - hangar   B. rain - snow
    C. cloth - cotton   D. hunger - food

Choice A is the answer to this sample question since of the choices given, the relationship between airplane and hangar is most similar to the relationship between boat and dock.

1. AUTOMOBILE - FACTORY   1.____

    A. tea - lemon   B. wheel - engine
    C. pot - flower   D. paper - mill

2. GIRDER - BRIDGE   2.____

    A. petal - flower   B. street - sidewalk
    C. meat - vegetable   D. sun - storm

3. RADIUS - CIRCLE   3.____

    A. brick - building   B. tie - tracks
    C. spoke - wheel   D. axle - tire

4. DISEASE - RESEARCH   4.____

    A. death - poverty   B. speech - audience
    C. problem - conference   D. invalid - justice

5. CONCLUSION - INTRODUCTION   5.____

    A. commencement - beginning   B. housing - motor
    C. caboose - engine   D. train - cabin

6. SOCIETY - LAW   6.____

    A. baseball - rules   B. jury - law
    C. cell - prisoner   D. sentence - jury

7. PLAN - ACCOMPLISHMENT 7.____

    A. deed - fact   B. method - success
    C. graph - chart   D. rules - manual

8. ORDER - GOVERNMENT 8.____

    A. chaos - administration   B. confusion - pandemonium
    C. rule - stability   D. despair - hope

9. TYRANNY - FREEDOM 9.____

    A. despot - mob   B. wealth - poverty
    C. nobility - commoners   D. dictatorship - democracy

10. TELEGRAM - LETTER 10.____

    A. hare - tortoise   B. lie - truth
    C. number - word   D. report - research

Questions 11-30.

DIRECTIONS: In Questions 11 through 30, the first two capitalized words have a relationship to each other. Determine the relationship, and then match the third capitalized word with the one of the lettered choice with which it has the same relationship as the words of the first pair have to each other.

11. CONGRESS is to SENATOR as CONVENTION is to 11.____

    A. election   B. chairman   C. delegate   D. nominee

12. DIVIDEND is to INVESTOR as WAGE is to 12.____

    A. employee   B. salary   C. consumer   D. price

13. TERMINATE is to COMMENCE as ADJOURN is to 13.____

    A. enact   B. convene   C. conclude   D. veto

14. SANITATION is to HEALTH as EDUCATION is to 14.____

    A. school   B. hygiene   C. knowledge   D. teacher

15. ADMINISTRATOR is to POLICY as CLERK is to 15.____

    A. subordinate   B. organization
    C. coordination   D. procedure

16. ALLEGIANCE is to LOYALTY as TREASON is to 16.____

    A. felony   B. faithful   C. obedience   D. rebellion

17. DIAMOND is to GLASS as PLATINUM is to 17.____

    A. jewelry   B. metal   C. aluminum   D. mine

18. WATER is to AQUEDUCT as ELECTRICITY is to 18.____

    A. meter   B. battery   C. fuse   D. wire

19. ORATORY is to FILIBUSTER as REIGN is to   19._____

    A. tyranny   B. terror   C. government   D. empire

20. GRAVITY is to GAIETY as TAUNT is to   20._____

    A. ridicule   B. console   C. avoid   D. amuse

21. ELECTRON is to ATOM as EARTH is to   21._____

    A. sun   B. solar system   C. moon   D. planet

22. FLATTERY is to PRAISE as CRUELTY is to   22._____

    A. pain   B. punishment   C. pleasantry   D. favoritism

23. ROWBOAT is to OAR as AUTOMOBILE is to   23._____

    A. land   B. engine   C. driver   D. passenger

24. FRICTION is to OIL as WAR is to   24._____

    A. conference   B. peace   C. munitions   D. satellite

25. DISEASE is to INFECTION as REACTION is to   25._____

    A. control   B. injury   C. relapse   D. stimulus

26. PERSECUTION is to MARTYR as SWINDLE is to   26._____

    A. embezzler   B. refugee   C. victim   D. bank

27. PHYSICIAN is to PATIENT as ATTORNEY is to   27._____

    A. court   B. client   C. counsel   D. judge

28. JUDGE is to SENTENCE as JURY is to   28._____

    A. court   B. foreman   C. defendant   D. verdict

29. REVERSAL is to AFFIRMANCE as CONVICTION is to   29._____

    A. appeal   B. acquittal   C. error   D. mistrial

30. GENUINE is to TRUE as SPURIOUS is to   30._____

    A. correct   B. conceived   C. false   D. speculative

KEY (CORRECT ANSWERS)

1.	D	16.	D
2.	A	17.	C
3.	C	18.	D
4.	C	19.	A
5.	C	20.	B
6.	A	21.	B
7.	B	22.	B
8.	C	23.	B
9.	D	24.	A
10.	A	25.	D
11.	C	26.	C
12.	A	27.	B
13.	B	28.	D
14.	C	29.	B
15.	D	30.	C

VERBAL ANALOGIES
EXAMINATION SECTION

DIRECTIONS: Each question or incomplete statement is followed by several suggested answers or completions. Select the one that BEST answers the question or completes the statement. *PRINT THE LETTER OF THE CORRECT ANSWER IN THE SPACE AT THE RIGHT.*

Questions 1-10.

DIRECTIONS: In each of Questions 1 through 10, a pair of related words written in capital letters is followed by four other pairs of words. For each question, select the pair of words which MOST closely expresses a relationship similar to that of the pair in capital letters.

SAMPLE QUESTION:

BOAT - DOCK
    A. airplane - hangar   B. rain - snow
    C. cloth - cotton   D. hunger - food

Choice A is the answer to this sample question since of the choices given, the relationship between airplane and hangar is most similar to the relationship between boat and dock.

1. AUTOMOBILE - FACTORY   1.____

    A. tea - lemon   B. wheel - engine
    C. pot - flower   D. paper - mill

2. GIRDER - BRIDGE   2.____

    A. petal - flower   B. street - sidewalk
    C. meat - vegetable   D. sun - storm

3. RADIUS - CIRCLE   3.____

    A. brick - building   B. tie - tracks
    C. spoke - wheel   D. axle - tire

4. DISEASE - RESEARCH   4.____

    A. death - poverty   B. speech - audience
    C. problem - conference   D. invalid - justice

5. CONCLUSION - INTRODUCTION   5.____

    A. commencement - beginning   B. housing - motor
    C. caboose - engine   D. train - cabin

6. SOCIETY - LAW   6.____

    A. baseball - rules   B. jury - law
    C. cell - prisoner   D. sentence - jury

7. PLAN - ACCOMPLISHMENT   7.____

    A. deed - fact   B. method - success
    C. graph - chart   D. rules - manual

8. ORDER - GOVERNMENT   8.____

    A. chaos - administration   B. confusion - pandemonium
    C. rule - stability   D. despair - hope

9. TYRANNY - FREEDOM   9.____

    A. despot - mob   B. wealth - poverty
    C. nobility - commoners   D. dictatorship - democracy

10. TELEGRAM - LETTER   10.____

    A. hare - tortoise   B. lie - truth
    C. number - word   D. report - research

Questions 11-30.

DIRECTIONS: In Questions 11 through 30, the first two capitalized words have a relationship to each other. Determine the relationship, and then match the third capitalized word with the one of the lettered choice with which it has the same relationship as the words of the first pair have to each other.

11. CONGRESS is to SENATOR as CONVENTION is to   11.____

    A. election   B. chairman   C. delegate   D. nominee

12. DIVIDEND is to INVESTOR as WAGE is to   12.____

    A. employee   B. salary   C. consumer   D. price

13. TERMINATE is to COMMENCE as ADJOURN is to   13.____

    A. enact   B. convene   C. conclude   D. veto

14. SANITATION is to HEALTH as EDUCATION is to   14.____

    A. school   B. hygiene   C. knowledge   D. teacher

15. ADMINISTRATOR is to POLICY as CLERK is to   15.____

    A. subordinate   B. organization
    C. coordination   D. procedure

16. ALLEGIANCE is to LOYALTY as TREASON is to   16.____

    A. felony   B. faithful   C. obedience   D. rebellion

17. DIAMOND is to GLASS as PLATINUM is to   17.____

    A. jewelry   B. metal   C. aluminum   D. mine

18. WATER is to AQUEDUCT as ELECTRICITY is to   18.____

    A. meter   B. battery   C. fuse   D. wire

19. ORATORY is to FILIBUSTER as REIGN is to   19.____

    A. tyranny   B. terror   C. government   D. empire

20. GRAVITY is to GAIETY as TAUNT is to   20.____

    A. ridicule   B. console   C. avoid   D. amuse

21. ELECTRON is to ATOM as EARTH is to   21.____

    A. sun   B. solar system   C. moon   D. planet

22. FLATTERY is to PRAISE as CRUELTY is to   22.____

    A. pain   B. punishment   C. pleasantry   D. favoritism

23. ROWBOAT is to OAR as AUTOMOBILE is to   23.____

    A. land   B. engine   C. driver   D. passenger

24. FRICTION is to OIL as WAR is to   24.____

    A. conference   B. peace   C. munitions   D. satellite

25. DISEASE is to INFECTION as REACTION is to   25.____

    A. control   B. injury   C. relapse   D. stimulus

26. PERSECUTION is to MARTYR as SWINDLE is to   26.____

    A. embezzler   B. refugee   C. victim   D. bank

27. PHYSICIAN is to PATIENT as ATTORNEY is to   27.____

    A. court   B. client   C. counsel   D. judge

28. JUDGE is to SENTENCE as JURY is to   28.____

    A. court   B. foreman   C. defendant   D. verdict

29. REVERSAL is to AFFIRMANCE as CONVICTION is to   29.____

    A. appeal   B. acquittal   C. error   D. mistrial

30. GENUINE is to TRUE as SPURIOUS is to   30.____

    A. correct   B. conceived   C. false   D. speculative

KEY (CORRECT ANSWERS)

1.	D	16.	D
2.	A	17.	C
3.	C	18.	D
4.	C	19.	A
5.	C	20.	B
6.	A	21.	B
7.	B	22.	B
8.	C	23.	B
9.	D	24.	A
10.	A	25.	D
11.	C	26.	C
12.	A	27.	B
13.	B	28.	D
14.	C	29.	B
15.	D	30.	C

———

FIGURE ANALOGIES

Figure analogies are a novel and differentiated measure of non-numerical mathematics reasoning.

This question takes the form of, and, indeed, is similar to, the one-blank verbal analogy. However, pictures or drawings are used instead of words.

SAMPLE QUESTIONS AND EXPLANATIONS

DIRECTIONS: Each question in this part consists of 3 drawings lettered A,B,C, followed by 5 alternative drawings, numbered 1 to 5. The first 2 drawings in each question are related in some way. Choose the number of the alternative that is related to the third drawing in the same way that the second drawing is related to the first, and mark the appropriate space on your answer sheet.

1.   1.____

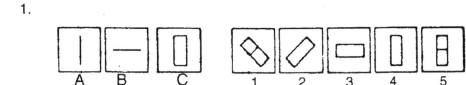

The CORRECT answer is 3. A vertical line has the same relationship to a horizontal line that a rectangle standing on its end has to a rectangle lying on its side.

2.   2.____

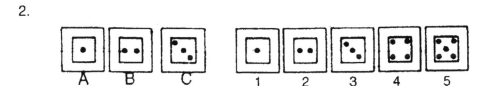

The second square has one more dot than the first square. Therefore the CORRECT answer is alternative 4, which has one more dot than the third square.

                                                                                                      3.____

3.

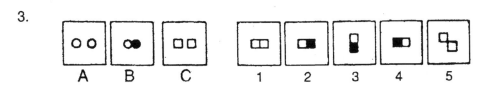

In the second drawing the circles are moved together and the circle on the right darkened. Therefore the CORRECT answer is 2 , in which the squares are moved together and the right-hand square darkened.

                                                                                                      4.____

4.

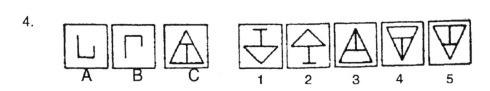

ABSTRACT REASONING

COMMENTARY

The mathematical or quantitative ability of the candidate is generally measured through the form of questions and/or problems involving arithmetical reasoning, algebraic problem solving, and the interpretation of visual materials graphs, charts, tables, diagrams, maps, cartoons, and pictures.

A more recent development, which attempts to assay facets of quantitative ability not ordinarily discernible or measurable, is the nonverbal test of reasoning of the type commonly designated as the figure analogy. Figure analogies are novel and differentiated measures of non-numerical mathematics reasoning.

Since intelligence exists in many forms or phases and the theory of differential aptitudes is now firmly established in testing, other manifestations and measurements of intelligence than verbal or purely arithmetical must be identified and measured.

Classification inventory, or figure classification, involves the aptitude of form perception, i.e., the ability to perceive pertinent detail in objects or in pictorial or graphic material. It involves making visual comparisons and discriminations and discerning slight differences in shapes and shading figures and widths and lengths of lines.

One aspect of this type of nonverbal question takes the form of a *positive* requirement to find the *COMPATIBLE PATTERN* (i.e., the one that *does* belong) from among two (2) sets of figure groups. The prescription for this question-type is as follows:

A group of three drawings lettered A, B, and C, respectively, is presented, followed on the same line by five (5) numbered alternative drawings labeled 1, 2, 3, 4, and 5, respectively.

The first two (2) drawings (A, B) in each question are related in some way.

The candidate is then to decide what characteristic *each* of the figures labeled A and B has that causes them to be related, and is then to select the one alternative from the five (5) numbered figures that is related to figure C in the same way that drawing B is related to drawing A.

Leading examples of presentation are the figure analogy and the figure classification. The section that follows presents progressive and varied samplings of this type of question.

The CORRECT answer is 5. The second drawing is the inverted version of the first; alternative 5 is the inverted version of the third drawing.

5.
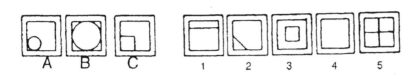

5.____

The CORRECT answer is 4. Drawing A has a small circle within a square; drawing B contains a circle completely filling the square. Drawing C has a small square within a square; in alternative 4, this small square has been magnified to its complete size within the square so that this magnified square coincides with the enclosing square, leaving the outline of only one square.

6.____

6.
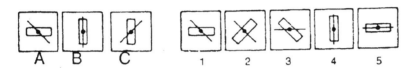

The CORRECT answer is 5. Drawing A appears in a horizontal position, with a diagonal line drawn through the center dot; drawing B appears in a vertical position, with a straight line drawn through the center dot. Drawing C is similar to drawing A, except that it appears in a vertical position; drawing 5 is similar to drawing B, except that it appears in a horizontal position. Our analogy may, therefore, be verbally expressed as
A:B:C:5.

SUGGESTIONS FOR ANSWERING THE FIGURE ANALOGY QUESTION

1. In doing the actual questions, there can be little practical gain in rationalizing each answer that you attempt. What is needed is a quick and ready perceptive sense in this matter.

2. The BEST way to prepare for this type of question is to do the "Tests" in figure analogies that follow. By this method, you will gain enough functional skill to enable you to cope successfully with this type of question on the Examination.

PLEASE NOTE -- In the tests which begin on page 5, after the sample questions, the three (3) drawings are unlabeled and the answers have four (4) choices instead of five (5) labeled A, B, C and D. They are to be answered in the same way.

SAMPLE TEST

1.
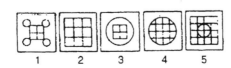

1.____

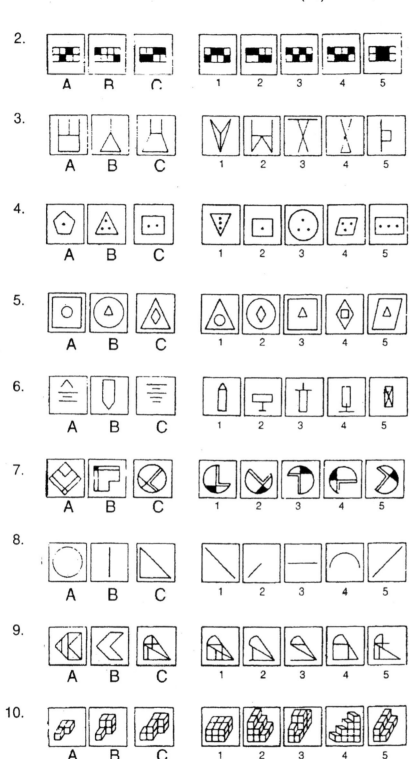

2. A B C   1 2 3 4 5

2._____

3. A B C   1 2 3 4 5

3._____

4. A B C   1 2 3 4 5

4._____

5. A B C   1 2 3 4 5

5._____

6. A B C   1 2 3 4 5

6._____

7. A B C   1 2 3 4 5

7._____

8. A B C   1 2 3 4 5

8._____

9. A B C   1 2 3 4 5

9._____

10. A B C   1 2 3 4 5

10._____

KEY(CORRECT ANSWERS)

1.	2	5.	4
2.	2	6.	3
3.	4	7.	3
4.	1	8.	2

———

EXPLANATION OF ANSWERS

1. In the second figure, the squares are changed to circles and the circles to squares.

2. In the second figure, the upper darkened area has moved two squares to left; the lower, two squares to right.

3. The second figure has a flat base, like the first.

4. The sum of sides and dots in the second figure equals that of the first.

5. The outside part of the second figure is the inside part of the first.

6. The second figure is constructed from the lines given in the first.

7. The second figure is obtained from the first by rotating it 135 clockwise, darkening the smaller area and deleting the larger.

8. The second figure is the bisector of the area of the first.

9. The second figure is obtained from the first by deleting all the vertical lines.

10. The second figure contains two blocks more than the first.

EXAMINATION SECTION

PROBLEM FIGURES

ANSWER FIGURES

1.

A   B   C   D

2.

A   B   C   D

3.

A   B   C   D

4.

A   B   C   D

5.

A   B   C   D

6.

A   B   C   D

7.

A   B   C   D

8.

A   B   C   D

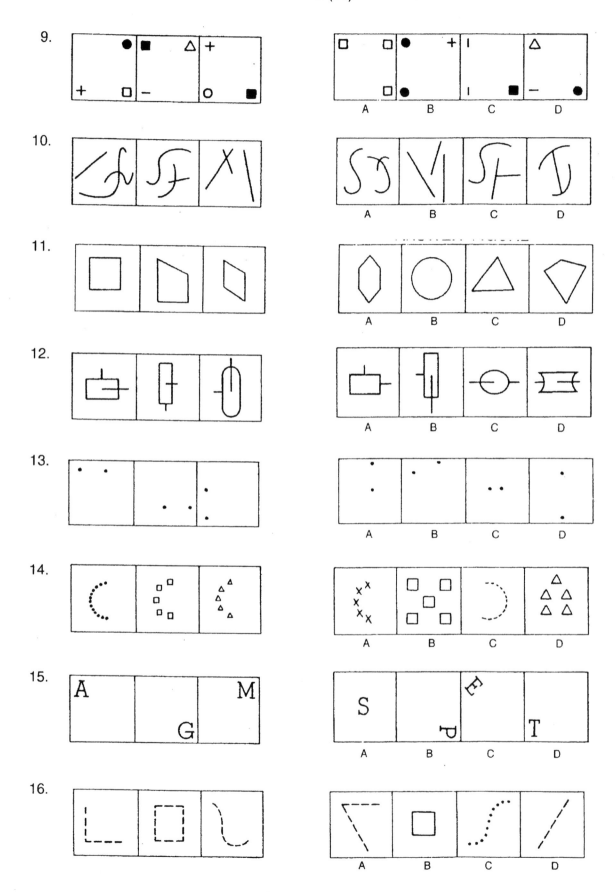

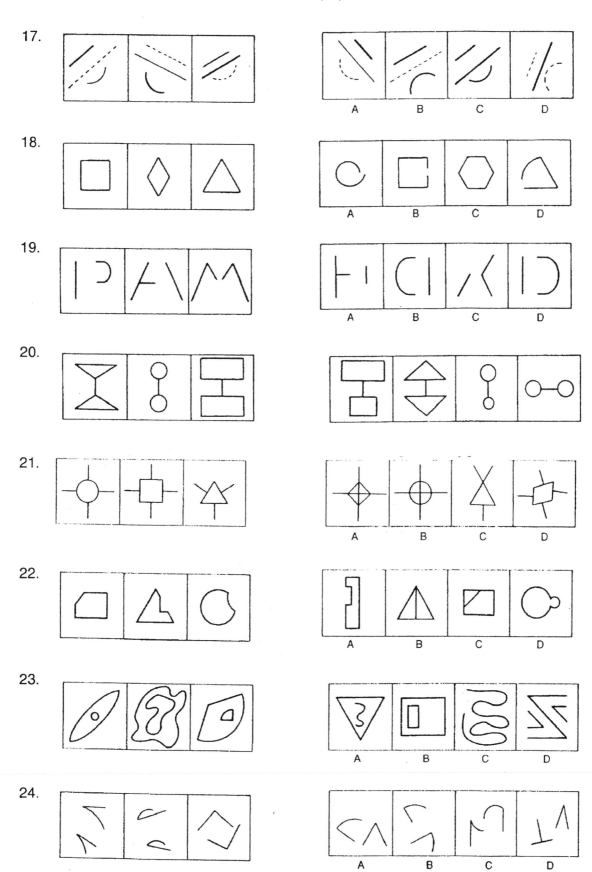

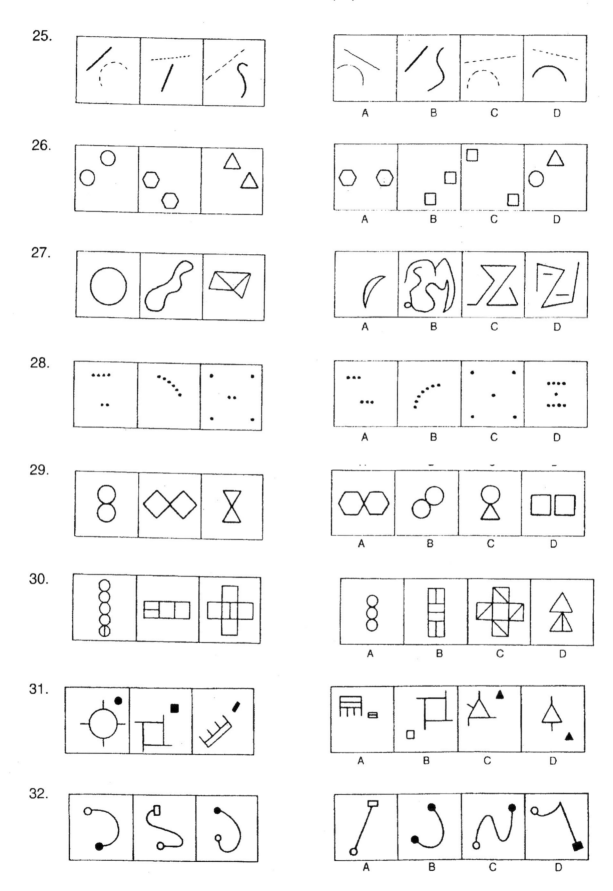

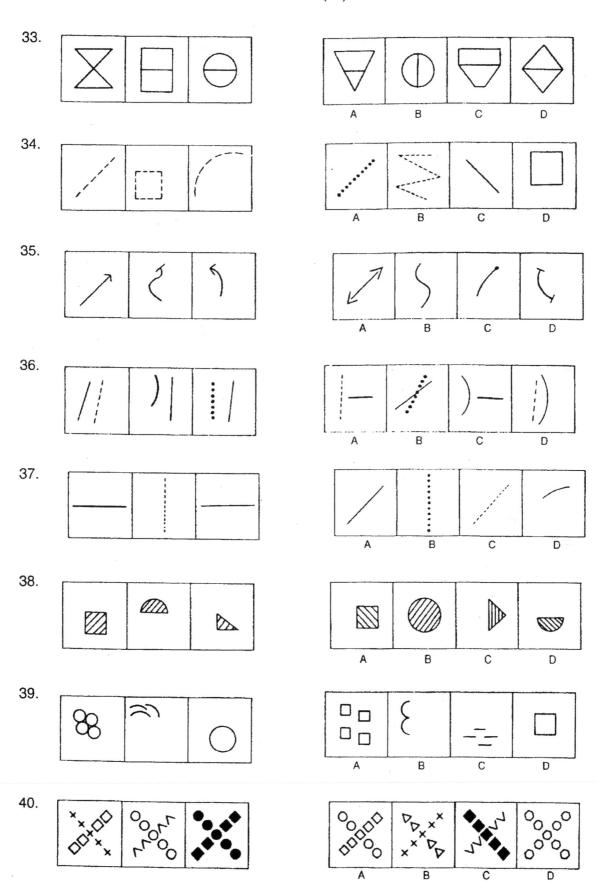

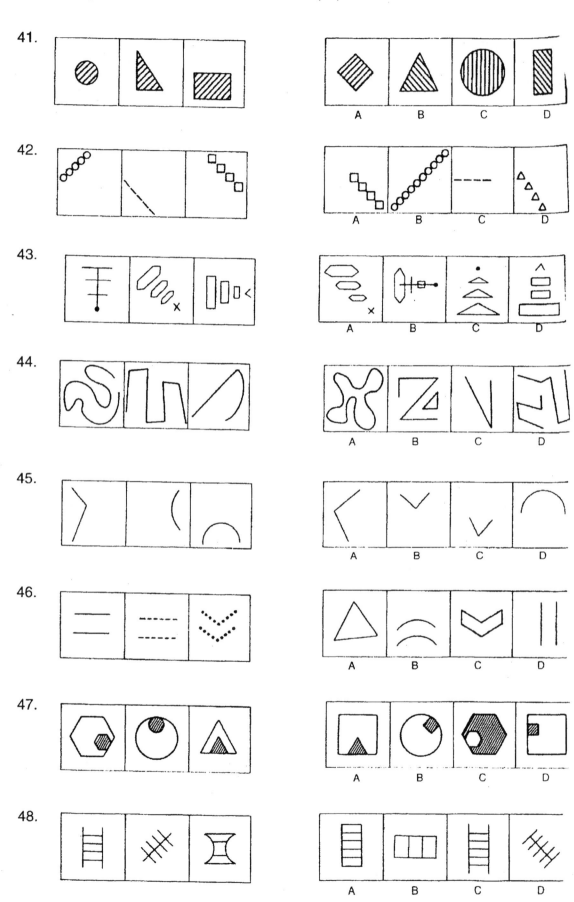

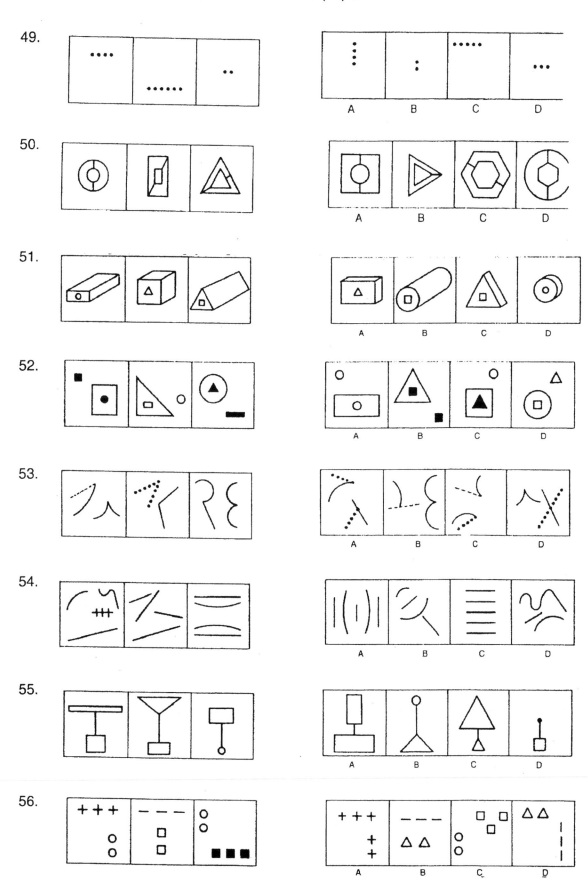

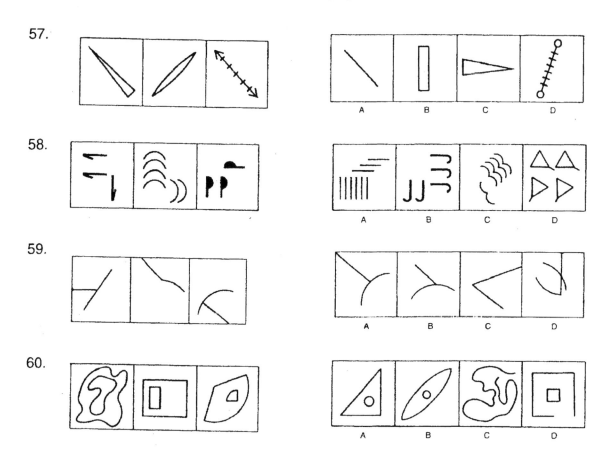

57.
58.
59.
60.

KEY (CORRECT ANSWERS)

1. C	11. D	21. D	31. C	41. A	51. B
2. B	12. B	22. A	32. C	42. D	52. D
3. A	13. A	23. B	33. D	43. C	53. C
4. C	14. A	24. B	34. B	44. C	54. B
5. D	15. D	25. D	35. C	45. B	55. C
6. B	16. A	26. B	36. D	46. B	56. D
7. C	17. A	27. A	37. B	47. D	57. A
8. C	18. C	28. A	38. B	48. B	58. A
9. D	19. D	29. A	39. B	49. D	59. C
10. A	20. B	30. D	40. C	50. C	60. B

ARITHMETICAL COMPUTATION AND REASONING
EXAMINATION SECTION
TEST 1

DIRECTIONS: Each question or incomplete statement is followed by several suggested answers or completions. Select the one that BEST answers the question or completes the statement. *PRINT THE LETTER OF THE CORRECT ANSWER IN THE SPACE AT THE RIGHT.*

1. 3/8 less than $40 is   1.____
   A. $25   B. $65   C. $15   D. $55

2. 27/64 expressed as a percent is   2.____
   A. 40.625%   B. 42.188%   C. 43.750%   D. 45.313%

3. 1/6 more than 36 gross is _____ gross.   3.____
   A. 6   B. 48   C. 30   D. 42

4. 15 is 20% of   4.____

5. The number which when increased by 1/3 of itself equals 96 is   5.____
   A. 128   B. 72   C. 64   D. 32

6. 0.16 3/4 written as percent is   6.____
   A. 16 3/4%   B. 16.3/4%   C. .016 3/4%   D. .0016 3/4%

7. 55% of 15 is   7.____
   A. 82.5   B. 0.825   C. 0.0825   D. 8.25

8. The number which when decreased by 1/3 of itself equals 96 is   8.____
   A. 64   B. 32   C. 128   D. 144

9. A carpenter used a board 15 3/4 ft. long from which 3 footstools were made with suffi-   9.____
cient lumber left over for half of another footstool.
If the lumber cost 24 1/2¢ per foot, the cost of EACH footstool was
   A. $1.54   B. $3.86   C. $1.10   D. $1.08

10. In one year, a luncheonette purchased 1231 gallons of milk for $907.99.   10.____
The AVERAGE cost per half pint was
   A. $0.046   B. $0.045   C. $0.047   D. $0.044

11. The product of 23 and 9 3/4 is   11.____
   A. 191 2/3   B. 224 1/4   C. 213 3/4   D. 32 3/4

12. An order for 345 machine bolts at $4.15 per hundred will cost   12.____
   A. $0.1432   B. $1.1432   C. $14.32   D. $143.20

13. The fractional equivalent of .0625 is 13._____

    A.   1/16   B.   1/15   C.   1/14   D.   1/13

14. The number 0.03125 equals 14._____

    A.   3/64   B.   1/16   C.   1/64   D.   1/32

15. 21.70 divided by 1.75 equals 15._____

    A.   124   B.   12.4   C.   1.24   D.   .124

16. The average cost of school lunches for 100 children varied as follows: Monday, $0.285; Tuesday, $0.237; Wednesday, $0.264; Thursday, $0.276; Friday, $0.292. The AVERAGE lunch cost 16._____

    A. $0.136   B. $0.270   C. $0.135   D. $0.271

17. The cost of 5 dozen eggs at $8.52 per gross is 17._____

    A. $3.50   B. $42.60   C. $3.55   D. $3.74

18. 410.07 less 38.49 equals 18._____

    A.   372.58   B.   371.58   C.   381.58   D.   382.68

19. The cost of 7 3/4 tons of coal at $20.16 per ton is 19._____

    A. $15.12   B. $151.20   C. $141.12   D. $156.24

20. The sum of 90.79, 79.09, 97.90, and 9.97 is 20._____

    A.   277.75   B.   278.56   C.   276.94   D.   277.93

KEY (CORRECT ANSWERS)

1.	A	11.	B
2.	B	12.	C
3.	D	13.	A
4.	C	14.	D
5.	B	15.	B
6.	A	16.	D
7.	D	17.	C
8.	D	18.	B
9.	C	19.	D
10.	A	20.	A

SOLUTIONS TO PROBLEMS

1. ($40)(5/8) = $25

2. 27/64 = .421875 ≈ 42.188%

3. (36)(1 1/6) = 42

4. Let x = missing number. Then, 15 = .20x. Solving, x = 75

5. Let x = missing number. Then, x + 1/3 x = 96. Simplifying, 4/3 x = 96. Solving, x = 96 ÷ 4/3 = 72

6. .16 3/4 = 16 3/4% by simply moving the decimal point two places to the right.

7. (.55)(15) = 8.25

8. Let x = missing number. Then, x - 1/3 x = 96. Simplifying, 2/3 x = 96. Solving, x = 96 ÷ 2/3 = 144

9. 15 3/4 ÷ 3 1/2 = 4.5 feet per footstool. The cost of one footstool is ($.245)(4.5) = $1.1025 ≈ $1.10

10. $907.99 ÷ 1231 = $.7376 per gallon. Since there are 16 half-pints in a gallon, the average cost per half-pint is $.7376 ÷ 16 ≈ $.046

11. (23)(9 3/4) = (23)(9.75) = 224.25 or 224 1/4

12. ($4.15)(3.45) = $14.3175 = $14.32

13. .0625 = 625/10,000 = 1/16

14. .03125 = 3125/100,000 = 1/32

15. 21.70 ÷ 1.75 = 12.4

16. The sum of these lunches is $1.354. Then, $1.354 ÷ 5 = $.2708 = $.271

17. $8.52 ÷ 12 = $.71 per dozen. Then, the cost of 5 dozen is ($.71)(5) = $3.55

18. 410.07 - 38.49 = 371.58

19. ($20.16)(7.75) = $156.24

20. 90.79 + 79.09 + 97.90 + 9.97 = 277.75

TEST 2

DIRECTIONS: Each question or incomplete statement is followed by several suggested answers or completions. Select the one that BEST answers the question or completes the statement. *PRINT THE LETTER OF THE CORRECT ANSWER IN THE SPACE AT THE RIGHT.*

1. 1600 is 40% of what number?   1.____

    A. 6400   B. 3200   C. 4000   D. 5600

2. An executive's time card reads: Arrived 9:15 A.M., Left 2:05 P.M.   2.____
How many hours was he in the office? _____ hours _____ minutes.

    A. 5; 10   B. 4; 50   C. 4; 10   D. 5; 50

3. .4266 times .3333 will have the following number of decimals in the product: 3.____

    A. 8   B. 4   C. 1   D. None of these

4. An office floor is 25 ft. wide by 36 ft. long.   4.____
To cover this floor with carpet will require _____ square yards.

    A. 100   B. 300   C. 900   D. 25

5. 1/8 of 1% expressed as a decimal is   5.____

    A. .125   B. .0125   C. 1.25   D. .00125

6. $\dfrac{6 \div 4}{6 \times 4}$ equals 6x4   6.____

    A. 1/16   B. 1   C. 1/6   D. 1/4

7. 1/25 of 230 equals   7.____

    A. 92.0   B. 9.20   C. .920   D. 920

8. 4 times 3/8 equals   8.____

    A. 1 3/8   B. 3/32   C. 12.125   D. 1.5

9. 3/4 divided by 4 equals   9.____

    A. 3   B. 3/16   C. 16/3   D. 16

10. 6/7 divided by 2/7 equals   10.____

    A. 6   B. 12/49   C. 3   D. 21

11. The interest on $240 for 90 days ' 6% is   11.____

    A. $4.80   B. $3.40   C. $4.20   D. $3.60

12. 16 2/3% of 1728 is   12.____

    A. 91   B. 288   C. 282   D. 280

13. 6 1/4% of 6400 is   13.____
    A.   2500   B.   410   C.   108   D.   400

14. 12 1/2% of 560 is   14.____
    A.   65   B.   40   C.   50   D.   70

15. 2 yards divided by 3 equals   15.____
    A.   2 feet   B.   1/2 yard   C.   3 yards   D.   3 feet

16. A school has 540 pupils. 45% are boys. How many girls are there in this school?   16.____
    A.   243   B.   297   C.   493   D.   394

17. .1875 is equivalent to   17.____
    A.   18 3/4   B.   75/18   C.   18/75   D.   3/16

18. A kitchen cabinet listed at $42 is sold for $33.60. The discount allowed is   18.____
    A.   10%   B.   15%   C.   20%   D.   30%

19. 3 6/8 divided by 8 1/4 equals   19.____
    A.   9 1/8   B.   12   C.   5/11   D.   243.16

20. An agent sold goods to the amount of $1480. His commission at 5 1/2% was   20.____
    A. $37.50   B. $81.40   C.   76.70   D. $81.10

KEY (CORRECT ANSWERS

1.	C	11.	D
2.	B	12.	B
3.	A	13.	D
4.	A	14.	D
5.	D	15.	A
6.	A	16.	B
7.	B	17.	D
8.	D	18.	C
9.	B	19.	C
10.	C	20.	B

SOLUTIONS TO PROBLEMS

1. Let x = missing number. Then, 1600 = .40x. Solving, x = 4000

2. 2:05 PM - 9:15 AM = 4 hours 50 minutes

3. The product of two 4-decimal numbers is an 8-decimal number.

4. (25 ft)(36 ft) = 900 sq.ft. = 100 sq.yds.

5. (1/8)(1%) = (.125)(.01) = .00125

6. (6 ÷ 4) ÷ (6 x 4) = 3/2 ÷ 24 = (3/2)(1/24)= (1/16)

7. (1/25)(230) = 9.20

8. (4)(3/8) = 12/8 = 1.5

9. 3/4 ÷ 4 = (3/4)(1/4) = 3/16

10. 6/7 / 2/7 = (6/7)(7/2) = 3

11. ($240)(.06)(90/360) = $3.60

12. (16 2/3%)(1728) = (1/6)(1728) = 288

13. (6 1/4%)(6400) = (1/16)(6400) = 400

14. (12 1/2%)(560) = (1/8)(560) = 70

15. 2 yds ÷ 3 = 2/3 yds = (2/3)(3) = 2 ft.

16. If 45% are boys, then 55% are girls. Thus, (540)(.55) = 297

17. .1875 = 1875/10,000 = 3/16

18. $42 - $33.60 = $8.40.
    The discount is $8.40 ÷ $42 = .20 = 20%

19. 3 6/8 - 8 1/4 = (30/8)(4/33) = 5/11

20. ($1480)(.055) = $81.40

TEST 3

DIRECTIONS: Each question or incomplete statement is followed by several suggested answers or completions. Select the one that BEST answers the question or completes the statement. *PRINT THE LETTER OF THE CORRECT ANSWER IN THE SPACE AT THE RIGHT.*

1. 93.648 divided by 0.4 is

    A. 23.412   B.   234.12   C.   2.3412   D.   2341.2

1.____

2. Add 4.3682, .0028, 34., 9.92, and from the sum subtract 1.992. The remainder is

    A. .46299   B.   4.6299   C.   462.99   D.   46.299

2.____

3. At $2.88 per gross, three dozen will cost

    A. $8.64   B. $0.96   C. $0.72   D. $11.52

3.____

4. 13 times 2.39 times 0.024 equals

    A. 745.68   B.   74.568   C.   7.4568   D.   .74568

4.____

5. A living room suite is marked $64 less 25 percent. A cash discount of 10 percent is allowed.
The cash price is

    A. $53.20   B. $47.80   C. $36.00   D. $43.20

5.____

6. 1/8 of 1 percent expressed as a decimal is

    A. .125   B.   .0125   C.   1.25   D.   .00125

6.____

7. 16 percent of 482.11 equals

    A. 77.1376   B.   771.4240   C.   7714.2400   D.   7.71424

7.____

8. A merchant sold a chair for $60. This was at a profit of 25 percent of what it cost him. The chair cost him

    A. $48   B. $45   C. $15   D. $75

8.____

9. Add 5 hours 13 minutes, 3 hours 49 minutes, and 14 minutes. The sum is _____ hours _____ minutes.

    A. 9; 16   B.   9;76   C.   8;16   D.   8;6

9.____

10. 89 percent of $482 is

    A. $428.98   B. $472.36   C. $42.90   D. $47.24

10.____

11. 200 percent of 800 is

    A. 16   B.   1600   C.   2500   D.   4

11.____

12. Add 2 feet 3 inches, 4 feet 11 inches, 8 inches, 6 feet 6 inches. The sum is _____ feet _____ inches.

    A. 12; 4   B.   12; 14   C.   14; 4   D.   14; 28

12.____

13. A merchant bought dresses at $15 each and sold them at $20 each. His overhead expenses are 20 percent of cost. His net profit on each dress is   13._____

    A. $1   B. $2   C. $3   D. $4

14. 0.0325 expressed as a percent is   14._____

    A. 325%   B. 3 1/4%   C. 32 1/2%   D. 32.5%

15. Add 3/4, 1/8, 1/32, 1/2; and from the sum subtract 4/8. The remainder is   15._____

    A. 2/32   B. 7/8   C. 29/32   D. 3/4

16. A salesman gets a commission of 4 percent on his sales. If he wants his commission to amount to $40, he will have to sell merchandise totaling   16._____

    A. $160   B. $10   C. $1,000   D. $100

17. Jones borrowed $225,000 for five years at 3 1/2 percent. The annual interest charge was   17._____

    A. $1,575   B. $1,555   C. $7,875   D. $39,375

18. A kitchen cabinet listed at $42 is sold for $33.60. The discount allowed is _____ percent.   18._____

    A. 10   B. 15   C. 20   D. 30

19. The exact number of days from May 5, 2007 to July 1, 2007 is _____ days.   19._____

    A. 59   B. 58   C. 56   D. 57

20. A dealer sells an article at a loss of 50% of the cost. Based on the selling price, the loss is   20._____

    A. 25%   B. 50%   C. 100%   D. none of these

KEY (CORRECT ANSWERS)

1.	B	11.	B
2.	D	12.	C
3.	C	13.	B
4.	D	14.	B
5.	D	15.	C
6.	D	16.	C
7.	A	17.	C
8.	A	18.	C
9.	A	19.	D
10.	A	20.	C

SOLUTIONS TO PROBLEMS

1. $93.648 \div .4 = 234.12$

2. $4.368 + .0028 + 34 + 9.92 - 1.992 = 48.291 - 1.992 = 46.299$

3. $2.88 for 12 dozen means $.24 per dozen. Three dozen will cost $(3)($.24) = $.72$

4. $(13)(2.39)(.024) = .74568$

5. $($64)(.75)(.90) = 43.20

6. $(1/8)(1\%) = (.125)(.01) = .00125$

7. $(.16)(482.11) = 77.1376$

8. Let x = cost. Then, $1.25x = 60. Solving, $x = 48

9. 5 hrs. 13 min. + 3 hrs. 49 min. + 14 min = 8 hrs. 76 min.

10. $(.89)($482) = 428.98

11. $200\% = 2$. So, $(200\%)(800) = (2)(800) = 1600$

12. 2 ft. 3 in. + 4 ft. 11 in. + 8 in. + 6 ft. 6 in. + 12 ft. 28 in. = 14 ft. 4 in.

13. Overhead is $(.20)($15) = 3. The net profit is $20 - $15 - $3 = 2

14. $.0325 = 3.25\% = 3\ 1/4\%$

15. $3/4 + 1/8 + 1/32 + 1/2 - 4/8 = 45/32 - 4/8 = 29/32$

16. Let x = sales. Then, $40 = .04x$. Solving, $x = 1000

17. Annual interest is $($225,000)(.035) \times 1 = 7875$

18. $42 - $33.60 = 8.40. Then, $8.40 \div $42 = .20 = 20\%$

19. The number of days left for May, June, July is 26, 30, and 1. Thus, $26 + 30 + 1 = 57$

20. Let x = cost, so that $.50x$ = selling price. The loss is represented by $.50x \div .50x = 1 = 100\%$ on the selling price. (Note: The loss in dollars is $x - .50x = .50x$)

ARITHMETICAL REASONING
EXAMINATION SECTION
TEST 1

DIRECTIONS: Each question or incomplete statement is followed by several suggested answers or completions. Select the one that BEST answers the question or completes the statement. *PRINT THE LETTER OF THE CORRECT ANSWER IN THE SPACE AT THE RIGHT.*

Questions 1-4.

DIRECTIONS: In answering questions 1-4, assume that you are working in a medical facility and are responsible for maintaining inventory and stock.

1. The following quantities of disposable syringes were used during the first six weeks of the year: 840, 756, 772, 794, 723, and 789.
   If the cost of a disposable syringe is seventy cents, the average weekly cost for disposable syringes is MOST NEARLY

   A. $550 B. $780 C. $850 D. $3,270   1._____

2. Four pieces of glass tubing measuring 4 feet 3 inches, 6 feet 8 inches, 7 feet 2 inches, and 7 feet 6 inches are to be cut into 5-inch pieces.
   The TOTAL number of 5-inch pieces that can be cut from the four pieces is

   A. 60 B. 61 C. 62 D. 63   2._____

3. Assume that a 55-gallon drum of disinfectant is to be distributed equally among eight work stations.
   The amount of disinfectant that each work station should receive is

   A. 7.5 gallons   B. 27.5 pints
   C. 55 pints   D. 55 quarts   3._____

4. On June 30, an inventory indicated that there were 13 dozen petri dishes in the stockroom. During the next four weeks in July, the following quantities of petri dishes were given out by the stockroom: 23, 56, 37, and 31. On August 1, no petri dishes were given out, but 9 dozen were delivered to the stockroom.
   The number of petri dishes in the stockroom AFTER delivery on August 1 is

   A. 18 B. 108 C. 110 D. 117   4._____

5. A table of composition of foods lists the protein value of a 100 gram portion of hamburger at 22 grams. The protein value of a 45 gram portion of hamburger is, therefore, _____ grams.

   A. 5 B. 9.9 C. 11.3 D. 12.4   5._____

6. To cover a room 15' x 18' with wall-to-wall carpeting requires _____ square yards.

   A. 25 B. 30 C. 35 D. 90   6._____

7. Assume that you are in a hospital whose x-ray department is open from 8 A.M. to 12 Noon and from 1 P.M. to 6 P.M. You have assigned one of your technicians to schedule all the x-ray appointments for the clinic cases. Your instructions to him are not to make more than 12 appointments per half hour in the morning session and not more 15 per hour for the afternoon session.
The GREATEST number of patients he can schedule in the entire day will be

    A. 75   B. 96   C. 123   D. 171

7._____

8. 1,000,000 may be represented as

    A. 10^3 B. 10^5 C. 10^6 D. 10^{10}

8._____

9. 35° Centigrade equals

    A. 70° F   B. 95° F   C. 100° F   D. 120° F

9._____

10. $10^3 \times 10^4$ equals

    A. 10^7 B. 10^{12} C. 100^7 D. 100^{12}

10._____

11. If a mixture is made up of one part Substance A, 3 parts Substance B, and 12 parts Substance C, the proportion of Substance A in the mixture is

    A. 4%   B. 6 1/4%   C. 16%   D. 62 1/2%

11._____

12. If 5 grams of a chemical are enough to perform a certain laboratory test 9 times, the quantity of the chemical needed to perform this test 1,350 times would be _____ grams.

    A. 30   B. 150   C. 270   D. 750

12._____

13. If it takes 7 grams of a certain substance to make 5 liters of a solution, the quantity of the substance needed to make 4 liters of the solution is _____ grams.

    A. 2.85   B. 4.70   C. 5.60   D. 8.75

13._____

14. If it takes 3 grams of Substance A and 7 grams of Substance B to make 4 liters of a solution, how many grams of Substances A and B does it take to make 5 liters of the solution?
_____ of Substance A and _____ of Substance B.

    A. 3.35; 6.65   B. 3.50; 7.50
    C. 3.75; 8.75   D. 4; 7

14._____

15. A certain type of laboratory test can be performed by a laboratory technician in 20 minutes.
Three laboratory technicians can perform 243 such tests in _____ hours.

    A. 16   B. 20   C. 27   D. 81

15._____

16. Pairs of shatterproof plastic safety glasses cost $38.00 each, but an 8% discount is given on orders of six pairs or more. Pairs of straight blade dissecting scissors cost $144 a dozen with a 12% discount on orders of two dozen or more.
The TOTAL cost of eight pairs of safety glasses and 30 pairs of dissecting scissors is MOST NEARLY

    A. $596.50   B. $621.00   C. $664.00   D. $731.50

16._____

17. On July 1, your laboratory has 280 usable 20-gauge needles on hand. On August 1, 15% of these needles have been lost or damaged beyond repair. On August 15, a new shipment of 50 needles is received by the laboratory, but 10% of these arrive damaged and are returned to the seller.
At this point, the number of usable 20-gauge needles on hand would be

   17.____

   A. 238   B. 283   C. 288   D. 325

18. A certain laboratory procedure can be completed by a laboratory technician in 15 minutes.
If your lab is assigned 30 such tests, and they must be completed within 3 hours, the MINIMUM number of technicians that would have to be assigned to this task is

   18.____

   A. 2   B. 3   C. 4   D. 5

19. A patient's hospital bill is $24,600. The patient has three different medical insurance plans, each of which will make partial payment toward his bill. One plan will pay $6,500 of the patient's bill, another will pay $7,300 of the bill, and the third will pay $8,832 of the bill. The percentage of the bill that the patient's three insurance plans combined do NOT pay for is

   19.____

   A. 5%   B. 8%   C. 10%   D. 20%

20. A patient has stayed at a hospital for which the all-inclusive daily rate is $205.00. The patient was hospitalized for 27 days. The patient is covered by a private insurance plan that will pay the hospital 2/3 of the patient's total hospital bill.
The one of the following that MOST NEARLY indicates how much of the patient's hospital bill would NOT be covered by this insurance plan is

   20.____

   A. $1,845   B. $2,078   C. $3,690   D. $3,156

21. A hospital charges a flat daily rate for all hospital services. In February 2000, the hospital charged a patient $2,772 for 14 days of hospitalization. In April 2002, the same patient was charged for 16 days of hospitalization at the same hospital.
If the daily rate charged by the hospital increased by $7 between the patient's 2000 hospitalization and his 2002 hospitalization, the total amount that the patient must pay for the 2002 hospitalization is

   21.____

   A. $3,296   B. $3,280   C. $3,264   D. $3,248

22. A hospital insurance plan that previously covered 3/5 of the total hospital charges for its subscribers has recently been improved, and coverage for total hospital charges has been increased by 25% of the previous rate. A subscriber to this plan has just completed a hospital stay and has received a bill for total hospital charges of $6,200.
Assuming that the hospital stay is covered by the recently improved plan, the one of the following that MOST NEARLY indicates how much the plan now provides the patient toward the payment of the hospital bill is

   22.____

   A. $1,550   B. $3,720   C. $4,650   D. $5,270

Questions 23-25.

DIRECTIONS: Questions 23 through 25 are to be answered on the basis of the following situation.

You have been asked to keep records of the time spent with each patient by the doctors in the clinic where you are assigned. Your notes show that Dr. Jones spent the following amount of time with each patient he examined on a certain day: Patient A - 14 minutes, Patient B - 13 minutes, Patient C - 34 minutes, Patient D - 48 minutes, Patient E - 26 minutes, Patient F - 20 minutes, Patient G - 25 minutes.

23. The average number of minutes spent by Dr. Jones with each patient is MOST NEARLY   23.____

    A. 20   B. 25   C. 30   D. 35

24. If Dr. Jones is to take care of the seven patients mentioned above at one session, the   24.____
number of hours he will have to remain at the clinic is MOST NEARLY _____ hour(s).

    A. 1   B. 2   C. 3   D. 4

25. The one of the following groups of patients that required the LEAST time to examine is   25.____
Patients _____ and _____.

    A. A, C; E   B. B, D; F   C. C , E; G   D. A, D; G

KEY (CORRECT ANSWERS)

1.	A		11.	B
2.	B		12.	D
3.	C		13.	C
4.	D		14.	C
5.	B		15.	C
6.	B		16.	A
7.	D		17.	B
8.	C		18.	B
9.	B		19.	B
10.	A		20.	A

21.	B
22.	C
23.	B
24.	C
25.	A

SOLUTIONS TO PROBLEMS

1. $(840+756+772+794+723+789) \div 6 = 779$. Then, $(779)(.70) = \$545.30$ $\$550$

2. $4'3'' + 6'8'' + 7'2'' + 7'6'' = 25'7'' = 307''$. Then, $307 \div 5 = 61.4$, so 61 5-inch pieces exist.

3. $55 \div 8 = 6.875$ gallons = 55 pints

4. $(13)(12) - 23 - 56 - 37 - 31 + (9)(12) = 117$ dishes

5. Let x = protein value. Then, Solving, $x = 9.9$ grams

6. $(15')(18') = 270$ sq.ft. = 30 sq.yds.

7. Maximum number of appointments = $(12)(8) + (15)(5) = 171$

8. $1,000,000 = 10^6$

9. $F = 9/5\ C + 32$. If $C = 35$, $F = (9/5)(35) + 32 = 95$

10. $10^3 \times 10^4 = 10^7$. When multiplying with like bases, add the exponents.

11. $\dfrac{1}{1+3+2} = \dfrac{1}{16} = 6\dfrac{1}{4}\%$

12. Let x = grams needed. Then, $5/9 = x/1350$. Solving, $x = 750$

13. Let x = grams needed. Then, $7/5 = x/4$ Solving, $x = 5.6$

14. Let x = grams of A needed and y = grams of B needed.
    Then, $3/4 = x/5$ and $7/4 = y/5$ Solving, $x = 3.75$, $y = 8.75$

15. The test requires 1/3 technician-hrs. Now, $(243)(1/3) = 81$ technician-hrs., and $81 \div 3 = 27$ hours

16. $(8)(\$38.00)(.92) + (2\ 1/2)(\$144)(.88) = \$596.48 \approx \$596.50$

17. $280 - (.15)(280) + 50 - (.10)(50) = 283$ needles on hand

18. The test requires 1/4 technician-hrs., so 30 tests require 7 1/2 technician-hrs. Since 3 hrs. is the time limit for these 30 tests, $7\ 1/2 \div 3 = 2.5$ or 3 technicians at a minimum are needed.

19. $\$24,600 - (\$6500+\$7300+\$8832) = \$1968$, and $1968/24,600 = 8\%$

20. Amount not covered = $(1/3)(\$205)(27) = \$1845$

21. Daily rate for 2000 = $\$2772\ 14 = \$198$, so for 2002 the daily rate = $\$205$. Finally, $(\$205)(16) = \$3280$

22. The new plan covers $(.60)(1.25) = .75$ or 75% of the bill. Then, $(.75)(\$6200) = \$4650$

23. $(14+13+34+48+26+20+25) \div 7 \approx 26$ min., closest to 25 min.

24. 180 min. = 3 hours

25. Patients A, C, E: 74 min.; patients B, D, F: 81 min.; patients C, E, G: 85 min.; patients A, D, G: 87 min. So, the 1st group requires the least time.

_____

TEST 2

DIRECTIONS: Each question or incomplete statement is followed by several suggested answers or completions. Select the one that BEST answers the question or completes the statement. *PRINT THE LETTER OF THE CORRECT ANSWER IN THE SPACE AT THE RIGHT.*

1. A stack of cartons containing pesticides is 10 cartons long, 9 cartons wide, and 5 cartons high.
The number of cartons in the stack is

    A. 24   B. 55   C. 95   D. 450

1._____

2. Assume that you have bags of corn meal, each of the same weight. The total weight of 25 bags is 125 pounds.
How many of these bags would it take to make a TOTAL weight of 50 pounds?

    A. 2   B. 5   C. 6   D. 10

2._____

3. You are working in the sub-basement of a project building, and the foreman tells you to get two boards from the maintenance shop to stand on. One of the boards is 5 yards long, and the other 3 1/2 feet long.
The TOTAL length, in feet, of the two boards is

    A. 8 1/2   B. 9 1/2   C. 17 1/2   D. 18 1/2

3._____

4. Three hundred plastic bags of rat-mix, each bag weighing four ounces, are packed in a carton. The carton weighed one pound before the rat-mix was packed in it.
The TOTAL weight of the filled carton is _____ pounds.

    A. 37 1/2   B. 38 1/2   C. 75   D. 76

4._____

5. Of 180 families that relocated in a given month, 1/5 moved into Finder's Fee apartments, 1/4 moved into tenant-found apartments, 1/3 moved into public housing, and the rest moved out of the city.
How many moved out of the city?

    A. 36   B. 39   C. 45   D. 60

5._____

6. If a space treatment device covers 1,000 cubic feet in six seconds, how long should it run in order to treat a room that is 30 feet long, 20 feet wide, and 15 feet high?

    A. 18 seconds   B. 54 seconds
    C. 1 minute 24 seconds   D. 1 minute 48 seconds

6._____

7. If you have to prepare five gallons of 0.5 Diazinon emulsion using water and 20% Diazinon emulsifiable concentrate, what is the amount of concentrate that is necessary?
_____ ounces.

    A. 1.6   B. 3.2   C. 16.0   D. 64.0

7._____

8. Suppose you have 15 5/6 ounces of a certain chemical on hand.
If you later receive shipments of 6 1/2 ounces and 8 3/4 ounces of this chemical, the TOTAL number of ounces you should then have on hand is

    A. 29 7/8   B. 30 5/6   C. 31 1/12   D. 31 3/4

8._____

9. You are told to prepare 60 pounds of 2% pyrethrum dust using talc and 5% pyrethrum   9._____
dust concentrate.
What is the amount of concentrate that is required in the mixture?
_____ pounds.

   A. 24   B. 28   C. 30 1/2   D. 36

10. In the pest control shop of a certain housing development, there is a supply of 4 one-gal-   10._____
lon containers of insecticide. This week, the exterminator will use up five quarts of this
insecticide in his work, and for each week thereafter he will use up five quarts. Deliveries
are made on the first day of the week.
Next week, and each week thereafter, the shop will get a delivery of one gallon of
insecticide. The exterminator will need an additional supply of insecticide by the end of
the _____ week.

   A. 4th   B. 12th   C. 24th   D. 29th

11. There are 22 boxes of rat mix in a certain pest control shop.   11._____
If each box contains 7 1/2 pounds of rat mix, the TOTAL amount of rat mix in the shop
is _____ pounds.

   A. 165   B. 172 1/2   C. 180   D. 182 1/2

12. A pest control shop has a supply of 26 one-gallon cans of insecticide.   12._____
If the exterminator works 5 days a week and uses 32 ounces of the liquid a day, the
number of work weeks this supply of insecticide will last is MOST NEARLY

   A. 10   B. 20   C. 28   D. 32

13. A certain supplier packs two dozen mousetraps to a box. If the exterminator gets a deliv-   13._____
ery of 20 boxes and finds that two of these boxes are half-full, the TOTAL number of traps
the exterminator received from this supplier is

   A. 408   B. 432   C. 456   D. 480

14. Assume that a truck which contains a shipment of pesticides is parked outside your   14._____
exterminating shop. You are able to unload the truck in one hour.
How long would it take four exterminators, starting at the same time and working at the
same rate as you, to unload four trucks similar to the one you unloaded?

   A. 15 minutes   B. 1 hour   C. 2 hours   D. 4 hours

15. A certain building in a housing development has 142 apartments. It takes one extermina-   15._____
tor an average of six minutes to treat one apartment.
At that rate, approximately how long should it take him to treat all 142 apartments?
_____ hours.

   A. 2   B. 14   C. 24   D. 85

16. A crate contains 3 pieces of pesticide equipment weighing 73, 84, and 47 pounds,   16._____
respectively.
If the crate is lifted by 4 exterminators, each lifting one corner of the crate, the average
number of pounds, in addition to the weight of the crate, lifted by each of the exterminators is

   A. 51   B. 65   C. 71   D. 78

17. Of the following, the pair that is NOT a set of equivalents is   17.____

    A. .014%; .00014   B. 1/5%; .002   C. 1.5%; 3/200   D. 115%; .115

18. 10^{-2} is equal to   18.____

    A. 0.001   B. 0.01   C. 0.1   D. 100.0

19. $10^2 \times 10^3$ is equal to   19.____

    A. 10^5 B. 10^6 C. 100^5 D. 100^6

20. The length of two objects are in the ratio of 2:1.   20.____
If each were 3 inches shorter, the ratio would be 3:1.
The longer object is _____ inches.

    A. 8   B. 10   C. 12   D. 14

21. If the weight of water is 62.4 pounds per cubic foot, the weight of the water that fills a   21.____
rectangular container 6 inches by 6 inches by 1 foot is pounds.

    A. 7.8   B. 15.6   C. 31.2   D. 46.8

22. The formula for converting degrees Centigrade to degrees Fahrenheit is as follows: 22.____
    Fahrenheit = 9/5 of Centigrade + 32°, or
    multiply the number of degrees Centigrade by 9, divide by 5 and add 32).
If the Centigrade thermometer reads 25°, the temperature in degrees Fahrenheit is

    A. 13   B. 45   C. 53   D. 77

23. To make a certain preparation, you have been told to mix one ounce of Liquid A and 3   23.____
ounces of Liquid B.
If you have used 18 ounces of Liquid B in preparing a larger amount, the number of
ounces of Liquid A you should use is

    A. 6   B. 15   C. 21   D. 54

24. If one inch is equal to approximately 2.5 centimeters, the number of inches in fifteen cen-   24.____
timeters is MOST NEARLY

    A. 1.6   B. 6   C. 12.5   D. 37.5

25. You are in charge of a small lawn area of 1,850 sq. ft. You are asked to apply lime on this   25.____
lawn at the rate of 40 pounds per 1,000 sq. ft.
The number of pounds of lime you will need to cover the entire area of the lawn is
MOST NEARLY _____ pounds.

    A. 74   B. 86   C. 87   D. 89

KEY (CORRECT ANSWERS)

1.	D	11.	A
2.	D	12.	B
3.	D	13.	C
4.	D	14.	B
5.	B	15.	B
6.	B	16.	A
7.	C	17.	D
8.	C	18.	B
9.	A	19.	A
10.	B	20.	C

21.	B
22.	D
23.	A
24.	B
25.	A

SOLUTIONS TO PROBLEMS

1. (10)(9)(5) = 450 cartons

2. Let x = number of bags. Then, 25/125 = x/50 . Solving, x = 10

3. 5 yds. + 3 1/2 ft. = 15 ft. + 3 1/2 ft. = 18 1/2 ft.

4. Total weight = 1 + (300) (4/16) = 76 pounds

5. 1-1/5-1/4-1/3=13/60. Then, (180)(13/60) = 39 families

6. (30')(20')(15') = 9000 cu.ft. Let x = number of seconds , Then, $\dfrac{1000}{6} = \dfrac{9000}{X}$. Solving, x = 54

7. 1 qt. of concentrate = 16 oz.

8. 15 5/6 + 6 1/2 + 8 3/4 = 29 25/12 = 31 1/12 ounces

9. .05x = .02(60)
    x = 24

10. For the 1st week (end), there will be 16 - 5 = 11 qts. left. For each additional week, since 4 qts. are delivered but 5 qts. are used, there will be a net loss of 1 qt. Thus, at the end of 12 weeks, the supply of insecticide will be gone.

11. (22)(7 1/2) = 165 pounds

12. (26)(128) = 3328 oz., and (32)(5) = 160 oz. used each week. Finally, 3328 ÷ 160 = 20.8, closest to 20 oz.

13. (24) (18) + (12)(2) = 456 mousetraps

14. 4 trucks require 4 man-hours. Then, 4 ÷ 4=1 hour

15. (142)(6) = 852 min. = 14.2 hrs. ≈ 14 hrs.

16. Total weight = 204 lbs. Then, 204 ÷ 4 = 51 lbs.

17. 115% = 1.15, not .115

18. 10^{-2} = 1/100 = .01

19. 10^2 x 10^3 = 10^5. When multiplying with like bases, add the exponents.

20. Let x, 1/2x = lengths of the longer and shorter objects. Then, x - 3 = 3(1/2x-3). Simplifying, x - 3 = 3/2x - 9. Solving, x = 12 in.

21. (1/2'))(1/2')(1') = 1/4 cu.ft. Then, (62.4)(1/4) = 15.6 pounds

22. F = (9/5)(25^0) + 32^0 = 77^0

23. Let x = number of ounces of liquid A. Then, 1/3 = x/18. Solving, x = 6

24. 15 cm. = $\dfrac{15}{\approx 2.5}$ or approx. 6 in.

25. (40)(1850/1000) = 74 pounds

———

SCIENCE READING COMPREHENSION
EXAMINATION SECTION
TEST 1

DIRECTIONS: Each question or incomplete statement is followed by several suggested answers or completions. Select the one that BEST answers the question or completes the statement. *PRINT THE LETTER OF THE CORRECT ANSWER IN THE SPACE AT THE RIGHT.*

PASSAGE

Photosynthesis is a complex process with many intermediate steps. Ideas differ greatly as to the details of these steps, but the general nature of the process and its outcome are well established. Water, usually from the soil, is conducted through the xylem of root, stem and leaf to the chlorophyl-containing cells of a leaf. In consequence of the abundance of water within the latter cells, their walls are saturated with water. Carbon dioxide, diffusing from the air through the stomata and into the intercellular spaces of the leaf, comes into contact with the water in the walls of the cells which adjoin the intercellular spaces. The carbon dioxide becomes dissolved in the water of these walls, and in solution diffuses through the walls and the plasma membranes into the cells. By the agency of chlorophyl in the chloroplasts of the cells, the energy of light is transformed into chemical energy. This chemical energy is used to decompose the carbon dioxide and water, and the products of their decomposition are recombined into a new compound. The compound first formed is successively built up into more and more complex substances until finally a sugar is produced.

Questions 1-8.

1. The union of carbon dioxide and water to form starch results in an excess of   1.____

   A. hydrogen   B. carbon   C. oxygen
   D. carbon monoxide   E. hydrogen peroxide

2. Synthesis of carbohydrates takes place   2.____

   A. in the stomata
   B. in the intercellular spaces of leaves
   C. in the walls of plant cells
   D. within the plasma membranes of plant cells
   E. within plant cells that contain chloroplasts

3. In the process of photosynthesis, chlorophyl acts as a   3.____

   A. carbohydrate   B. source of carbon dioxide
   C. catalyst   D. source of chemical energy
   E. plasma membrane

4. In which of the following places are there the GREATEST number of hours in which photosynthesis can take place during the month of December?   4.____

   A. Buenos Aires, Argentina   B. Caracas, Venezuela
   C. Fairbanks, Alaska   D. Quito, Ecuador
   E. Calcutta, India

5. During photosynthesis, molecules of carbon dioxide enter the stomata of leaves because   5.___

    A. the molecules are already in motion
    B. they are forced through the stomata by the son's rays
    C. chlorophyl attracts them
    D. a chemical change takes place in the stomata
    E. oxygen passes out through the stomata

6. Besides food manufacture, another USEFUL result of photosynthesis is that it   6.___

    A. aids in removing poisonous gases from the air
    B. helps to maintain the existing proportion of gases in the air
    C. changes complex compounds into simpler compounds
    D. changes certain waste products into hydrocarbons
    E. changes chlorophyl into useful substances

7. A process that is almost the exact reverse of photosynthesis is the   7.___

    A. rusting of iron   B. burning of wood
    C. digestion of starch   D. ripening of fruit
    E. storage of food in seeds

8. The leaf of the tomato plant will be unable to carry on photosynthesis if the   8.___

    A. upper surface of the leaf is coated with vaseline
    B. upper surface of the leaf is coated with lampblack
    C. lower surface of the leaf is coated with lard
    D. leaf is placed in an atmosphere of pure carbon dioxide
    E. entire leaf is coated with lime

———

TEST 2

PASSAGE

The only carbohydrate which the human body can absorb and oxidize is the simple sugar glucose. Therefore, all carbohydrates which are consumed must be changed to glucose by the body before they can be used. There are specific enzymes in the mouth, the stomach, and the small intestine which break down complex carbohydrates. All the monosaccharides are changed to glucose by enzymes secreted by the intestinal glands, and the glucose is absorbed by the capillaries of the villi.

The following simple test is used to determine the presence of a reducing sugar. If Benedict's solution is added to a solution containing glucose or one of the other reducing sugars and the resulting mixture is heated, a brick-red precipitate will be formed. This test was carried out on several substances and the information in the following table was obtained. "P" indicates that the precipitate was formed and "N" indicates that no reaction was observed.

Material Tested	Observation
Crushed grapes in water	P
Cane sugar in water	N
Fructose	P
Molasses	N

Questions 1-2.

1. From the results of the test made upon crushed grapes in water, one may say that grapes contain   1.____

    A. glucose   B. sucrose   C. a reducing sugar
    D. no sucrose   E. no glucose

2. Which one of the following foods probably undergoes the LEAST change during the process of carbohydrate digestion in the human body?   2.____

    A. Cane sugar   B. Fructose   C. Molasses
    D. Bread   E. Potato

TEST 3

DIRECTIONS: Each question or incomplete statement is followed by several suggested answers or completions. Select the one that BEST answers the question or completes the statement. *PRINT THE LETTER OF THE CORRECT ANSWER IN THE SPACE AT THE RIGHT.*

PASSAGE

The British pressure suit was made in two pieces and joined around the middle in contrast to the other suits, which were one-piece suits with a removable helmet. Oxygen was supplied through a tube, and a container of soda lime absorbed carbon dioxide and water vapor. The pressure was adjusted to a maximum of 2 1/2 pounds per square inch (130 millimeters) higher than the surrounding air. Since pure oxygen was used, this produced a partial pressure of 130 millimeters, which is sufficient to sustain the flier at any altitude.

Using this pressure suit, the British established a world's altitude record of 49,944 feet in 1936 and succeeded in raising it to 53,937 feet the following year. The pressure suit is a compromise solution to the altitude problem. Full sea-level pressure can not be maintained, as the suit would be so rigid that the flier could not move arms or legs. Hence a pressure one third to one fifth that of sea level has been used. Because of these lower pressures, oxygen has been used to raise the partial pressure of alveolar oxygen to normal.

Questions 1-9.

1. The MAIN constituent of air not admitted to the pressure suit described was   1._____

   A. oxygen   B. nitrogen   C. water vapor
   D. carbon dioxide   E. hydrogen

2. The pressure within the suit exceeded that of the surrounding air by an amount equal to   2._____
   130 millimeters of

   A. mercury   B. water   C. air
   D. oxygen   E. carbon dioxide

3. The normal atmospheric pressure at sea level is   3._____

   A. 130 mm   B. 250 mm   C. 760 mm
   D. 1000 mm   E. 1300 mm

4. The water vapor that was absorbed by the soda lime came from   4._____

   A. condensation
   B. the union of oxygen with carbon dioxide
   C. body metabolism
   D. the air within the pressure suit
   E. water particles in the upper air

5. The HIGHEST altitude that has been reached with the British pressure suit is about   5._____

   A. 130 miles   B. 2 1/2 miles   C. 6 miles
   D. 10 miles   E. 5 miles

6. If the pressure suit should develop a leak, the   6._____

    A.   oxygen supply would be cut off
    B.   suit would fill up with air instead of oxygen
    C.   pressure within the suit would drop to zero
    D.   pressure within the suit would drop to that of the surrounding air
    E.   suit would become so rigid that the flier would be unable to move arms or legs

7. The reason why oxygen helmets are unsatisfactory for use in efforts to set higher altitude   7._____
records is that

    A.   it is impossible to maintain a tight enough fit at the neck
    B.   oxygen helmets are too heavy
    C.   they do not conserve the heat of the body as pressure suits do
    D.   if a parachute jump becomes necessary, it can not be made while such a helmet is being worn
    E.   oxygen helmets are too rigid

8. The pressure suit is termed a compromise solution because   8._____

    A.   it is not adequate for stratosphere flying
    B.   aviators can not stand sea-level pressure at high altitudes
    C.   some suits are made in two pieces, others in one
    D.   other factors than maintenance of pressure have to be accommodated
    E.   full atmospheric pressure can not be maintained at high altitudes

9. The passage implies that   9._____

    A.   the air pressure at 49,944 feet is approximately the same as it is at 53,937 feet
    B.   pressure cabin planes are not practical at extremely high altitudes
    C.   a flier's oxygen requirement is approximately the same at high altitudes as it is at sea level
    D.   one-piece pressure suits with removable helmets are unsafe
    E.   a normal alveolar oxygen supply is maintained if the air pressure is between one third and one fifth that of sea level

TEST 4

DIRECTIONS: Each question or incomplete statement is followed by several suggested answers or completions. Select the one that BEST answers the question or completes the statement. *PRINT THE LETTER OF THE CORRECT ANSWER IN THE SPACE AT THE RIGHT.*

PASSAGE

Chemical investigations show that during muscle contraction the store of organic phosphates in the muscle fibers is altered as energy is released. In doing so, the organic phosphates (chiefly adenoisine triphosphate and phospho-creatine) are transformed anaerobically to organic compounds plus phosphates. As soon as the organic phosphates begin to break down in muscle contraction, the glycogen in the muscle fibers also transforms into lactic acid plus free energy; this energy the muscle fiber uses to return the organic compounds plus phosphates into high-energy organic phosphates ready for another contraction. In the presence of oxygen, the lactic acid from the glycogen decomposition is changed also. About one-fifth of it is oxidized to form water and carbon dioxide and to yield another supply of energy. This time the energy is used to transform the remaining four-fifths of the lactic acid into glycogen again.

Questions 1-5.

1.   The energy for muscle contraction comes directly from the   1.__

   A.   breakdown of lactic acid into glycogen
   B.   resynthesis of adenosine triphosphate
   C.   breakdown of glycogen into lactic acid
   D.   oxidation of lactic acid
   E.   breakdown of the organic phosphates

2.   Lactic acid does NOT accumulate in a muscle that   2.__

   A.   is in a state of lacking oxygen
   B.   has an ample supply of oxygen
   C.   is in a state of fatigue
   D.   is repeatedly being stimulated
   E.   has an ample supply of glycogen

3.   The energy for the resynthesis of adenosine triphosphate and phospho-creatine comes   3.__
     from the

   A.   oxidation of lactic acid
   B.   synthesis of organic phosphates
   C.   change from glycogen to lactic acid
   D.   resynthesis of glycogen
   E.   change from lactic acid to glycogen

4.   The energy for the resynthesis of glycogen comes from the   4.__

   A.   breakdown of organic phosphates
   B.   resynthesis of organic phosphates
   C.   change occurring in one-fifth of the lactic acid

D. change occurring in four-fifths of the lactic acid
E. change occurring in four-fifths of glycogen

5. The breakdown of the organic phosphates into organic compounds plus phosphates is an   5.____

  A. anobolic reaction   B. aerobic reaction
  C. endothermic reaction   D. exothermic reaction
  E. anaerobic reaction

———

TEST 5

DIRECTIONS: Each question or incomplete statement is followed by several suggested answers or completions. Select the one that BEST answers the question or completes the statement. *PRINT THE LETTER OF THE CORRECT ANSWER IN THE SPACE AT THE RIGHT.*

PASSAGE

And with respect to that theory of the origin of the forms of life peopling our globe, with which Darwin's name is bound up as closely as that of Newton with the theory of gravitation, nothing seems to be further from the mind of the present generation than any attempt to smother it with ridicule or to crush it by vehemence of denunciation. "The struggle for existence," and "natural selection," have become household words and everyday conceptions. The reality and the importance of the natural processes on which Darwin founds his deductions are no more doubted than those of growth and multiplication; and, whether the full potency attributed to them is admitted or not, no one is unmindful of or at all doubts their vast and far-reaching significance. Wherever the biological sciences are studied, the "Origin of Species" lights the path of the investigator; wherever they are taught it permeates the course of instruction. Nor has the influence of Darwinian ideas been less profound beyond the realms of biology. The oldest of all philosophies, that of evolution, was bound hand and foot and cast into utter darkness during the millennium of theological scholasticism. But Darwin poured new life-blood into the ancient frame; the bonds burst, and the revivified thought of ancient Greece has proved itself to be a more adequate expression of the universal order of things than any of the schemes which have been accepted by the credulity and welcomed by the superstition of seventy later generations of men.

Questions 1-7.

1. Darwin's theory of the origin of the species is based on   1.___

    A.   theological deductions
    B.   the theory of gravitation
    C.   Greek mythology
    D.   natural processes evident in the universe
    E.   extensive reading in the biological sciences

2. The passage implies that   2.___

    A.   thought in ancient Greece was dead
    B.   the theory of evolution is now universally accepted
    C.   the "Origin of Species" was seized by the Church
    D.   Darwin was influenced by Newton
    E.   the theories of "the struggle for existence" and "natural selection" are too evident to be scientific

3. The idea of evolution   3.___

    A.   was suppressed for 1,000 years
    B.   is falsely claimed by Darwin
    C.   has swept aside all superstition
    D.   was outworn even in ancient Greece
    E.   has revolutionized the universe

4. The processes of growth and multiplication   4.____

    A.   have been replaced by others discovered by Darwin
    B.   were the basis for the theory of gravitation
    C.   are "the struggle for existence" and "natural selection"
    D.   are scientific theories not yet proved
    E.   are accepted as fundamental processes of nature

5. Darwin's treatise on evolution   5.____

    A.   traces life on the planets from the beginning of time to the present day
    B.   was translated from the Greek
    C.   contains an ancient philosophy in modern, scientific guise
    D.   has had a profound effect on evolution
    E.   has had little notice outside scientific circles

6. The theory of evolution   6.____

    A.   was first advanced in the "Origin of Species"
    B.   was suppressed by the ancient Greeks
    C.   did not get beyond the monasteries during the millennium
    D.   is philosophical, not scientific
    E.   was elaborated and revived by Darwin

7. Darwin has contributed GREATLY toward   7.____

    A.   a universal acceptance of the processes of nature
    B.   reviving the Greek intellect
    C.   ending the millennium of theological scholasticism
    D.   a satisfactory explanation of scientific theory
    E.   easing the struggle for existence

———

TEST 6

DIRECTIONS: Each question or incomplete statement is followed by several suggested answers or completions. Select the one that BEST answers the question or completes the statement. *PRINT THE LETTER OF THE CORRECT ANSWER IN THE SPACE AT THE RIGHT.*

PASSAGE

The higher forms of plants and animals, such as seed plants and vertebrates, are similar or alike in many respects but decidedly different in others. For example, both of these groups of organisms carry on digestion, respiration, reproduction, conduction, growth, and exhibit sensitivity to various stimuli. On the other hand, a number of basic differences are evident. Plants have no excretory systems comparable to those of animals. Plants have no heart or similar pumping organ. Plants are very limited in their movements. Plants have nothing similar to the animal nervous system. In addition, animals can not synthesize carbohydrates from inorganic substances. Animals do not have special regions of growth, comparable to terminal and lateral meristems in plants, which persist through-out the life span of the organism. And, finally, the animal cell "wall" is only a membrane, while plant cell walls are more rigid, usually thicker, and may be composed of such substances as cellulose, lignin, pectin, cutin, and suberin. These characteristics are important to an understanding of living organisms and their functions and should, consequently, be carefully considered in plant and animal studies

Questions 1-7.

1. Which of the following do animals lack?   1.___

   A. Ability to react to stimuli
   B. Ability to conduct substances from one place to another
   C. Reproduction by gametes
   D. A cell membrane
   E. A terminal growth region

2. Which of the following statements is false?   2.___

   A. Animal cell "walls" are composed of cellulose.
   B. Plants grow as long as they live.
   C. Plants produce sperms and eggs.
   D. All vertebrates have hearts.
   E. Wood is dead at maturity.

3. Respiration in plants takes place   3.___

   A. only during the day
   B. only in the presence of carbon dioxide
   C. both day and night
   D. only at night
   E. only in the presence of certain stimuli

4. An example of a vertebrate is the   4.___

   A. earthworm   B. starfish   C. amoeba
   D. cow   E. insect

5. Which of the following statements is true?   5.____

    A. All animals eat plants as a source of food.
    B. Respiration, in many ways, is the reverse of photo-synthesis.
    C. Man is an invertebrate animal.
    D. Since plants have no hearts, they can not develop high pressures in their cells.
    E. Plants can not move.

6. Which of the following do plants lack?   6.____

    A. A means of movement
    B. Pumping structures
    C. Special regions of growth
    D. Reproduction by gametes
    E. A digestive process

7. A substance that can be synthesized by green plants but NOT by animals is   7.____

    A. protein   B. cellulose   C. carbon dioxide
    D. uric acid   E. water

———

TEST 7

DIRECTIONS: Each question or incomplete statement is followed by several suggested answers or completions. Select the one that BEST answers the question or completes the statement. *PRINT THE LETTER OF THE CORRECT ANSWER IN THE SPACE AT THE RIGHT.*

PASSAGE

Sodium chloride, being by far the largest constituent of the mineral matter of the blood, assumes special significance in the regulation of water exchanges in the organism. And, as Cannon has emphasized repeatedly, these latter are more extensive and more important than may at first thought appear. He points out "there are a number of circulations of the fluid out of the body and back again, without loss." Thus, by example, it is estimated that from a quart and one-half of water daily "leaves the body" when it enters the mouth as saliva; another one or two quarts are passed out as gastric juice; and perhaps the same amount is contained in the bile and the secretions of the pancreas and the intestinal wall. This large volume of water enters the digestive processes; and practically all of it is reabsorbed through the intestinal wall, where it performs the equally important function of carrying in the digested foodstuffs. These and other instances of what Cannon calls "the conservative use of water in our bodies" involve essentially osmotic pressure relationships in which the concentration of sodium chloride plays an important part.

Questions 1-11.

1. This passage implies that   1.___

    A. the contents of the alimentary canal are not to be considered within the body
    B. sodium chloride does not actually enter the body
    C. every particle of water ingested is used over and over again
    D. water can not be absorbed by the body unless it contains sodium chloride
    E. substances can pass through the intestinal wall in only one direction

2. According to this passage, which of the following processes requires MOST water? The   2.___

    A. absorption of digested foods
    B. secretion of gastric juice
    C. secretion of saliva
    D. production of bile
    E. concentration of sodium chloride solution

3. A body fluid that is NOT saline is   3.___

    A. blood   B. urine   C. bile
    D. gastric juice   E. saliva

4. An organ that functions as a storage reservoir from which large quantities of water are   4.___
    reabsorbed into the body is the

    A. kidney   B. liver   C. large intestine
    D. mouth   E. pancreas

5. Water is reabsorbed into the body by the process of 5.____

    A. secretion   B. excretion   C. digestion
    D. osmosis   E. oxidation

6. Digested food enters the body PRINCIPALLY through the 6.____

    A. mouth   B. liver   C. villi
    D. pancreas   E. stomach

7. The metallic element found in the blood in compound form and present there in larger 7.____
quantities than any other metallic element is

    A. iron   B. calcium   C. magnesium
    D. chlorine   E. sodium

8. An organ that removes water from the body and prevents its reabsorption for use in the 8.____
body processes is the

    A. pancreas   B. liver   C. small intestine
    D. lungs   E. large intestine

9. In which of the following processes is sodium chloride removed MOST rapidly from the 9.____
body?

    A. Digestion   B. Breathing   C. Oxidation
    D. Respiration   E. Perspiration

10. Which of the following liquids would pass from the alimentary canal into the blood MOST 10.____
rapidly?

    A. A dilute solution of sodium chloride in water
    B. Gastric juice
    C. A concentrated solution of sodium chloride in water
    D. Digested food
    E. Distilled water

11. The reason why it is unsafe to drink ocean water even under conditions of extreme thirst 11.____
is that it

    A. would reduce the salinity of the blood to a dangerous level
    B. contains dangerous disease germs
    C. contains poisonous salts
    D. would greatly increase the salinity of the blood
    E. would cause salt crystals to form in the blood stream

TEST 8

DIRECTIONS: Each question or incomplete statement is followed by several suggested answers or completions. Select the one that BEST answers the question or completes the statement. *PRINT THE LETTER OF THE CORRECT ANSWER IN THE SPACE AT THE RIGHT.*

PASSAGE

The discovery of antitoxin and its specific antagonistic effect upon toxin furnished an opportunity for the accurate investigation of the relationship of a bacterial antigen and its antibody. Toxin-antitoxin reactions were the first immunological processes to which experimental precision could be applied, and the discovery of principles of great importance resulted from such studies. A great deal of the work was done with diphtheria toxin and antitoxin and the facts elucidated with these materials are in principle applicable to similar substances.

The simplest assumption to account for the manner in which an antitoxin renders a toxin innocuous would be that the antitoxin destroys the toxin. Roux and Buchner, however, advanced the opinion that the antitoxin did not act directly upon the toxin, but affected it indirectly through the mediation of tissue cells. Ehrlich, on the other hand, conceived the reaction of toxin and antitoxin as a direct union, analogous to the chemical neutralization of an acid by a base.

The conception of toxin destruction was conclusively refuted by the experiments of Calmette. This observer, working with snake poison, found that the poison itself (unlike most other toxins) possessed the property of resisting heat to 100 degrees C, while its specific antitoxin, like other antitoxins, was destroyed at or about 70 degrees C. Nontoxic mixtures of the two substanues, when subjected to heat, regained their toxic properties. The natural inference from these observations was that the toxin in the original mixture had not been destroyed, but had been merely inactiviated by the presence of the antitoxin and again set free after destruction of the antitoxin by heat.

Questions 1-10.

1. Both toxins and antitoxins ORDINARILY   1.__

    A.   are completely destroyed at body temperatures
    B.   are extremely resistant to heat
    C.   can exist only in combination
    D.   are destroyed at 180° F
    E.   are products of nonliving processes

2. MOST toxins can be destroyed by   2.__

    A.   bacterial action   B.   salt solutions
    C.   boiling   D.   diphtheria antitoxin
    E.   other toxins

3. Very few disease organisms release a true toxin into the blood stream. It would follow,   3.__
    then, that

    A.   studies of snake venom reactions have no value
    B.   studies of toxin-antitoxin reactions are of little importance

174

C.   the treatment of most diseases must depend upon information obtained from study of a few
D.   antitoxin plays an important part in the body defense against the great majority of germs
E.   only toxin producers are dangerous

4.   A person becomes susceptible to infection again immediately after recovering from   4.____

   A.   mumps   B.   tetanus   C.   diphtheria
   D.   smallpox   E.   tuberculosis

5.   City people are more frequently immune to communicable diseases than country people   5.____
     are because

   A.   country people eat better food
   B.   city doctors are better than country doctors
   C.   the air is more healthful in the country
   D.   country people have fewer contacts with disease carriers
   E.   there are more doctors in the city than in the country

6.   The substances that provide us with immunity to disease are found in the body in the   6.____

   A.   blood serum   B.   gastric juice   C.   urine
   D.   white blood cells   E.   red blood cells

7.   A person ill with diphtheria would MOST likely be treated with   7.____

   A.   diphtheria toxin   B.   diphtheria toxoid
   C.   dead diphtheria germs   D.   diphtheria antitoxin
   E.   live diphtheria germs

8.   To determine susceptibility to diphtheria, an individual may be given the   8.____

   A.   Wassermann test   B.   Schick test
   C.   Widal test   D.   Dick test
   E.   Kahn test

9.   Since few babies under six months of age contract diphtheria, young babies PROBABLY   9.____

   A.   are never exposed to diphtheria germs
   B.   have high body temperatures that destroy the toxin if acquired
   C.   acquire immunity from their mothers
   D.   acquire immunity from their fathers
   E.   are too young to become infected

10.   Calmette's findings   10.____

   A.   contradicted both Roux and Buchner's opinion and Ehrlich's conception
   B.   contradicted Roux and Buchner, but supported Ehrlich
   C.   contradicted Ehrlich, but supported Roux and Buchner
   D.   were consistent with both theories
   E.   had no bearing on the point at issue

TEST 9

DIRECTIONS: Each question or incomplete statement is followed by several suggested answers or completions. Select the one that BEST answers the question or completes the statement. *PRINT THE LETTER OF THE CORRECT ANSWER IN THE SPACE AT THE RIGHT.*

PASSAGE

In the days of sailing ships, when voyages were long and uncertain, provisions for many months were stored without refrigeration in the holds of the ships. Naturally no fresh or perishable foods could be included. Toward the end of particularly long voyages the crews of such ships became ill and often many died from scurvy. Many men, both scientific and otherwise, tried to devise a cure for scurvy. Among the latter was John Hall, a son-in-law of William Shakespeare, who cured some cases of scurvy by administering a sour brew made from scurvy grass and water cress.

The next step was the suggestion of William Harvey that scurvy could be prevented by giving the men lemon juice. He thought that the beneficial substance was the acid contained in the fruit.

The third step was taken by Dr. James Lind, an English naval surgeon, who performed the following experiment with 12 sailors, all of whom were sick with scurvy: Each was given the same diet, except that four of the men received small amounts of dilute sulfuric acid, four others were given vinegar and the remaining four were given lemons. Only those who received the fruit recovered.

Questions 1-7.

1. Credit for solving the problem described above belongs to   1.___

    A. Hall, because he first devised a cure for scurvy
    B. Harvey, because he first proposed a solution of the problem
    C. Lind, because he proved the solution by means of an experiment
    D. both Harvey and Lind, because they found that lemons are more effective than scurvy grass or water cress
    E. all three men, because each made some contribution

2. A good substitute for lemons in the treatment of scurvy is   2.___

    A. fresh eggs   B. tomato juice   C. cod-liver oil
    D. liver   E. whole-wheat bread

3. The number of control groups that Dr. Lind used in his experiment was   3.___

    A. one   B. two   C. three   D. four   E. none

4. A substance that will turn blue litmus red is   4.___

    A. aniline   B. lye   C. ice
    D. vinegar   E. table salt

5. The hypothesis tested by Lind was: 5.___

    A. Lemons contain some substance not present in vinegar.
    B. Citric acid is the most effective treatment for scurvy.

C. Lemons contain some unknown acid that will cure scurvy.
D. Some specific substance, rather than acids in general, is needed to cure scurvy.
E. The substance needed to cure scurvy is found only in lemons.

6. A problem that Lind's experiment did NOT solve was: 6.____

A. Will citric acid alone cure scurvy?
B. Will lemons cure scurvy?
C. Will either sulfuric acid or vinegar cure scurvy?
D. Are all substances that contain acids equally effective as a treatment for scurvy?
E. Are lemons more effective than either vinegar or sulfuric acid in the treatment of scurvy?

7. The PRIMARY purpose of a controlled scientific experiment is to   7.____

A. get rid of superstitions
B. prove a hypothesis is correct
C. disprove a theory that is false
D. determine whether a hypothesis is true or false
E. discover new facts

TEST 10

DIRECTIONS: Each question or incomplete statement is followed by several suggested answers or completions. Select the one that BEST answers the question or completes the statement. *PRINT THE LETTER OF THE CORRECT ANSWER IN THE SPACE AT THE RIGHT.*

PASSAGE

The formed elements of the blood are the red corpuscles or erythrocytes, the white corpuscles or leucocytes, the blood platelets, and the so-called blood dust or hemoconiae. Together, these constitute 30-40 per cent by volume of the whole blood, the remainder being taken up by the plasma. In man, there are normally 5,000,000 red cells per cubic millimeter of blood; the count is somewhat lower in women. Variations occur frequently, especially after exercise or a heavy meal, or at high altitudes. Except in camels, which have elliptical corpuscles, the shape of the mammalian corpuscle is that of a circular, nonnucleated, bi-concave disk. The average diameter usually given is 7.7 microns, a value obtained by examining dried preparations of blood and considered by Ponder to be too low. Ponder's own observations, made on red cells in the fresh state, show the human corpuscle to have an average diameter of 8.8 microns. When circulating in the blood vessels, the red cell does not maintain a fixed shape but changes its form constantly, especially in the small capillaries. The red blood corpuscles are continually undergoing destruction, new corpuscles being formed to replace them. The average life of red corpuscles has been estimated by various investigators to be between three and six weeks. Preceding destruction, changes in the composition of the cells are believed to occur which render them less resistant. In the process of destruction, the lipids of the membrane are dissolved and the hemoglobin which is liberated is the most important, though probably not the only, source of bilirubin. The belief that the liver is the only site of red cell destruction is no longer generally held. The leucocytes, of which there are several forms, usually number between 7000 and 9000 per cubic millimeter of blood. These increase in number in disease, particularly when there is bacterial infection.

Questions 1-10.

1. Leukemia is a disease involving the   1.__

    A. red cells   B. white cells   C. plasma
    D. blood platelets   E. blood dust

2. Are the erythrocytes in the blood increased in number after a heavy meal? The paragraph implies that this   2.__

    A. is true   .   B. holds only for camels
    C. is not true   D. may be true
    E. depends on the number of white cells

3. When blood is dried, the red cells   3.__

    A. contract   B. remain the same size   C. disintegrate
    D. expand   E. become elliptical

4. Ponder is probably classified as a professional   4.__

    A. pharmacist   B. physicist   C. psychologist
    D. physiologist   E. psychiatrist

5. The term "erythema" when applied to skin conditions signifies   5.____

    A. redness   B. swelling   C. irritation

    D. pain   E. roughness

6. Lipids are insoluble in water and soluble in such solvents as ether, chloroform and ben-   6.____
zene. It may be inferred that the membranes of red cells MOST closely resemble

    A. egg white   B. sugar   C. bone

    D. butter   E. cotton fiber

7. Analysis of a sample of blood yields cell counts of 4,800,000 erythrocytes and 16,000   7.____
leucocytes per cubic millimeter. These data suggest that the patient from whom the
blood was taken

    A. is anemic

    B. has been injuriously invaded by germs

    C. has been exposed to high-pressure air

    D. has a normal cell count

    E. has lost a great deal of blood

8. Bilirubin, a bile pigment, is   8.____

    A. an end product of several different reactions

    B. formed only in the liver

    C. formed from the remnants of the cell membranes of erythrocytes

    D. derived from hemoglobin exclusively

    E. a precursor of hemoglobin

9. Bancroft found that the blood count of the natives in the Peruvian Andes differed from   9.____
that usually accepted as normal. The blood PROBABLY differed in respect to

    A. leucocytes   B. blood platelets   C. cell shapes

    D. erythrocytes   E. hemoconiae

10. Hemoglobin is probably NEVER found   10.____

    A. free in the blood stream

    B. in the red cells

    C. in women's blood

    D. in the blood after exercise

    E. in the leucocytes

TEST 11

Questions 1-7.

DIRECTIONS: Each question or incomplete statement is followed by several suggested answers or completions. Select the one that BEST answers the question or completes the statement. *PRINT THE LETTER OF THE CORRECT ANSWER IN THE SPACE AT THE RIGHT.*

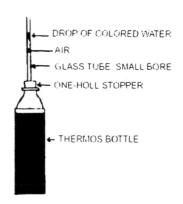

1. The device shown in the diagram above indicates changes that are measured more accurately by a(n)   1.__

   A. thermometer   B. hygrometer   C. anemometer
   D. hydrometer   E. barometer

2. If the device is placed in a cold refrigerator for 72 hours, which of the following is MOST likely to happen?   2.__

   A. The stopper will be forced out of the bottle.
   B. The drop of water will evaporate.
   C. The drop will move downward.
   D. The drop will move upward.
   E. No change will take place.

3. When the device was carried in an elevator from the first floor to the sixth floor of a building, the drop of colored water moved about 1/4 inch in the tube. Which of the following is MOST probably true? The drop moved   3.__

   A. *downward* because there was a decrease in the air pressure
   B. *upward* because there was a decrease in the air pressure
   C. *downward* because there was an increase in the air temperature
   D. *upward* because there was an increase in the air temperature
   E. *downward* because there was an increase in the temperature and a decrease in the pressure

4. The part of a thermos bottle into which liquids are poured consists of   4.__

   A. a single-walled, metal flask coated with silver
   B. two flasks, one of glass and one of silvered metal
   C. two silvered-glass flasks separated by a vacuum
   D. two silver flasks separated by a vacuum
   E. a single-walled, glass flask with a silver-colored coating

5. The thermos bottle is MOST similar in principle to   5.____

    A. the freezing unit in an electric refrigerator
    B. radiant heaters
    C. solar heating systems
    D. storm windows
    E. a thermostatically controlled heating system

6. In a plane flying at an altitude where the air pressure is only half the normal pressure at   6.____
sea level, the plane's altimeter should read, *approximately,*

    A. 3000 feet   B. 9000 feet   C. 18000 feet
    D. 27000 feet   E. 60000 feet

7. Which of the following is the POOREST conductor of heat?   7.____

    A. Air under a pressure of 1.5 pounds per square inch
    B. Air under a pressure of 15 pounds per square inch
    C. Unsilvered glass
    D. Silvered glass
    E. Silver

———

TEST 12

DIRECTIONS: Each question or incomplete statement is followed by several suggested answers or completions. Select the one that BEST answers the question or completes the statement. *PRINT THE LETTER OF THE CORRECT ANSWER IN THE SPACE AT THE RIGHT.*

PASSAGE

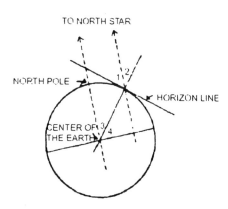

The latitude of any point on the earth's surface is the angle between a plumb line dropped to the center of the earth from that point and the plane of the earth's equator. Since it is impossible to go to the center of the earth to measure latitude, the latitude of any point may be determined indirectly as shown in the accompanying dia gram.

It will be recalled that the axis of the earth, if extended out-ward, passes very near the North Star. Since the North Star is, for all practical purposes, infinitely distant, the line of sight to the North Star of an observer on the surface of the earth is virtually parallel with the earth's axis. Angle 1, then, in the diagram represents the angular distance of the North Star above the horizon. Angle 2 is equal to angle 3, because when two parallel lines are intersected by a straight line, the corresponding angles are equal. Angle 1 plus angle 2 is a right angle and so is angle 3 plus angle 4. Therefore, angle 1 equals angle 4 because when equals are sub-tracted from equals the results are equal.

Questions 1-10.

1. If an observer finds that the angular distance of the North Star above the horizon is 30, his latitude is   1.____

    A. 15° N   B. 30° N   C. 60° N   D. 90° N   E. 120° N

2. To an observer on the equator, the North Star would be   2.____

    A. 30° above the horizon   B. 60° above the horizon
    C. 90° above the horizon   D. on the horizon
    E. below the horizon

3. To an observer on the Arctic Circle, the North Star would be

    A. directly overhead
    B. 23 1/2° above the horizon
    C. 66 1/2° above the horizon
    D. on the horizon
    E. below the horizon

3.____

4. The distance around the earth along a certain parallel of latitude is 3600 miles. At that latitude, how many miles are there in one degree of longitude?

    A. 1 mile   B. 10 miles   C. 30 miles
    D. 69 miles   E. 100 miles

4.____

5. At which of the following latitudes would the sun be DIRECTLY overhead at noon on June 21?

    A. 0°   B. 23 1/2°S   C. 23 1/2°N
    D. 66 1/2°N   E. 66 1/2°S

5.____

6. On March 21 the number of hours of daylight at places on the Arctic Circle is

    A. none   B. 8   C. 12   D. 16   E. 24

6.____

7. The distance from the equator to the 45th parallel, measured along a meridian, is, *approximately,*

    A. 450 miles   B. 900 miles   C. 1250 miles
    D. 3125 miles   E. 6250 miles

7.____

8. The difference in time between the meridians that pass through longitude 45°E and longitude 105°W

    A. 6 hours   B. 2 hours   C. 8 hours
    D. 4 hours   E. 10 hours

8.____

9. Which of the following is NOT a great circle or part of a great circle?

    A. Arctic Circle
    B. 100th meridian
    C. Equator
    D. Shortest distance between New York and London
    E. Greenwich meridian

9.____

10. At which of the following places does the sun set EARLIEST on June 21?

    A. Montreal, Canada   B. Santiago, Chile
    C. Mexico City, Mexico   D. Lima, Peru
    E. Manila, P.I.

10.____

KEY (CORRECT ANSWERS)

TEST 1		**TEST 2**	**TEST 3**		**TEST 4**
1. C	5. A	1. C	1. B	6. D	1. A
2. E	6. B	2. B	2. A	7. D	2. B
3. C	7. B		3. C	8. E	3. C
4. A	8. C		4. C	9. C	4. C
			5. D		5. D

TEST 5		**TEST 6**		**TEST 7**		**TEST 8**	
1. D	5. D	1. E	5. B	1. A	6. C	1. D	6. A
2. B	6. E	2. A	6. B	2. A	7. E	2. C	7. D
3. A	7. A	3. C	7. B	3. D	8. D	3. C	8. B
4. E		4. D		4. C	9. E	4. E	9. C
				5. D	10. E	5. D	10. D
					11. D		

TEST 9		**TEST 10**		**TEST 11**		**TEST 12**	
1. E	5. D	1. B	6. D	1. A	5. D	1. B	6. C
2. B	6. A	2. D	7. B	2. C	6. C	2. D	7. D
3. B	7. D	3. A	8. A	3. B	7. A	3. C	8. E
4. D		4. D	9. D	4. C		4. B	9. A
		5. A	10. E			5. C	10. B

EXAMINATION SECTION
TEST 1

DIRECTIONS: Each question or incomplete statement is followed by several suggested answers or completions. Select the one that BEST answers the question or completes the statement. *PRINT THE LETTER OF THE CORRECT ANSWER IN THE SPACE AT THE RIGHT.*

Questions 1-8.

DIRECTIONS: Questions 1-8 refer to the passage that follows. Base your choice on the info mation given in the selection and on your own understanding of science.

Whenever micro-organisms have successfully invaded the body and are growing at the expense of the tissues, the process is called an infection. The term *infection* should always imply the existence of an abnormal state or unnatural condition resulting from the harmful action of micro-organisms. In other words, the simple presence of an organism is not suffi- cient to cause disease. .

Infection may arise from the admission of microorganisms to the tissues through the gas- trointestinal tract, through the upper air passages, through wounds made by contaminated teeth or claws of animals or by contaminated weapons, and by the bite of suctorial insects. Another type of infection sometimes occurs when for some reason the body has become vul- nerable to the pathogenic action of bacteria whose normal habitat is the body.

The reaction of the body to the attack of an invading organism results in the formation of substances of a specific nature. Those reaction bodies which circulate mainly in the blood serum are known as antibodies and are classified according to their activity. Some known as antitoxins, neutralize poisonous substances produced by the infecting organism. Others, called bacteriolysins, destroy bacteria by dissolving them. Opsonins or bacteriotropins pre- pare the bacteria for destruction by phagocytes, while precipitins and agglutinins have the property of grouping the invading agents into small clumps or precipitates. The formation of defensive substances is specific for each organism.

1. The passage states "the formation of defensive substances is specific for each organ- ism." This implies that

    A. organisms inherit the ability to produce antibodies
    B. only specific organisms can produce antibodies
    C. the same organism cannot cause the production of two kinds of antibodies
    D. diphtheria antitoxin will not neutralize tetanus toxin
    E. only specific microorganisms can cause the production of antibodies in the human body

1.____

2. The passage you have read defines the term *infection*. In the light of what it says, which of the following conditionswould illustrate an infection?

    A. A guinea pig is injected with diphtheria toxin. It becomes very ill and dies.
    B. A nurse taking care of a tubercular patient inhales some tuberculosis bacilli.
    C. A man cuts his finger with a dirty knife. He uses no antiseptic.

2.____

D. A student examines his saliva with a microscope. Under high power he observes some streptococci.

E. An anopheles mosquito bites a healthy soldier. Some time thereafter, the soldier experiences alternate periods of chin and fever.

3. Phagocytes are mentioned in the last paragraph of the passage. Of the following, the statement that is TRUE of phagocytes is:

    3.____

    A. All white corpuscles are phagocytes.
    B. Some white corpuscles are phagocytes.
    C. Phagocytes are always red corpuscles.
    D. Phagocytes are usually platelets.
    E. Parasitic amebas are phagocytes.

4. In their control of infection the phagocytes are aided by

    4.____

    A. enzymes   B. insulin   C. fibrinogen   D. lipids
    E. lymph glands

5. The passage mentions several ways in which germs may enter the body. One of those mentioned is by way of the gastrointestinal tract. A disease that enters in this way is

    5.____

    A. beriberi   B. typhoid   C. typhus
    D. yellow fever   E. cancer of the stomach

6. With which of the following statements would the author of the passage agree?

    6.____

    A. The white blood corpuscles help ward off infection by distributing antibodies to all parts of the body.
    B. A disease organism may live in the body of a person without having any bad effect on the person.
    C. Antibodies are classified according to the type of organism they attack.
    D. Infection is usually accompanied by swelling and the formation of pus.
    E. Antitoxins are formed against every organism which enters the body.

7. A child comes down with diphtheria. His brother, who has never had diphtheria and has never been immunized against it, should receive

    7.____

    A. the Shick test
    B. injections of diphtheria toxin
    C. injections of diphtheria antitoxin
    D. injections of diphtheria toxoid
    E. nothing, as any treatment would be ineffective

8. Not long ago a child in a large city died of diphtheria. The following opinions were expressed by different people when they read about this. Which opinion is in best keeping with modern medical knowledge and practice?

    8.____

    A. In the struggle for existence the weak die off. Therefore, the death of this child is of advantage to society because the child was probably a weakling.
    B. Diphtheria is a disease of childhood and some children must die of it.
    C. In a large city some deaths from diphtheria must be expected despite all precautions.

D. This death was unnecessary. The child could have been saved if the proper medical care had been provided while the child was ill.

E. No child should sicken with diphtheria, much less die of it. Where children still die of diphtheria, either the parents are ignorant of the fact that it is preventable or they are negligent of the welfare of their children.

9. Accidents in the home occur MOST frequently from   9.____

   A. burns   B. falls   C. firearms   D. poisons
   E. suffocation

10. When a motor car is going 20 miles per hour, its brakes can stop it in 40 feet. When the   10.____
    same car is going 40 miles per hour, its brakes ought to stop it in about

   A. 40 ft.   B. 80 ft.   C. 160 ft.   D. 200 ft.
   E. 240 ft.

11. Emotional stability is a characteristic of mental health that is MOST important to   11.____

   A. clearness of complexion
   B. digestion
   C. muscle tone
   D. resistance to infectious disease
   E. respiration

12. Anne and Margaret went to a restaurant for lunch. Anne had a cup of consomm?, four   12.____
    saltines , a square of butter, a serving of plain jello and a gingersnap. Margaret had a cup
    of tomato soup, two slices of buttered toast, a glass of milk and a baked apple. Compari-
    son of their lunches indicated that

   A. Margaret's lunch was a poorer source of calcium than Anne's
   B. Margaret's lunch was a poorer source of vitamin C
   C. Anne's lunch was higher in caloric value than Margaret's
   D. Anne's lunch was a better source of iron than Margaret's
   E. Anne's lunch was a poorer source of vitamin A

13. A family consists of father, mother and three children aged fifteen, thirteen and five. The   13.____
    MINIMUM amount of milk the family should buy per week is

   A. 7 quarts   B. 14 quarts   C. 21 quarts
   D. 28 quarts   E. 35 quarts

14. In buying citrus fruit for juice it is MOST economical to select the fruit   14.____

   A. with thick skins   B. heavy for their size
   C. extra large in size   D. small in size
   E. with most highly colored skins

15. In selecting eggs for the family, it is BEST to buy those that   15.____

   A. are fertile   B. are whitest in color
   C. seem light in the hand   D. have smooth, shiny shells
   E. have rough, dull shells

16. In caring for plastics (such as bakelite), it is important to know that
    A. an abrasive is a good cleanser for them
    B. they can be subjected to high temperatures
    C. they are resistant to water and most chemicals
    D. they are molded
    E. their colors are apt to fade

16.____

17. Which of the following circuits could you wire from this diagram?

17.____

    A. code oscillator
    C. electric chime
    E. electric train signal
    B. doorbell system
    D. radio receiving set

18. Which process does the illustration represent?

18.____

    A. heading a rivet
    C. setting a nail
    E. forming the head of a screw
    B. flattening a bolt
    D. clinching a nail

19. Which drawing illustrates a wired edge in sheet metal work?

19.____

    A.   B.   C.   D.   E.

20. Which symbol represents an electrical ground connection?

20.____

    A.   B.   C.   D.   E.

21. With what kind of saw should the type of curve illustrated below be cut?

21.____

    A. back saw
    D. key-hole saw
    B. coping saw
    E. rip saw
    C. dovetail saw

22. In squaring up a piece of rough lumber, which of the surfaces indicated would you plane first?   22._____

23. Which diagram illustrates the CORRECT method of determining the position of a circle?   23._____

A.   B.   C.   D.   E.

24. All of the following are drawing instruments EXCEPT   24._____

   A. T-square   B. compass   C. triangle
   D. scale rule   E. plumb bob

25. The instrument used to regulate the temperature of a refrigerator is a   25._____

   A. thermocouple   B. thermograph
   C. thermometer   D. thermoscope
   E. thermostat

26. The source from which MOST electromagnetic waves radiate is   26._____

   A. electromagnets   B. power plants   C. the spectrum
   D. the sun   E. uranium 235

27. If the bulb of a glass thermometer is plunged into hot water, the mercury first falls before rising because the   27._____

   A. air above the mercury expands
   B. mercury contracts from the shock
   C. glass expands faster than the mercury
   D. mercury has a negative coefficient of expansion
   E. expanding glass absorbs heat from the mercury

28. A Diesel engine operates without   28._____

   A. a crankshaft   B. a cooling system
   C. an ignition coil   D. a flywheel
   E. pistons

29. Electric clocks commonly used in homes rarely need setting because they   29._____

   A. are well regulated at the factory
   B. keep in step with carefully regulated generators
   C. are manufactured with such fine tolerances
   D. contain ingenious governors
   E. are kept wound by small motors

30. The fuse in a household wiring circuit is a metal with a high   30._____

    A. capacity   B. combustion point
    C. coefficient of expansion   D. melting point.
    E. resistance

31. The area of a regular-size postage stamp is about   31._____

    A. 8 square millimeters   B. 1 square centimeter
    C. 5 square centimeters   D. 50 square centimeters
    E. 2.4 square decimeters

32. The spectroscope is used to   32._____

    A. calibrate periscopes
    B. study the interior of the lungs
    C. magnify small objects enormously
    D. analyze the composition of hot materials
    E. discover the defects in large castings

33. The Beaufort scale is used in the measurement of   33._____

    A. wind velocity
    B. very low temperatures
    C. earthquake intensities
    D. light intensity
    E. small changes in gravitational forces

34. Electrons are   34._____

    A. neutral particles   B. the nuclei of atoms
    C. negative particles   D. neutralized protons
    E. positive particles

35. The differential in an automobile is a device that allows   35._____

    A. a continuous change of gear ratio
    B. the rear wheels to turn independently of each other
    C. a variable battery-charging voltage
    D. traction for one rear wheel when the other is on a slippery surface
    E. compensation for gasolines of various octane ratings

36. A railroad locomotive stopped with a crankshaft on dead center is started forward by   36._____

    A. an auxiliary engine
    B. the stored inertia from previous motion
    C. the opposite piston
    D. cranking the crankshaft off center
    E. first backing up

37. The exhaust gas of an automobile is mainly carbon, carbon dioxide, carbon monoxide, nitrogen, and   37._____

    A. hydrogen   B. oxygen   C. steam
    D. gasoline vapor   E. silicon carbide

38. A woman bought a navy blue dress with white polka dots in a store illuminated with a   38.____
    pure yellow light. The colors of the dress as they appeared in the store were

    A. blue with yellow polka dots
    B. black with white polka dots
    C. black with yellow polka dots
    D. green with white polka dots
    E. green with yellow polka dots

39. Of the following, the one that weighs MOST is   39.____

    A. 50 grams of feathers
    B. 1 pound of cotton
    C. 12 ounces of lead
    D. 1 cubic centimeter of mercury
    E. 600,000 milligrams of sulfur

40. Water is obtained from an artesian well   40.____

    A. with a shallow lift pump   B. with a shallow force pump
    C. with a deep lift pump   D. with a deep force pump
    E. without a pump

41. Which one of the following items would NOT have to be seriously considered by a group   41.____
    of scientists exploring on the moon?

    A. Effects of insolation
    B. Effects of gravity
    C. Temperature changes after nightfall
    D. Changing weather conditions
    E. Communication with the earth

42. Each day between March 21 and June 21, the sun appears to set a tiny bit farther north   42.____
    of west than it rose north of east because the

    A. days are getting longer
    B. earth has moved on its orbit during the day
    C. earth's axis tilts a little more each day
    D. earth rotates on its axis
    E. earth is coming closer to the sun

43. The twinkling of a star is caused by   43.____

    A. the star itself
    B. interplanetary dust
    C. defects in the structure of the human eye
    D. objects passing between the star and our eyes
    E. turbulence within the atmosphere

44. The Aurora borealis and the Aurora australis are indications that   44.____

    A. the earth's atmosphere is more than 200 miles in depth
    B. large ice sheets reflect considerable light
    C. the earth's orbit and its axis are not mutually perpendicular
    D. moonlight is reflected from cirrus clouds
    E. moonlight is reflected from nimbus clouds

45. A point on the earth's surface diametrically opposite latitude 40° N, longitude 70° W is   45._____

    A. 40° N 70° E   B. 40° S 70° E   C. 50° S 110° E
    D. 40° S 110° E   E. 50° S 70° E

46. The BEST estimate of the age of the earth comes from studies of   46._____

    A. the total thickness of sedimentary rocks
    B. certain changes in radioactive minerals
    C. the amount of salt in the ocean
    D. the amount of erosion
    E. the mineralization of the lowest fossil-bearing rock

47. Which of the following elements related to the process of nuclear fission does NOT occur   47._____
in nature?

    A. barium   B. curium   C. radium   D. thorium
    E. uranium

48. The nucleus of an atom of uranium 235 contains   48._____

    A. 235 protons
    B. 235 neutrons
    C. 92 protons and 143 neutrons
    D. 90 protons and 146 neutrons
    E. 146 protons and 89 neutrons

49. A mineral mined in large quantities in the East is   49._____

    A. aluminum   B. coal   C. magnesium   D. salt
    E. sulfur

50. Certain metals are added to increase the hardness and toughness of steel. A group of   50._____
such metals is

    A. magnesium, cadmium, antimony
    B. manganese, chromium, nickel
    C. carbon, tin, copper
    D. zinc, lead, aluminum
    E. nickel, tin, zinc

KEY (CORRECT ANSWERS)

1.	D	11.	B	21.	B	31.	C	41.	D
2.	E	12.	E	22.	E	32.	D	42.	B
3.	B	13.	D	23.	A	33.	A	43.	E
4.	E	14.	B	24.	E	34.	C	44.	A
5.	B	15.	E	25.	E	35.	B	45.	D
6.	B	16.	C	26.	D	36.	C	46.	B
7.	C	17.	D	27.	C	37.	C	47.	B
8.	E	18.	A	28.	C	38.	C	48.	C
9.	B	19.	C	29.	B	39.	E	49.	D
10.	C	20.	C	30.	E	40.	E	50.	B

———

TEST 2

DIRECTIONS: Each question or incomplete statement is followed by several suggested answers or completions. Select the one that *BEST* answers the question or completes the statement. *PRINT THE LETTER OF THE CORRECT ANSWER IN THE SPACE AT THE RIGHT.*

1. A relatively inert gas, such as argon, is included in many incandescent electric lamps because the gas

    A.   excludes oxygen, which would corrode the filament
    B.   glows when electrically excited
    C.   reacts with the filament to cause the glow
    D.   permits rapid vaporization around the filament
    E.   prevents rapid vaporization around the filament

1.____

2. Wet wood will usually burn but does *NOT* make good tinder because

    A.   water does not burn
    B.   so much heat is needed to evaporate the water
    C.   wet wood has a higher kindling temperature than dry wood
    D.   the water vapor produced smothers the fire
    E.   wet wood has a lower kindling temperature than dry wood

2.____

3. When coal burns in a furnace, the weight of all the substances derived from the burning will be equal to the weight of

    A.   the coal
    B.   the ashes taken from the furnace
    C.   all the air entering the furnace
    D.   the air entering the furnace plus the weight of the ashes
    E.   the oxygen entering the furnace plus the weight of the coal

3.____

4. Hard coal burns with less smoke than soft coal because hard coal

    A.   is more nearly pure carbon
    B.   contains more volatile materials
    C.   has a lower kindling temperature
    D.   undergoes chemical change more readily
    E.   contains more smoke-reducing compounds

4.____

5. A metal much used in the construction of permanent magnets is

    A.   brass   B.   copper   C.   nickel
    D.   tin   E.   zinc

5.____

6. The frequency of visible light falls between that of

    A.   infrared rays and radio waves
    B.   X rays and cosmic rays
    C.   ultraviolet rays and X rays
    D.   short radio waves and long radio waves
    E.   ultraviolet rays and infrared waves

6.____

7. In the visible spectrum, yellow is between 7._____

    A.   red and orange   B.   orange and green
    C.   green and blue   D.   green and blue
    E.   blue and violet

8. The centripetal force that holds the earth in a nearly circular orbit is 8._____

    A.   the momentum of the earth
    B.   the inertia of the earth
    C.   the gravitational attraction of the earth and sun for each other
    D.   the atomic energy of the sun
    E.   the electromagnetic attraction of the sun for the iron core of the earth

9. A light year is a measure of 9._____

    A.   acceleration   B.   distance
    C.   intensity   D.   time
    E.   velocity

10. The atmosphere contains about 1% 10._____

    A.   argon   B.   carbon dioxide
    C.   helium   D.   hydrogen
    E.   krypton

11. Air that has a relative humidity of 50% 11._____

    A.   has half as much water vapor as it can hold
    B.   is half water vapor and half air
    C.   has half its water vapor condensed
    D.   has its water vapor half way condensed
    E.   has half its water content condensed and half evaporated

12. As a mass of air rises 12._____

    A.   its temperature increases and its pressure increases
    B.   its temperature decreases and its pressure increases
    C.   its temperature decreases and its pressure decreases
    D.   its temperature increases and its pressure decreases
    E.   its temperature stays the same and its pressure increases

13. The meridian at which the time is 5 hours earlier than the time at Greenwich is 13._____

    A. 105° E   B. 105° W
    C. 75° E   D. 75° W
    E.   none of these answers

14. Which of the following will absorb *MOST* water per given volume? 14._____

    A.   gravel   B.   humus
    C.   quartz   D.   sand
    E.   sandy loam

15. Coal consists of organic matter which, during geologic ages, was   15._____

    A. thoroughly decayed   B. unable to oxidize
    C. thoroughly oxidized   D. preserved unchanged
    E. incompletely calcified

16. The plants of which of the following groups act as hosts to nitrogen-fixing bacteria?   16._____

    A. Wheat, oats, rye
    B. Corn, rye, barley
    C. Pumpkins, squash, cucumbers
    D. Beets, carrots, turnips
    E. Clover, alfalfa, soybeans

17. Of the following deciduous trees, the one that loses its leaves *LAST* after a summer's growing season is the   17._____

    A. box elder   B. elm
    C. oak   D. poplar
    E. sumac

18. Seedless orange trees are produced by   18._____

    A. planting oranges that contain no seeds
    B. cross-pollination
    C. careful breeding
    D. budding or grafting
    E. planting an orange segment that has no seeds

19. The oxygen absorbed from water by aquatic animals is   19._____

    A. dissolved in the water
    B. produced by the respiration of plants
    C. produced by the respiration of animals
    D. derived by breaking down water into hydrogen and oxygen
    E. produced by oxidation of decaying materials

20. Which of the following is the *BEST* definition of photosynthesis? The   20._____

    A. action of sunlight on chlorophyl
    B. process by which plants give off oxygen
    C. building of protoplasm by a plant
    D. manufacture of carbohydrate by a green plant
    E. process by which plants use carbon dioxide

21. Muskrats share with beavers the habit of   21._____

    A. cutting down trees
    B. building dams
    C. building lodges
    D. slapping the water with their tails when alarmed
    E. digging canals

22. The primary source of fish food in a pond is   22.____

    A. one-celled animals   B. one-celled plants
    C. crayfish and snails   D. large water plants
    E. insects falling in or washed in from the land

23. The principal food of our larger hawks is   23.____

    A. calves   B. chickens
    C. game birds   D. small rodents
    E. songbirds

24. The young of houseflies are   24.____

    A. caterpillars   B. cocoons
    C. small flies   D. gnats
    E. maggots

25. Of the following, the animal that is *MOST* dangerous to man in America is the   25.____

    A. black bear   B. housefly
    C. mountain lion   D. rattlesnake
    E. black widow spider

26. All of the following diseases are spread by animals *EXCEPT*   26.____

    A. bubonic plague   B. malaria
    C. scarlet fever   D. tularemia
    E. yellow fever

27. All of the following are parasitic diseases *EXCEPT*   27.____

    A. diabetes   B. malaria
    C. tuberculosis   D. typhoid fever
    E. streptococcic sore throat

28. A sharp blow in the front of the abdomen just below the ribs may cause a momentary   28.____
stoppage of breathing because

    A. so much air has been knocked from one's lungs
    B. the secretion of adrenalin has been temporarily ended
    C. the portion of the autonomic nervous system which is centered in the solar plexus
       is affected
    D. the aveoli of the lungs have collapsed
    E. the diaphragm muscles are no longer stimulated by the cerebrum

29. In the control of disease, it has been found that   29.____

    A. all diseases can be prevented by vaccines or serums
    B. all communicable diseases can be cured by specific drugs
    C. effective treatment for all diseases is not known at the present time
    D. an individual who follows hygienic practices will avoid illness.
    E. a low-caloric diet should be given to all who are seriously ill

30. Children are not being successfully immunized to prevent   30.____

    A. chicken pox   B. measles
    C. mumps   D. pneumonia
    E. whooping cough

31. A disease that is highly infectious, incurable if not immediately treated and transmissible   31.____
to unborn children is

    A. cancer   B. measles
    C. syphilis   D. tuberculosis
    E. infantile paralysis

32. The greatest danger from malaria is that it   32.____

    A. produces chills and a high fever
    B. attacks brain cells
    C. causes dysentery
    D. destroys red blood corpuscles
    E. upsets hormone distribution

33. Binocular vision is a type of eye functioning that   33.____

    A. is acquired at birth
    B. results in double vision
    C. is the simultaneous use of both eyes
    D. causes squinting
    E. is the result of discordant movements of the eyes

34. Infantile paralysis often causes immediate damage to   34.____

    A. blood vessels   B. bones
    C. muscles   D. the spinal cord
    E. connective tissues

35. In one type of treatment of hay fever, the patient is given, over a period of a month,   35.____
increasing doses of the pollen that causes his allergy. This type of treatment resembles
most closely

    A. the injection of antitoxin for curative purposes
    B. the Pasteur treatment for rabies
    C. vaccination against smallpox
    D. the toxoid treatment for tetanus
    E. the use of penicillin

36. When a person is confined to his bed by diphtheria,   36.____

    A. everything should be removed from the sickroom except the bed, table and chair
    B. a window should be kept open
    C. liquids should be given as the best nourishment
    D. anyone entering the room should wear a gown over the regular clothing
    E. the room should be fumigated immediately upon recovery

37. In many states, the health officer should be notified when a person has   37.____

    A. measles   B. pellagra
    C. mumps   D. scabies
    E. scurvy

38. Depilatories are used to   38.____

    A. relieve pain   B. overcome constipation
    C. remove hair   D. check perspiration
    E. remedy skin blemishes

39. The ultraviolet rays of the sun are especially beneficial in   39.____

    A. eczema   B. measles
    C. rickets   D. scabies
    E. scurvy

40. Safe drinking water in small quantities can be obtained quickly and economically 40.____

    A. from a spring   B. by chlorination
    C. by distillation   D. by filtration
    E. by exposure to the sun

41. The principal minerals that food should provide for building and preserving sound teeth 41.____
are

    A. iodine and phosphorus   B. iron and calcium
    C. calcium and phosphorus   D. magnesium and iron
    E. phosphorus and iron

42. The enamel of one's permanent teeth is   42.____

    A. formed entirely before eruption
    B. formed entirely after eruption
    C. partially formed before eruption and added constantly after eruption
    D. entirely formed before eruption and added as needed to replace damage
    E. partially formed before eruption and added at certain periods through one's life

43. The vitamin that affects the clotting of the blood is   43.____

    A. ascorbic acid   B. riboflavin
    C. thiamin   D. vitamin D
    E. vitamin K

44. One function of the liver is the   44.____

    A. secretion of adrenalin
    B. formation of red blood cells
    C. temporary storage of glycogen
    D. digestion and absorption of starches
    E. absorption of fats from the intestinal tract

45. The principal function of red blood cells is to   45.____

    A. destroy disease germs
    B. carry oxygen to cells
    C. act as toxins in the blood stream
    D. cause the blood to coagulate
    E. give the blood a red color

46. The use of iodine in the body is most closely related to the functioning of the   46._____

    A. gall bladder   B. kidneys
    C. lymph nodes   D. pancreas
    E. thyroid

47. One function of the projections (villi) of the small intestine is to   47._____

    A. produce digestive hormones
    B. aid in the grinding of foods
    C. synchronize the peristaltic action of the intestine
    D. increase the absorptive surface of the intestine
    E. reverse peristaltic action

48. One function of sweat is to   48._____

    A. cleanse the pores   B. lubricate the skin
    C. nourish the hair   D. cool the body
    E. produce perspiration

49. An example of an enzyme is   49._____

    A. adrenalin   B. ptyalin   C. thiamin   D. thyroxine
    E. trichinosis

50. The acid found in our stomachs is _____ acid.   50._____

    A. acetic   B. formic   C. hydrochloric   D. nitric
    E. sulfuric

———————

KEY (CORRECT ANSWERS)

No.	Ans	No.	Ans	No.	Ans	No.	Ans	No.	Ans
1.	E	11.	A	21.	C	31.	C	41.	C
2.	C	12.	C	22.	B	32.	D	42.	A
3.	E	13.	D	23.	D	33.	C	43.	E
4.	A	14.	B	24.	E	34.	D	44.	C
5.	C	15.	B	25.	B	35.	B	45.	B
6.	E	16.	E	26.	C	36.	D	46.	E
7.	B	17.	C	27.	A	37.	A	47.	D
8.	C	18.	D	28.	C	38.	C	48.	D
9.	B	19.	A	29.	C	39.	C	49.	B
10.	A	20.	D	30.	D	40.	B	50.	C

———————

TEST 3

DIRECTIONS: Each question or incomplete statement is followed by several suggested answers or completions. Select the one that BEST answers the question or completes the statement.

1.   Petroleum consists MAINLY of   1.____

   A.   carbon and hydrogen   B.   hydrogen and oxygen
   C.   oxygen and nitrogen   D.   nitrogen and carbon
   E.   carbon and oxygen

2.   If a strong solution of table salt is poured on the soil of a potted plant,   2.____

   A.   much salt will diffuse into the juices of the plant
   B.   the plant will be unaffected
   C.   minerals dissolved in the plant juices will diffuse into the salt solution
   D.   the plant will lose water through its roots
   E.   root pressure will be increased and the plant will become turgid

3.   The MAIN function of humus in soil is to   3.____

   A.   keep the soil "sweet"
   B.   provide carbon dioxide for photosynthesis in the roots
   C.   conserve moisture
   D.   absorb nitrogen from the air
   E.   live symbiotically with the plants

4.   Fungi procure their food   4.____

   A.   by photosynthesis
   B.   from the air
   C.   from materials produced by other organisms
   D.   from soil minerals
   E.   by combining inorganic materials

5.   A grain of wheat is PRIMARILY   5.____

   A.   a fertilized plant egg
   B.   an embryo plant plus a food supply
   C.   a developed pollen grain
   D.   a miniature of the adult plant
   E.   a food supply for the unfertilized plant egg

6.   An oak tree increases in diameter because of the growth that takes place   6.____

   A.   in the bark
   B.   just under the bark
   C.   in the center of the trunk
   D.   uniformly throughout the trunk
   E.   in the size of each cell in the tree

7. Grapefruit are so named because they   7.____

    A. are closely related to a species of tropical grapes
    B. grow in clusters
    C. are mutants of a domestic grape
    D. grow on trees whose leaves are almost indistinguishable from grape leaves
    E. are produced on vines

8. Of the following, the plant that requires two growing seasons to complete its life cycle is   8.____
the

    A. bean   B. cabbage   C. corn   D. tomato
    E. watermelon

9. The flounder   9.____

    A. swims in its unique manner from birth
    B. has a symmetrical head
    C. has one eye that migrates to the opposite side of its head
    D. is a surface feeder
    E. is the main enemy of the oyster

10. One can drink water from a brook with his head lower than his feet because of the   10.____

    A. peristaltic action of the esophagus
    B. capillary action in the throat
    C. difference in pressure between the stomach and the atmosphere
    D. pumping action of the diaphragm
    E. valvular action of the larynx

11. Radioactive isotopes have been used in medicine to   11.____

    A. trace the course of certain compounds through the body
    B. cure anema
    C. determine the amount of phosphorus in the body
    D. supplement the bactericidal action of streptomycin
    E. make vaccines for the treatment of cancer

12. The effect of a specific antibody in the blood is to cause   12.____

    A. disintegration of white blood corpuscles
    B. destruction of all disease-producing bacteria
    C. disintegration of most bacteria
    D. destruction of specific bacteria
    E. rapid blood-clotting in wounds

13. Expressed in the centigrade scale, the average normal temperature of the human body is   13.____

    A. 37° C   B. 55° C   C. 68° C   D. 98° C   E. 212° C

14. The incubation period of a disease is the   14.____

    A. time required for the bacterium to hatch
    B. time from infection until the appearance of symptoms
    C. length of the life cycle of the infecting organism

D. period during which the patient should be confined to bed
E. length of exposure necessary to acquire a disease

15. As individual may do much to protect himself against hookworm in an infected area by   15.____

    A. being vaccinated against hookworm
    B. taking preventive medicine
    C. avoiding all pork
    D. eating only food that has been cooked under pressure
    E. wearing shoes

16. The iron lung is a device that   16.____

    A. replaces one lobe of the lungs
    B. blows air into the lungs
    C. raises and lowers the pressure on the outside of the body
    D. supplies pure oxygen to invalids
    E. increases peristaltic action

17. Sir Alexander Fleming is BEST known for his work in connection with the   17.____

    A. discovery of insulin
    B. development of the iron lung
    C. use of X-rays in the treatment of cancer
    D. prevention of yellow fever
    E. discovery of penicillin

18. Radioactive isotopes produced by atomic energy have already been used successfully in the   18.____

    A. removal of superfluous hair
    B. treatment of certain types of goiter
    C. prevention of tooth decay
    D. treatment of certain forms of mental disease
    E. treatment of water supplies to kill dangerous bacteria

19. When caring for an invalid in the home, one should remember that   19.____

    A. unless a person is ill, the body temperature is always 98. 6° F.
    B. the red arrow point on a clinical thermometer is at 100° F.
    C. the normal body temperature may vary as much as one and one-half degrees during the day
    D. a rectal temperature of 98° F. is considered normal
    E. the body temperature is usually lowest at about 4 p.m. and highest at about 3 a.m.

20. Which of the following statements is TRUE?   20.____

    A. Salivation is a sign that a baby is teething.
    B. After a baby has had an accidental fall, the mother should try to put it to sleep as soon as possible.
    C. Breast-fed babies usually have greater immunity to contagious diseases than bottle-fed babies have.

D. Thumb sucking is a sign that a baby is not getting enough to eat.
E. Infant mortality is higher in females than in males.

21. A disease to which a person is USUALLY permanently immune after recovering from an attack is

21.____

A. influenza
D. poliomyelitis
B. malaria
E. syphilis
C. pneumonia

22. Of the following, the BEST treatment for someone who looks as if he were about to faint is to

22.____

A. have him sit down in a chair and close his eyes for a few minutes
B. have him hold his arms above his head
C. have someone take hold of him on either side and keep him walking
D. have him sit down on the floor or ground with his head between his knees
E. slap him vigorously on the back several times

23. Of the following, the BEST first-aid treatment for a person whose eyes have been exposed to irritating fumes is to

23.____

A. flush the eyes with water from a drinking fountain
B. put powdered boracic acid in the eyes
C. apply cold towels to the eyes
D. rub the eyes to stimulate the flow of tears
E. rush the patient to the nearest physician

24. The MOST serious type of fatigue is induced by

24.____

A. emotional strain
B. mental work
C. physical activity
D. sedentary occupations
E. inadequate sleep over several days

25. The BEST body position in going to sleep has been found to be

25.____

A. on the abdomen
C. on the right side
E. any way that is comfortable
B. on the left side
D. flat on one's back

26. The use of a common towel by two or more persons may result in the spread of

26.____

A. eczema
E. shingles
B. hives
C. impetigo
D. rickets

27. Legally prohibiting expectoration in public places helps prevent

27.____

A. cancer
E. typhoid fever
B. pneumonia
C. scabies
D. tetanus

28. When in need of a stimulant, one may BEST use

28.____

A. brandy
E. bicarbonate of soda in water
B. hot milk
C. orange juice
D. tea

29. Toasted bread is more digestible than untoasted bread because the toasting process changes a part of the carbohydrate into

    A. dextrin   B. heparin   C. melanin   D. opsonin
    E. palmitin

29.____

30. Insufficient calcium in the diet of a child may cause

    A. bowlegs   B. impaired vision   C. infantile paralysis
    D. wryneck   E. tuberculosis of the bones

30.____

31. A generous supply of vitamin C may be included in a day's diet by using a sufficient quantity of

    A. broiled mackerel   B. stewed prunes
    C. pork chops   D. tomato juice
    E. whole wheat bread or cereals

31.____

32. Of the following, the food nutrient that provides energy in the diet is

    A. cellulose   B. iron   C. protein   D. riboflavin
    E. thiamin

32.____

33. Of the foods listed below, the one that will contribute the GREATEST number of calories to the diet is

    A. one cup of milk
    B. two cups of cabbage
    C. one-half cup of cornstarch pudding
    D. four tablespoonfuls of mayonnaise
    E. two medium-sized white potatoes

33.____

34. In case of high price or shortage of meat, other foods rich in protein may be used. The BEST substitute from the following list is

    A. egg plant   B. dark rice   C. spaghetti
    D. string beans   E. red kidney beans

34.____

35. The BEST of the following lunches for a two-year old child would be

    A. egg yolk, baked potato, whole wheat toast, chopped peas, milk
    B. cream soup, cabbage, graham crackers, custard, milk
    C. meat loaf, cabbage salad, toast, chocolate pudding, milk
    D. soft cooked egg, pineapple and raw carrot salad, toast, junket, milk
    E. creamed corn, toast, weak cocoa, custard

35.____

36. Which of the following statements is TRUE?

    A. One can become physically ill from ailments that are purely imaginary.
    B. A receding chin usually indicates a weak will.
    C. Good and bad personality traits are sometimes inherited.
    D. Believing that a thing is true often makes it true.
    E. A person's intelligence can always be improved through education

36.____

37. Which of the following would be injured if a baking soda solution were allowed to stand in it overnight?

    A. An earthenware casserole
    B. An enamel saucepan
    C. A pyrex double boiler
    D. An aluminum saucepan
    E. A stainless steel pressure saucepan

37.____

38. The illustration below represents a

    A. brad   B. casing nail   C. common nail
    D. cut nail   E. finishing nail

38.____

39. A doorbell is USUALLY connected to the household circuit (A.C.) through a

    A. base plug   B. condenser   C. rectifier
    D. resistor   E. transformer

39.____

40. An ordinary automobile storage battery consists of

    A. one large dry cell   B. several dry cells
    C. one large wet cell   D. several wet cells
    E. a chemical rectifier

40.____

41. The tool illustrated below is used MOST often by

    A. an electrician   B. a machinist   C. a printer
    D. a plumber   E. a garage mechanic

41.____

42. The term "kiln dried" applies to

    A. linseed oil   B. lumber   C. plaster
    D. pottery   E. cold-rolled steel

42.____

43. A "stud" in a frame building is a part of the

    A. ceiling   B. floor   C. foundation
    D. roof   E. side wall

43.____

44. The joint shown below is a

    A. butt   B. dado   C. dovetail   D. half lap   E. rabbet

44.____

45. Which of the following prevents a saw from binding?

    A. set   B. sharpness   C. curve of back
    D. number of teeth   E. thickness of blade

45.____

46. Two men are pulling on ropes attached to a rock. It is found that their resultant force is less than that used by either man. It MUST be that the forces are

    46.____

    A.   acting at less than 90° to each other
    B.   acting at more than 90° to each other
    C.   acting at 90° to each other
    D.   both large
    E.   both small

47. An observer is moving away from a vibrating object with the speed of sound. The observer will

    47.____

    A.   hear a note an octave higher
    B.   hear a note an octave lower
    C.   hear the same note but more faintly
    D.   hear the same note emphasized
    E.   not hear the emitted note

48. The extraction of nitrogenous wastes from the blood is the CHIEF function of the

    48.____

    A.   bladder   B.   kidneys   C.   large intestine
    D.   liver   E.   lungs

49. The surface of the earth has been changed the MOST by

    49.____

    A.   winds   B.   glaciers   C.   running water
    D.   volcanos   E.   chemical action of the atmosphere

50. Molds are to spores as green plants are to

    50.____

    A.   flowers   B.   leaves   C.   roots   D.   seeds
    E.   stems

———

KEY (CORRECT ANSWERS)

1. A	11. A	21. D	31. D	41. D
2. D	12. D	22. D	32. C	42. B
3. C	13. A	23. A	33. D	43. E
4. C	14. B	24. A	34. E	44. B
5. B	15. E	25. E	35. A	45. A
6. B	16. C	26. C	36. A	46. B
7. B	17. E	27. B	37. D	47. E
8. B	18. B	28. D	38. C	48. B
9. C	19. C	29. A	39. E	49. C
10. A	20. C	30. A	40. D	50. D

———

TEST 4

DIRECTIONS: Each question or incomplete statement is followed by several suggested answers or completions. Select the one that BEST answers the question or completes the statement.

1. The dinosaur was a prehistoric   1._____

    A. amphibian   B. arthropod   C. mammal
    D. primate   E. reptile

2. Evidence indicating that great climatic changes have occurred in the past is found in   2._____

    A. the appearance of mountains
    B. the delta of the Mississippi
    C. coal deposits in Alaska
    D. lava deposits
    E. the records of the United States Department of Agriculture

3. A structure that helps to keep air pressure in the middle ear equal to atmospheric pressure is the   3._____

    A. eardrum   B. Eustachian tube
    C. Islands of Langerhans   D. nasal passage
    E. semicircular canal

4. One factor NOT necessary for photosynthesis is   4._____

    A. carbon dioxide   B. chlorophyll
    C. free oxygen   D. sunlight
    E. water

5. Carbon grains are an essential part of a   5._____

    A. doorbell   B. radio loudspeaker
    C. storage battery   D. transformer
    E. telephone transmitter

6. A container of water is placed on a scale and the scale reading is 100 pounds. If a block of wood weighing 25 pounds is then floated half submerged in the water, the scale will read   6._____

    A. 75 pounds   B. 87.5 pounds   C. 100 pounds
    D. 112.5 pounds   E. 125 pounds

7. Most evidence seems to indicate that the first vertebrate animal to appear on the earth was the   7._____

    A. amphibian   B. bird   C. fish   D. mammal   E. reptile

8. The earth's crust contains about 50% oxygen by weight. The next MOST abundant element in the earth's crust is   8._____

    A. aluminum   B. calcium   C. hydrogen   D. iron
    E. silicon

9. A large steel drum containing air at normal atmospheric pressure is found to float with 40% of its volume under water. When compressed air is forced into the drum until its pressure is doubled, the drum will

    A. float at the same level
    B. float higher in the water
    C. float lower in the water
    D. sink to a depth between the surface and the bottom
    E. sink to the bottom

9.____

10. When a bacterial cell is submerged in a strong salt solution, the cell shrinks because

    A. minerals enter the cell
    B. the cytoplasm within the cell decomposes
    C. the salt dissolves the cell wall
    D. the salt enters the cell
    E. water leaves the cell

10.____

11. Mosaic vision is characteristic of

    A. bacteria   B. bees
    C. earthworms   D. man
    E. robins

11.____

12. Ambergris, a substance used to make perfume, comes from

    A. an inflammation in the body of the sperm whale
    B. distilled attar of roses
    C. the hardened resin from pine trees
    D. the musk-producing organs of a deer
    E. the nectar-producing organs of the honeysuckle vine

12.____

13. Bloodplasma consists CHIEFLY of

    A. amino acids   B. fats   C. glucose   D. water
    E. urea and uric acids

13.____

14. Appendicitis is generally accompanied by

    A. daily fluctuation of red cell count
    B. high red cell count
    C. high white cell count
    D. low white cell count
    E. pain in the carotids

14.____

15. The dead red corpuscles in the blood stream are removed and decomposed by the

    A. heart   B. liver   C. lungs   D. small intestine
    E. white corpuscles

15.____

16. Auxins are

    A. growth hormones   B. insect poisons   C. new plastics
    D. new textiles   E. respiratory enzymes

16.____

17. On the desert the Arabs are able to keep water cool in earthenware jugs because 17.____

    A. particles of earthenware dissolve in the water and lower its temperature
    B. the attraction between the molecules of the jug and the water is a cooling process
    C. the change of some of the water to a vapor lowers the temperature
    D. the jug is a good conductor of heat
    E. the rough surface of the jug radiates heat more rapidly

18. An object weighs 10 pounds in air and floats in water with one half of its volume above the surface. The MINIMUM force that must be added to submerge the object is 18.____

    A. 5 pounds   B. 10 pounds   C. 20 pounds
    D. 31.25 pounds   E. 62.5 pounds

19. A hot stove poker is held near the face. The rays of light chiefly responsible for the sensation felt on the cheek are those of 19.____

    A. blue light   B. infrared light   C. red light
    D. ultraviolet light   E. white light

20. Plastic-coated screen is often used in place of glass in chicken coops and barns because 20.____

    A. glass filters out most of the infrared rays of sunlight
    B. glass filters out most of the ultraviolet rays of sunlight
    C. plastic filters out harmful rays of light
    D. plastic is far safer for the cattle or chickens since it will not shatter
    E. plastic transmits more of the rays of visible light

21. When smoke from a locomotive tends to settle to the ground, it may indicate that an area of rainy weather is approaching because 21.____

    A. the air is less dense and will not support the smoke particles
    B. the air is rising in a low pressure area
    C. the air is sinking near the low pressure area
    D. the smoke is sucked into the low pressure area
    E. there is less oxygen so that the smoke particles are not completely burned and are heavier

22. In order to overcome losses during long-distance transmission of electrical energy, it is common practice to 22.____

    A. decrease both the voltage and the current
    B. decrease the voltage and increase the current
    C. increase both the voltage and the current
    D. increase the voltage and keep the current constant
    E. increase the voltage and decrease the current

23. Oil is poured on water to reduce the height of waves because the 23.____

    A. added weight of the oil makes the waves break at a lesser height
    B. oil is a lubricant
    C. chemical action between oil and water produces a heavier substance
    D. oil fills up the troughs of the waves
    E. surface tension of the water will be weakened

24. The MOST penetrating of the following forms of radiation is   24.____

    A.   heat   B.   infrared light   C.   the cosmic ray
    D.   the X-ray   E.   ultraviolet light

25. A good index of the health of a community is its death rate from   25.____

    A.   arteriosclerosis   B.   diphtheria   C.   influenza
    D.   meningitis   E.   typhoid

26. Fehling's solution is added to a test tube containing a sample of breakfast cereal that has   26.____ been heated in water. If the Fehling's solution turns brick red, the breakfast food PROBA-BLY contains

    A.   animal fat   B.   grape sugar   C.   protein   D.   starch
    E.   vitamin C

27. The part of the eye that corresponds to the diaphragm of the camera is the   27.____

    A.   cornea   B.   iris   C.   lens   D.   pupil   E.   retina

28. The pneumothorax treatment is used in cases of   28.____

    A.   cancer   B.   heart disease   C.   tuberculosis
    D.   pneumonia   E.   paralysis of the upper thorax

29. In outer space, where there is no atmosphere, a jet-propelled rocket   29.____

    A.   cannot be stopped
    B.   cannot change its direction
    C.   will not operate since there is no air against which the expelled gases can push
    D.   will not operate since there is no air to supply oxygen for combustion of the fuel
    E.   will operate more efficiently because there is no air resistance

30. A man has a cup of hot coffee, a teaspoonful of sugar, an ounce of cream. He desires to   30.____ drink the combination at the lowest temperature possible at the end of three minutes. He should add the

    A.   cream at once and the sugar in three minutes
    B.   cream at once and the sugar slowly throughout the three-minute period
    C.   sugar and cream at the end of three minutes
    D.   sugar and cream immediately
    E.   sugar at once and the cream slowly throughout the three-minute period

31. In one state, the average temperature on August 6 is USUALLY higher than on June 21.   31.____ This is BEST explained by

    A.   the fact that August 6 is midway between June 21 and September 21
    B.   the fact that the humidity is higher on August 6
    C.   the reason that accounts for 2 p.m. usually being warmer than noon
    D.   the sun's rays being more vertical on August 6
    E.   the sun being farther away on August 6 than June 21

32. Ordinary photographic film is developed under a ruby-colored light because the film is   32.____

    A. not sensitive to long wave lengths of visible light
    B. not sensitive to short wave lengths of visible light
    C. not sensitive to ultraviolet light
    D. not sensitive to visible light
    E. sensitive to all wave lengths of visible light

33. In a plant the semipermeable membrane which surrounds the cell is the   33.____

    A. cell membrane   B. cell wall   C. vacuole membrane
    D. nuclear membrane   E. cytoplasmic inclusion

34. Tobacco mosaic is due to   34.____

    A. a bacterium   B. a lack of iron   C. too much sun
    D. a virus   E. a lack of magnesium

35. When sheets are washed, bluing is sometimes added to the water because   35.____

    A. a chemical change called bleaching will occur
    B. it destroys most water-borne bacteria
    C. it is a water softener
    D. its color is complementary to yellow
    E. the soap is made less harsh

36. The HIGHEST clouds are   36.____

    A. alto-cumulus   B. cirrus   C. cumulus   D. nimbus
    E. stratus

37. Acetylcholine is a substance that controls the   37.____

    A. absorption of vitamins   B. action of nerves
    C. digestion of food   D. germination of seeds
    E. storage of fat

38. The PRINCIPAL function of the white blood cells is to   38.____

    A. act as toxins in the blood stream
    B. carry away waste products
    C. carry oxygen to the cells
    D. destroy disease germs
    E. produce antitoxins

39. There are indications that decay is retarded by treating the teeth of children with a compound of   39.____

    A. bromine   B. chlorine   C. fluorine   D. iodine
    E. sulfur

40. Poisons manufactured by bacteria are called   40.____

    A. molds   B. phagocytes   C. septics   D. toxins
    E. viruses

41. Aero-embolism is a body disturbance commonly known as   41.____

   A. appendicitis   B. bends   C. infantile paralysis
   D. pneumonia   E. sugar diabetes

42. Diabetes is caused by the improper functioning of the   42.____

   A. adrenals   B. digestive juices   C. pancreas
   D. parathyroids   E. thyroid

43. The air we exhale, compared to the air we inhale, contains   43.____

   A. less carbon dioxide   B. less nitrogen
   C. more nitrogen   D. more oxygen
   E. more water vapor

44. Studies of sleep by psychologists and health specialists indicate that   44.____

   A. a tired, stuporous feeling sometimes following a profound sleep is attributed to tossing too much
   B. adults reveal considerable individual differences in their need of sleep, but infants and pre-school children reveal insignificant differences at a given age
   C. best rest is obtained from sleep when the stomach is empty
   D. the typically healthy sleeper usually changes from one gross bodily position to another between twenty and forty-five times during eight hours of sleep
   E. young children show more movements in sleep than older children and adults

45. Edward Jenner perfected a method of making people immune to   45.____

   A. anthrax   B. bubonic plague   C. diphtheria
   D. smallpox   E. yellow fever

46. A file clerk who has the habit of moistening her finger to facilitate the turning of pages can MOST easily break the habit by   46.____

   A. applying a bitter but harmless substance to her finger
   B. asking a co-worker to remind her when she puts her finger to her tongue
   C. making a practice of using the eraser of a pencil to turn pages
   D. placing a large sign in a conspicuous place on her desk
   E. putting a piece of adhesive plaster on her finger as a reminder

47. Ascorbic acid is the scientific name for   47.____

   A. a narcotic obtained from poppies
   B. a poisonous substance in tobacco
   C. acid in the stomach
   D. digitalis
   E. vitamin C

48. The HIGHEST concentration of oxygen is found in the   48.____

   A. hepatic vein   B. jugular vein   C. pulmonary artery
   D. pulmonary vein   E. right auricle

49. A workman was injured by a blunt piece of flying steel. The wound, close to his eye, was dirty and lacerated but there was only slight bleeding. In giving first aid, his co-worker should

    A. apply a mild tincture of iodine and cover the wound with sterile gauze
    B. clean the wound carefully with alcohol and cover with sterile gauze
    C. cover the wound with sterile gauze and leave the cleaning to a physician
    D. remove the specks of dirt with a sterile swab before covering the wound with sterile gauze
    E. wash the wound carefully with soap and water and cover it with sterile gauze

49.____

50. Which one of the following statements concerning first aid is TRUE?

    A. A tourniquet should be loosened every 30 or 40 minutes to prevent stoppage of circulation and possible gangrene.
    B. It is essential to wash the hands before applying digital pressure to an open wound.
    C. It is useless to continue artificial respiration for more than one hour of there is no sign of returning consciousness.
    D. The pulse of a person suffering from shock is rapid and weak.
    E. Whiskey is a good stimulant to give a person bitten by a poisonous snake.

50.____

———

KEY (CORRECT ANSWERS)

1.	E	11.	B	21.	A	31.	C	41.	B
2.	C	12.	A	22.	E	32.	A	42.	C
3.	B	13.	D	23.	E	33.	A	43.	E
4.	C	14.	C	24.	C	34.	D	44.	D
5.	E	15.	B	25.	E	35.	D	45.	D
6.	E	16.	A	26.	B	36.	B	46.	C
7.	C	17.	C	27.	B	37.	B	47.	E
8.	E	18.	B	28.	C	38.	D	48.	D
9.	C	19.	B	29.	E	39.	C	49.	C
10.	E	20.	B	30.	C	40.	D	50.	D

———

TEST 5

DIRECTIONS: Each question or incomplete statement is followed by several suggested answers or completions. Select the one that BEST answers the question or completes the statement. *PRINT THE LETTER OF THE CORRECT ANSWER IN THE SPACE AT THE RIGHT.*

1. Of the following, the BEST source of vitamin E is   1.____

   A. citrus fruits   B. cod liver oil
   C. halibut liver oil   D. wheat germ oil
   E. milk and milk products

2. Which one of the following may be caused by a plant?   2.____

   A. amoebic dysentery   B. influenza   C. malaria
   D. ringworm   E. yellow fever

3. Which one of the following parts of the circulatory system carries digested fats away from the intestines?   3.____

   A. arterial capillaries   B. lacteals
   C. pancreatic duct   D. pulmonary artery
   E. venal capillaries

4. At which one of the following points should digital pressure be applied to stop arterial bleeding in the hand or forearm?   4.____

   A. brachial   B. carotid   C. femoral   D. subclavian
   E. temporal

5. The hormone that regulates the general metabolism of the body is   5.____

   A. adrenalin   B. gastrin   C. insulin   D. pituitrin
   E. thyroxin

6. The small dipper seems to turn about the North Star once each day because   6.____

   A. all stars move in great circles on the celestial sphere
   B. the earth turns on its axis
   C. the North Star is the last star in the handle of the dipper
   D. the planets revolve around the sun
   E. the solar system rotates about a fixed star

7. The component of the atmosphere that shows the GREATEST percentage of variation is   7.____

   A. argon   B. carbon dioxide   C. nitrogen   D. oxygen
   E. water vapor

8. Slate is to shale as marble is to   8.____

   A. feldspar   B. gneiss   C. limestone   D. mica schist
   E. sandstone

9. A disease caused by the malfunction of the pancreas is　　　　　　　　　9.＿＿＿

    A. coronary thrombosis   B. diabetes   C. gallstones .
    D. rickets   E. tuberculosis

10. Respiration is to carbon dioxide as photosynthesis is to　　　　　　　　10.＿＿＿

    A. carbon dioxide   B. chlorophyll   C. oxygen
    D. starch   E. sunlight

11. When a machine that is 80% efficient does 1000 footpounds of work, the work input   11.＿＿＿
MUST be

    A. 80 foot-pounds   B. 800 foot-pounds
    C. 1000 foot-pounds   D. 1250 foot-pounds
    E. 1800 foot-pounds

12. A siphon is NOT used to empty the water out of the hold of a ship into the ocean because 12.＿＿＿

    A. a siphon does not create a sufficient vacuum
    B. a siphon will not operate at sea level
    C. salt water is heavier than fresh water
    D. the air pressure is less on the ocean's surface than it is in the hold
    E. the hold is beneath the ocean's surface

13. A full moon might be seen　　　　　　　　　　　　　　　　　　　　13.＿＿＿

    A. faintly at noon
    B. high in the sky at sunset
    C. low in the east in the evening
    D. low in the east in the morning
    E. low in the west at midnight

14. A kerosene lamp burns with a yellow flame due to the　　　　　　　　14.＿＿＿

    A. burning of hydrogen
    B. complete burning of the hydrocarbons
    C. heating of the wick
    D. incandescence of unburned carbon particles
    E. natural color of any burning kerosene

15. On which one of the following days will a person's shadow be LONGEST at noon in the 15.＿＿＿
East?

    A. Christmas   B. Easter Sunday   C. Fourth of July
    D. Labor Day   E. Thanksgiving

16. Perfume is made by dissolving oils containing the essence of the desired odor in 16.＿＿＿

    A. alcohol   B. banana oil   C. distilled water
    D. glycerin   E. volatile mineral oil

17. Which one of the following is produced naturally by living things?　　　　17.＿＿＿

    A. aspirin   B. atabrine   C. lysol   D. quinine
    E. sulfanilamide

18. Which one of the following terms is NOT associated with the others?   18.____

    A. beriberi   B. leukemia   C. rickets   D. scurvy
    E. xerophthalmia

19. Like most great caverns, the Howe Caverns of New York State   19.____

    A. are made of sandstone   B. are the result of glaciation
    C. occur in limestone rock   D. were formed by earthquakes
    E. were formed by wind erosion

20. The unrelated member of the following group is   20.____

    A. cyclotron   B. deuteron   C. electron   D. neutron
    E. positron

21. Fossils are MOST likely to be found in   21.____

    A. igneous rocks   B. marble quarries
    C. metamorphic rocks   D. D, ocean deeps
    E. sedimentary rocks

22. The watershed of a river has reference to   22.____

    A. its delta
    B. its flood plain
    C. the body of water into which the river drains
    D. the land from which water drains into the river
    E. the river and its tributaries

23. An increase of temperature from 10° C. to 30° C. is equivalent to an increase of   23.____

    A. $11\ 1/2^\circ$ F.   B. 36° F.   C. $43\ 1/2^\circ$ F.   D. 68° F.
    E. 86° F.

24. The body proper of all insects consists of three parts, namely, the head, the abdomen   24.____
and the

    A. antennae   B. legs   C. shell   D. thorax
    E. wings

25. The rate of sugar storage in the liver may be studied by using radioactive   25.____

    A. calcium   B. carbon   C. carbon dioxide   D. iron
    E. nitrogen

26. A water table is   26.____

    A. a flat rock mass eroded by waves   B. a rain gauge
    C. a river flood stage   D. the sea level
    E. an underground water level

27. We can see only one side of the moon because the period of the moon's   27.____

    A. revolution about the earth equals that of the earth's revolution about the sun
    B. rotation is equal to its period of revolution about the earth
    C. rotation is equal to that of the earth's rotation

D. rotation is half that of the earth's rotation
E. rotation is twice that of the earth's rotation

28. The term that includes all others in the following group is   28.____

    A. absorption   B. assimilation   C. circulation
    D. digestion   E. nutrition

29. The unrelated member of the following group is   29.____

    A. adrenin   B. amylopsin   C. insulin
    D. parathormone   E. thyroxin

30. An object that weighs 500 pounds in air appears to lose 200 pounds when submerged in   30.____
water to a depth of 10 feet. If the object is then lowered to a depth of 20 feet, its apparent
weight will be

    A. 100 lb.   B. 200 lb.   C. 300 lb.   D. 400 lb.
    E. 500 lb.

31. The color of the sky is blue because   31.____

    A. blue light is reflected from the Heaviside layer
    B. cosmic rays transmit blue light
    C. dust particles are blue in color
    D. the short wave lengths of visible light are scattered most
    E. there is an excess of ultraviolet rays in the stratosphere

32. If you were placed in the middle of a room where the floor was perfectly frictionless, the   32.____
BEST method to use in betting to a side wall would be to

    A. crawl over
    B. roll over
    C. throw an object horizontally
    D. walk over
    E. wave your arms violently up and down

33. A disease caused by a protozoan is   33.____

    A. arteriosclerosis   B. endocarditis   C. malaria
    D. poliomyelitis   E. tuberculosis

34. A one-cubic meter, closed, rigid tank contains air and 11 grams of water vapor at a tem-   34.____
perature of 20° C. If the temperature of the confined air is raised to 35° C., which one of
the following will result?

    A. The absolute himidity will rise.
    B. The absolute humidity will fall.
    C. The relative humidity will rise.
    D. The relative humidity will fall.
    E. No change will occur in either absolute or relative humidity

35. The use of a soda-acid type fire extinguisher is recommended for putting out fires involving burning

    A. dry chemicals   B. fats or vegetable oils
    C. gasoline   D. painted woodwork
    E. insulation on wires carrying 110-220 volts

36. The alloy, alnico, is widely used in making

    A. aluminum utensils   B. cutting tools
    C. permanent magnets   D. springs
    E. thermostats

37. A container is filled to the brim with ice water in which is floating an ice cube with 10 cc. of its volume above the surface. The specific gravity of ice is about 0.9. After the ice has completely melted,

    A. about one cc. of water will have overflowed
    B. about nine cc. of water will have overflowed
    C. about ten cc. of water will have overflowed
    D. the water level will have dropped
    E. the water level will have remained constant

38. A sextant is an instrument used to determine by a single observation the

    A. direction of true north
    B. elevation of a given place
    C. exact time at a given place
    D. latitude of a given place
    E. longitude of a given place

39. A 5-pound pail containing 25 pounds of water stands on a platform scale. A 4-pound piece of cork with a specific gravity of 0.25 is floated on the water. Weights are then placed on the piece of cork until it floats flush with the surface of the water. The platform scale now reads

    A. 30 lb.   B. 34 lb.   C. 37 lb.   D. 46 lb.   E. 50 lb.

40. The north pole of a magnet attracted one end of a freely swinging bar of metal marked *A*. This shows that the bar is

    A. made of a magnetic material
    B. made of iron
    C. made of iron with a south pole at *A*
    D. magnetized with a north pole at *A*
    E. unmagnetized

41. The corn plant produces its pollen and ovules

    A. at the same node
    B. in different rows
    C. on different plants
    D. on different flowering structures
    E. on the same flowering structure

42. Which one of the following prehistoric men appeared the LATEST chronologically? 42.____

    A. Cro-Magnon   B. Java   C. Neanderthal
    D. Peking   E. Piltdown

43. Tissues are to cells as organs are to 43.____

    A. blood   B. human beings   C. organisms   D. tissues
    E. vessels

44. The number of people who die each year from cancer is increasing because 44.____

    A. communicable diseases are better controlled and more people live longer
    B. it is a communicable disease
    C. it is an inherited disease
    D. malignant tumors are more prevalent than benign or harmless tumors
    E. medical science knows less about the disease than about any other disease

45. At noon on shipboard, a chronometer reads 10:00 p.m., Greenwich time. The longitude 45.____
    of the ship is

    A. 10° east   B. 150° east   C. 10° west   D. 100° west
    E. 150° west

46. In the East, hailstorms are MOST likely to occur in 46.____

    A. fall   B. late winter   C. midwinter   D. summer
    E. very early spring

47. An unused electric refrigerator was placed in a room which was surrounded with a per- 47.____
    fect heat insulator. The refrigerator was put into opeation by connecting it to an external
    electrical circuit and at the same time its door was left open. During the first hour the tem-
    perature of the room would

    A. fall continuously
    B. fall somewhat and remain at this temperature
    C. fall somewhat and then return to its original temperature
    D. remain constant
    E. rise

48. The *Rh* factor is of importance in the study of 48.____

    A. fingerprinting   B. the acidity of a solution
    C. the blood   D. the determination of sex
    E. the resistance to infection

49. Which one of the following is the GREATEST advantage of growing up in a large family? 49.____

    A. Each member may be able to borrow articles from other members.
    B. Each member may be easily provided with recreation within his family circle.
    C. Each member may be required to give and receive financial support.
    D. Each member may have a chance to make adjustments to himself and to other
       people early in life.
    E. Each member may have fewer responsibilities.

50. Small arteries branch to form a network of capillaries. In turn, the capillaries unite to form 50.____

    A. alveoles   B. arteries   C. auricles   D. D, veins
    E. ventricles

KEY (CORRECT ANSWERS)

1.	D	11.	D	21.	E	31.	D	41.	D
2.	D	12.	E	22.	D	32.	C	42.	A
3.	B	13.	C	23.	B	33.	C	43.	D
4.	A	14.	D	24.	D	34.	D	44.	A
5.	E	15.	A	25.	B	35.	D	45.	E
6.	B	16.	A	26.	E	36.	C	46.	D
7.	E	17.	D	27.	B	37.	E	47.	E
8.	C	18.	B	28.	E	38.	D	48.	C
9.	B	19.	C	29.	B	39.	D	49.	D
10.	C	20.	A	30.	C	40.	A	50.	D

EXAMINATION SECTION
TEST 1

DIRECTIONS: Each question or incomplete statement is followed by several suggested answers or completions. Select the one that BEST answers the question or completes the statement. *PRINT THE LETTER OF THE CORRECT ANSWER IN THE SPACE AT THE RIGHT.*

1. Photosynthesis is a process whereby a plant　　　　　　　　　　　　　　1.＿＿＿＿

    A. gives off oxygen   B. takes in carbon dioxide
    C. makes food   D. makes starch

2. ＿＿＿＿＿＿ does NOT make its own food.　　　　　　　　　　　　　　2.＿＿＿＿

    A. Mushroom   B. Geranium
    C. African violet   D. Corn

3. The key chemical necessary for plants to make their own food is　　　　　3.＿＿＿＿

    A. oxygen   B. chlorophyll
    C. carbon dioxide   D. starch

4. One substance spreading EVENLY through another is called　　　　　　　4.＿＿＿＿

    A. mixing   B. combining   C. diffusion   D. blending

5. The outer covering on the leaf of a plant is called　　　　　　　　　　　5.＿＿＿＿

    A. stomates   B. chloroplasts
    C. guard cell   D. epidermis

6. The BEST soil for growing a garden is　　　　　　　　　　　　　　　　6.＿＿＿＿

    A. sand   B. clay   C. loam   D. humus

7. When distilled water is thoroughly mixed with soil and the water filtered off and heated　　7.＿＿＿＿
until all the water has been evaporated, a whitish material will be found in the evaporating dish.
This is an example of

    A. carbon dioxide in water
    B. soil residue left in water
    C. soil water having dissolved minerals in it
    D. a poor filter

8. Asexual reproduction involves ＿＿＿＿＿＿ parent(s).　　　　　　　　　8.＿＿＿＿

    A. no   B. two
    C. one   D. two or more

9. ＿＿＿＿＿＿ is NOT a structure of a flower.　　　　　　　　　　　　　　9.＿＿＿＿

    A. Pollen   B. Stamen   C. Pistol   D. Ovary

10. One of the following pairs is MOST necessary for fertilization in a flower to take place:　　　10.____

    A. petals and limbs   B. stamens and pistols
    C. ovules and ovary   D. none of the above

11. A scientist cuts the tails off of two parent rats. Their offspring will　　　11.____

    A. have no tails
    B. have shorter tails
    C. some will have tails; others will not
    D. have normal tails

12. The BEST example of an acquired trait would be　　　12.____

    A. a rat with its tail cut off
    B. long legs
    C. a long nose
    D. a white crow

13. An early scientist who experimented to find out what traits in peas could be inherited was　　　13.____

    A. Helmont   B. Pasteur   C. Frosch   D. Mendel

14. Two pink flowers are mated. Of the four offspring, one is red, two are pink, and one is white.　　　14.____
This is the result of a

    A. dominant trait
    B. hybrid
    C. recessive trait
    D. dominant and recessive trait

15. An inherited trait in offspring is decided by the　　　15.____

    A. parents   B. sperm cell
    C. genes   D. ovary

16. An archer who releases an arrow from a drawn bow provides an example of _____ energy.　　　16.____

    A. radiant   B. mechanical
    C. chemical   D. heat

17. A can of gasoline is BEST described as an example of _____ energy.　　　17.____

    A. kinetic   B. mechanical
    C. heat   D. potential

18. All energy that is of practical use in our world comes from _____ energy.　　　18.____

    A. radiant   B. mechanical
    C. chemical   D. heat

19. Striking a match so that it bursts into flame is an example of _____ energy.　　　19.____

    A. heat   B. potential
    C. transformed   D. kinetic

20. What gas in the atmosphere is ESSENTIAL for burning?   20.____

    A. Oxygen   B. Nitrogen
    C. Water vapor   D. Carbon dioxide

21. Chemicals A and B are to be mixed in a ratio of 3 to 4. If 12 grams of Chemical B are   21.____
used, how many grams of Chemical A will be needed?

    A. 6   B. 8   C. 9   D. 16

22. A meter is a unit of length CLOSEST to a(n)   22.____

    A. inch   B. foot   C. yard   D. mile

23. _____ does NOT affect the length of time it takes a planet to revolve around the sun.   23.____

    A. Size of planet
    B. Length of orbit
    C. Distance from sun
    D. Gravitational pull of sun

24. The volume of a box that is 3 cm long, 3 cm wide, and 2 cm high is _____ cm^3.   24.____

    A. 8   B. 9   C. 11   D. 18

25. An instrument used to record movements in the earth's crust is a   25.____

    A. barograph   B. seismograph
    C. thermograph   D. spectrograph

KEY (CORRECT ANSWERS)

1.	C	11.	D
2.	A	12.	A
3.	B	13.	D
4.	C	14.	B
5.	D	15.	C
6.	C	16.	B
7.	C	17.	D
8.	C	18.	A
9.	A	19.	C
10.	B	20.	A

21.	C
22.	C
23.	A
24.	D
25.	B

TEST 2

DIRECTIONS: Each question or incomplete statement is followed by several suggested answers or completions. Select the one that BEST answers the question or completes the statement. *PRINT THE LETTER OF THE CORRECT ANSWER IN THE SPACE AT THE RIGHT.*

1. Work is done when   1.___

   A. you exert a force upon an object
   B. you expend energy
   C. a force moves an object
   D. all of the above

2. Work is measured by the   2.___

   A. amount of force exerted to move an object
   B. amount of energy used to move an object
   C. distance an object is moved
   D. amount of force multiplied by the distance an object is moved

3. A boy's car runs out of gas. He struggles to push it to a gas station.   3.___
   He is attempting to overcome

   A. gravity   B. resistance   C. friction   D. inertia

4. John had a flat tire, but had no jack. He used a fence post and a large rock to raise the   4.___
   car.
   This illustrates

   A. the lever   B. the fulcrum
   C. John's strength   D. the auto's resistance

5. Energy can be BEST explained as the   5.___

   A. capacity to do work
   B. amount of work done
   C. amount of force expended
   D. amount of force times the distance an object is moved

6. One of the oldest and simplest machines is the   6.___

   A. crow bar   B. inclined plane
   C. pulley   D. steam engine

7. The useful work one gets from a machine is _____ the work put in.   7.___

   A. always less than   B. always equal to
   C. always greater than   D. sometimes greater than

8. Efficiency is measured by   8.___

   A. the amount of useful work obtained from a machine
   B. the amount of work put in a machine
   C. A times B
   D. A divided by B

9. A block and tackle can be used to lift extremely heavy weight because it   9._____

    A. is fixed
    B. is movable
    C. has a large mechanical advantage
    D. has no friction

10. Inertia is BEST described as   10._____

    A. the tendency of an object to remain at rest
    B. the tendency of an object in motion to keep on going
    C. both of the above
    D. none of the above

11. Very rapid burning of fuel is BEST described as   11._____

    A. spontaneous combustion   B. an explosion
    C. ignition   D. work

12. A gasoline engine produces a dangerous gas called   12._____

    A. nitrogen   B. carbon monoxide
    C. carbon dioxide   D. carbon-nitrate

13. The man who invented the diesel engine was   13._____

    A. Rudolf Diesel   B. James Watt
    C. Charles Parsons   D. Thomas Savery

14. Static electricity is caused by   14._____

    A. a dynamo   B. a mechanical generator
    C. friction   D. electrons

15. An atom has   15._____

    A. the same number of electrons and protons
    B. more electrons than protons
    C. more protons than electrons
    D. a number of protons and electrons equal to one-half the number of neutrons

16. A gasoline truck drags a chain on the ground in order to   16._____

    A. discharge neutrons   B. discharge electrons
    C. discharge protons   D. take on protons

17. Another name for a battery is   17._____

    A. voltmeter   B. amperstand
    C. Gilberts box   D. Voltaic pile

18. An electric current can BEST be described as   18._____

    A. protons moving to neutrons   B. a flow of protons
    C. a flow of neutrons   D. a flow of electrons

19. A TRUE statement about magnets is: 19.____

    A. Magnets attract iron
    B. One end of a bar magnet will point north
    C. Like poles of magnets repel each other
    D. All of the above

20. Soil is DIFFERENT from rock because soil 20.____

    A. is dark in color   B. supports plant life
    C. is heavier than rock   D. does not contain minerals

21. The LARGEST river drainage system in the United States is the _____ River and its 21.____
tributaries.

    A. Hudson   B. Amazon
    C. Columbia   D. Mississippi

22. All invertebrate animals lack 22.____

    A. a brain   B. a backbone
    C. arms or legs   D. sensory organs

23. _____ is the HARDEST substance. 23.____

    A. Calcite   B. Quartz   C. Copper   D. Graphite

24. _____ CANNOT be classified as a fossil. 24.____

    A. A shell of a clam washed ashore on a beach
    B. A grasshopper preserved in volcanic ash
    C. The impression of a fern leaf in a piece of coal
    D. The footprint of a dinosaur found in a solid rock

25. An object that orbits a planet is called a(n) 25.____

    A. star   B. meteorite
    C. satellite   D. asteroid

KEY (CORRECT ANSWERS)

1.	C		11.	B
2.	D		12.	B
3.	B		13.	A
4.	A		14.	C
5.	A		15.	A
6.	B		16.	B
7.	A		17.	D
8.	D		18.	D
9.	C		19.	D
10.	C		20.	B

21.	D
22.	B
23.	B
24.	A
25.	C

TEST 3

DIRECTIONS: Each question or incomplete statement is followed by several suggested answers or completions. Select the one that BEST answers the question or completes the statement. *PRINT THE LETTER OF THE CORRECT ANSWER IN THE SPACE AT THE RIGHT.*

1. According to the metric system, the _____ is a unit of measure for weight.   1._____

   A. meter   B. pound   C. kilogram   D. liter

2. A germ killer made by a living organism is called a(n)   2._____

   A. toxin   B. antitoxin   C. anopheles   D. antibiotic

3. The position of a satellite at a point in its orbit when it is FURTHEST away from the earth is called its   3._____

   A. altitude   B. apogee   C. perigee   D. attitude

4. Men in outer space need LEAST worry about   4._____

   A. oxygen   B. radiation   C. gravity   D. meteors

5. When traveling from Philadelphia to San Francisco, one's watch should be set _____ hours.   5._____

   A. back three   B. ahead four
   C. ahead three   D. back four

6. The amount of water vapor present in air is called   6._____

   A. precipitation   B. BTU
   C. humidity   D. evaporation

7. A surface which reflects NEARLY all visible wave lengths appears as   7._____

   A. black   B. white   C. red   D. violet

8. The surface of the earth is covered by _____% of land.   8._____

   A. 70   B. 75   C. 65   D. 30

9. An element NOT known until made by scientists is   9._____

   A. uranium   B. radium   C. helium   D. plutonium

10. Cement is made by mixing clay and   10._____

   A. concrete   B. gravel   C. limestone   D. sand

11. Soft coal, heated in a test tube, does NOT produce   11._____

   A. coal tar   B. charcoal   C. coke   D. gas

12. Of the following traits, _____ are inherited.   12._____

   A. likes and dislikes   B. opinions
   C. eye color   D. handwriting

13. Nitrogen can BEST be added to the soil by planting   13._____

     A. clover   B. corn   C. potatoes   D. wheat

14. The dinosaur provides an example of lack of   14._____

     A. balance   B. adaptation
     C. fertilization   D. maneuverability

15. Because herons were thought to be destroying fishing grounds, a bounty was offered for   15._____
every heron killed. After most of the herons were killed, fishing improved for a while, but
then began to decrease.
This is an example of the need for

     A. balance   B. adaptation
     C. better food supply   D. fewer fishermen

16. One can describe lightning as being   16._____

     A. the result of thunder
     B. usually harmful
     C. a kind of electric spark
     D. a vacuum

17. If three 1 1/2 volt dry cell batteries are connected in series and measured by a voltmeter,   17._____
the reading would be _____ volts.

     A. 1 1/2   B. 3   C. 3 1/2   D. 4 1/2

18. Newton's third law of motion is BEST illustrated by a(n)   18._____

     A. apple falling from a tree
     B. rocket taking off
     C. can of gasoline
     D. radio transmitter

19. In a gasoline engine, combustion is caused by   19._____

     A. compression
     B. gasoline
     C. a mixture of air and gasoline
     D. a spark plug

20. A light-year is a measure of   20._____

     A. time   B. speed   C. distance   D. brightness

21. The classification of rocks into three major groups is PRIMARILY based upon differences   21._____
in

     A. age   B. size   C. origin   D. hardness

22. Isobars on a weather map connect points of equal   22._____

     A. temperature   B. air pressure
     C. precipitation   D. wind direction

23. The negatively-charged particle within an atom is called a(n)   23._____

    A. photon   B. proton   C. neutron   D. electron

24. In the ocean, MOST surface waves are a result of   24._____

    A. tides   B. wind action
    C. earthquakes   D. the revolution of the earth

25. Which of these is a unit of volume?   25._____

    A. Ton   B. Gram   C. Liter   D. Kilometer

KEY (CORRECT ANSWERS)

1.	C		11.	B
2.	D		12.	C
3.	B		13.	A
4.	C		14.	B
5.	A		15.	A
6.	C		16.	C
7.	B		17.	D
8.	D		18.	B
9.	D		19.	D
10.	C		20.	C

21.	C
22.	B
23.	D
24.	B
25.	C

EXAMINATION SECTION
TEST 1

DIRECTIONS: Each question or incomplete statement is followed by several suggested answers or completions. Select the one that BEST answers the question or completes the statement. *PRINT THE LETTER OF THE CORRECT ANSWER IN THE SPACE AT THE RIGHT.*

1. Respiration in plants occurs　　　　　　　　　　　　　　　　　　　　1.＿＿＿＿
   - A. only on cloudy days
   - B. only in the night
   - C. only in the daytime
   - D. all the time

2. The complex chemical ATP is necessary to produce　　　　　　　　2.＿＿＿＿
   - A. fats
   - B. sugars
   - C. proteins
   - D. amino acids

3. A medicine obtained from the bark of the cinchona tree is　　　　3.＿＿＿＿
   - A. atabrine
   - B. pentaquine
   - C. chloroquine
   - D. quinine

4. A radioactive element used to study photosynthesis in green plants is　　4.＿＿＿＿
   - A. I^{131}
   - B. C^{14}
   - C. N^{16}
   - D. U^{233}

5. The selectivity of a cell depends upon the　　　　　　　　　　　　5.＿＿＿＿
   - A. cell membrane
   - B. nucleus
   - C. cytoplasm
   - D. mitochondria

6. The zoologist who helped formulate the cell theory was　　　　　　6.＿＿＿＿
   - A. Schleiden
   - B. Hooke
   - C. Purkinje
   - D. Schwann

7. The brown spots on the back of fern fronds produce　　　　　　　　7.＿＿＿＿
   - A. pollen
   - B. spores
   - C. scales
   - D. seeds

8. Plants without true roots, stems, or leaves are called　　　　　　　8.＿＿＿＿
   - A. bryophytes
   - B. spermatophytes
   - C. thallophytes
   - D. pteridophytes

9. Of the following, the CLOSEST biological relative of the whale is the　　9.＿＿＿＿
   - A. shark
   - B. toad
   - C. crocodile
   - D. horse

10. The process LEAST likely to result in vitamin loss is　　　　　　　10.＿＿＿＿
    - A. bleaching celery
    - B. refining flour
    - C. quick freezing fruits
    - D. peeling vegetables

11. A trait determined by two identical alleles is said to be　　　　　　11.＿＿＿＿
    - A. homologous
    - B. analogous
    - C. heterozygous
    - D. homozygous

12. The nutrient that produces the LARGEST number of calories per gram of weight is   12.____

    A. protein   B. starch   C. carbohydrate   D. fat

13. A method used to condition the soil by spreading straw, manure, or peat moss over it is   13.____

    A. fallowing   B. terracing   C. leaching   D. mulching

14. The plant that acts as an alternate host for the wheat rust is   14.____

    A. gooseberry   B. white pine
    C. red cedar   D. barberry

15. In the process of respiration in a plant,   15.____

    A. potential energy is stored
    B. chlorophyll is necessary
    C. stored food is utilized
    D. protein is synthesized

16. The insect that feeds on the cottony cushion scale is the   16.____

    A. Ladybird bettle   B. Boll weevil
    C. Tachina fly   D. Hessian fly

17. Food made in the leaves moves to all parts of a green plant through the   17.____

    A. stomates   B. phloem   C. pith   D. xylem

18. Deamination of proteins occurs MAINLY in the   18.____

    A. small intestine   B. liver
    C. spleen   D. pancreas

19. The chemical that plays a part in the passage of nerve impulses across the space between two connecting neurons is   19.____

    A. auxin   B. colchicine
    C. reserpine   D. acetylcholine

20. The gathering of white blood cells around bacteria is an example of   20.____

    A. thigmotropism   B. chemotropism
    C. geotropism   D. hydrotropism

21. The Islets of Langerhans are located in the   21.____

    A. testis   B. pancreas   C. pituitary   D. thyroid

22. The adrenal cortex is stimulated to secrete cortisone by   22.____

    A. ATP   B. ACTH   C. 2, 4-D   D. PAS

23. Liquid wastes are carried from the kidneys to the urinary bladder by the   23.____

    A. ureters   B. urethras
    C. oviducts   D. Fallopian tubes

24. The part of the brain that controls the breathing rate is the

    A. medulla   B. cerebrum
    C. cerebellum   D. hypothalamus

24.____

25. The chemicals that cause clumping of the erythrocytes in the blood are

    A. platelets   B. red corpuscles
    C. white corpuscles   D. plasma

25.____

26. An organism with an *open circuit* system of circulation is the

    A. frog   B. earthworm   C. crayfish   D. fish

26.____

27. The heart chamber that pumps blood to the aorta is the

    A. right auricle   B. right ventricle
    C. left auricle   D. left ventricle

27.____

28. The substances that are absorbed into the lacteals of the villi are

    A. amino acids   B. vitamins
    C. simple sugars   D. fatty acids

28.____

29. A chemical that has been used with great success in the treatment of tuberculosis is

    A. isoniazid   B. chloromycetin
    C. sulfanilamide   D. radioactive phosphorus

29.____

30. Ringworm disease is caused by a

    A. lichen   B. roundworm
    C. segmented worm   D. fungus

30.____

31. The organism that causes typhus fever is a(n)

    A. fungus   B. Rickettsia   C. bacterium   D. virus

31.____

32. Emotional behavior is controlled in the

    A. hypothalamus   B. cerebrum
    C. cerebellum   D. medulla

32.____

33. In a given sample of blood, clumping occurred with both A serum and B serum. The blood type was

    A. A   B. B   C. O   D. AB

33.____

34. Of the following vitamins, the one that does NOT aid in cellular oxidation is

    A. thiamin   B. niacin
    C. ascorbic acid   D. riboflavin

34.____

35. The cyton of a motor neuron is found in the

    A. posterior root ganglion
    B. anterior root ganglion
    C. gray matter of the spinal cord
    D. white matter of the spinal cord

35.____

36. An instrument that records the electrical impulses developed in the brain is the   36.___

    A. kymograph   B. electrocardiograph
    C. polygraph   D. electroencephalograph

37. The relationship between clover plants and nitrogen-fixing bacteria is a form of   37.___

    A. parasitism   B. saprophytism
    C. commensalism   D. symbiosis

38. The number of pairs of cranial nerves in man is   38.___

    A. 12   B. 31   C. 48   D. 206

39. Water pollination occurs in the   39.___

    A. water lily   B. corn
    C. spruce   D. duckweed

40. A vegetative structure that consists of an underground stem surrounded by storage-leaves is a   40.___

    A. slip   B. rhizome   C. bulb   D. tuber

41. If a planarium is cut in half, each part will grow eventually into a complete organism. This process of forming a new organism is called   41.___

    A. conjugation   B. parthenogenesis
    C. meiosis   D. regeneration

42. Passive immunity GENERALLY lasts a   42.___

    A. few weeks   B. few months
    C. few years   D. lifetime

43. Septic tanks are used in waste disposal to   43.___

    A. break down solid wastes   B. dilute sewage
    C. aerate sewage   D. filter sewage

44. The development of the polio vaccine was made possible, in part, by the discovery that the polio viruses could be cultured in test tubes on one of the following organs of Old World monkeys: 44.___

    A. Liver   B. Thyroid gland
    C. Kidney   D. Lung

45. The scientist who discovered streptomycin was   45.___

    A. Enders   B. Fleming   C. Florey   D. Waksman

46. A sex-linked disease in man is   46.___

    A. leukemia   B. anemia
    C. hemophilia.   D. erythroblastosis fetalis

47. Destruction of the red blood cells of a developing embryo may occur when the embryo is Rh _____ and the mother is Rh _____.   47.____

    A. positive; positive   B. positive; n egative
    C. negative; negative   D. negative; positive

48. The scientist who FIRST used the word mutation to describe changes that he found in the evening primrose plant was   48.____

    A. Morgan   B. Muller   C. DeVries   D. Mendel

49. The study of the functioning of living organisms is called   49.____

    A. anatomy   B. pathology   C. ecology   D. physiology

50. The fact that a white guinea pig resulted from a cross between two hybrid black guinea pigs illustrates the law of   50.____

    A. segregation   B. dominance
    C. linkage   D. independent assortment

KEY (CORRECT ANSWERS)

1.	D	11.	D	21.	B	31.	B	41.	D
2.	B	12.	D	22.	B	32.	A	42.	A
3.	D	13.	D	23.	A	33.	D	43.	A
4.	B	14.	D	24.	A	34.	C	44.	C
5.	A	15.	C	25.	D	35.	C	45.	D
6.	D	16.	A	26.	C	36.	D	46.	C
7.	B	17.	B	27.	D	37.	D	47.	B
8.	C	18.	B	28.	D	38.	A	48.	C
9.	D	19.	D	29.	A	39.	D	49.	D
10.	C	20.	B	30.	D	40.	C	50.	A

TEST 2

DIRECTIONS: Each question or incomplete statement is followed by several suggested answers or completions. Select the one that BEST answers the question or completes the statement. *PRINT THE LETTER OF THE CORRECT ANSWER IN THE SPACE AT THE RIGHT.*

1.   When a blue Andalusian rooster is crossed with a blue Andalusian hen, the phenotypic ratio expected among the offspring will be   1.____

   A.   100% blue
   B.   50% black and 50% white
   C.   75% black and 25% white
   D.   25% white, 25% black, 50% blue

2.   A vitamin that contains cobalt as part of its chemical structure is vitamin   2.____

   A.   A   B. B_2 C. B_{12} D.   C

3.   The two-layered cup stage that forms during cleavage is called the   3.____

   A.   morula   B.   gastrula   C.   blastula   D.   mesoderm

4.   The one term that includes all the others is   4.____

   A.   equational division   B.   gamete
   C.   maturation   D.   reduction division

5.   Organizers are chemicals that influence   5.____

   A.   differentiation   B.   mitosis
   C.   fertilization   D.   maturation

6.   The developing embryo of a mammal is protected by a liquid-filled sac called the   6.____

   A.   placenta   B.   amnion   C.   uterus   D.   allantois

7.   The seedless orange is propagated by   7.____

   A.   self-pollination   B.   cross-pollination
   C.   hybridization   D.   grafting

8.   One similarity between reflexes and habits is that they are BOTH   8.____

   A.   inborn acts   B.   autonomic acts
   C.   learned acts   D.   automatic

9.   The MOST ancient of the following prehistoric men is   9.____

   A.   Heidelberg   B.   Neanderthal
   C.   Pithecantropus   D.   Cro-Magnon

10.   The theory of *Use and Disuse* was developed by   10.____

   A.   Weismann   B.   Darwin   C.   Wallace   D.   Lamarck

11. The micturating membrane in man is an example of a(n)   11.____

   A. mutation   B. vestigial structure
   C. malformation   D. embryonic structure

12. The LATEST of the geological eras is called the   12.____

   A. cenozoic   B. paleozoic
   C. proterozoic   D. mesozoic

13. Liquids are transported through stems and roots by the   13.____

   A. epidermis   B. cortex
   C. vascular bundles   D. pith

14. An animal that is PROBABLY a link between the fish and amphibia is the   14.____

   A. archeopteryx   B. coelacanth
   C. trilobite   D. lamprey

15. The hormone that stimulates the change of glycogen to glucose in the liver is   15.____

   A. insulin   B. progestin   C. cortin   D. adrenin

16. The haploid chromosome number in the fruit fly, Drosophila, is   16.____

   A. 4   B. 8   C. 24   D. 48

17. The plant in which seed dispersal by animals occurs is the   17.____

   A. cherry   B. coconut
   C. witch hazel   D. milkweed

18. Blood tissue differentiates from the primary germ layer known as the   18.____

   A. endoderm   B. endosperm   C. mesoderm   D. ectoderm

19. Of the following types of tissue, the one which is NOT classified as connective tissue is   19.____

   A. blood   B. bone   C. cartilage   D. tendon

20. A chrysalis is a   20.____

   A. pupa case   B. nymph   C. larva   D. cocoon

21. The one term that includes all the others is _____ plant.   21.____

   A. herbaceous   B. flowering
   C. spermatophyte   D. annual

22. Nitrogen from the air is made available to plants by   22.____

   A. decay   B. fixation
   C. denitrification   D. nitrate bacteria

23. The series of muscular waves of contraction in the alimentary canal is called   23.____

   A. pylorus   B. peristalsis
   C. symbiosis   D. parthenogenesis

24. The corals belong to the phylum

    A. Mollusca
    C. Arthropoda
    B. Porifera
    D. Coelenterata

24.____

25. Three of the following substances are narcotics. The one that is NOT is

    A. chlorpromazine
    C. morphine
    B. nicotine
    D. cocaine

25.____

26. Hydrogen sulfide is USUALLY prepared in the laboratory by the action of

    A. hydrogen on hot sulfur
    B. hydrochloric acid on ferrous sulfide
    C. acid on sulfite
    D. sulfuric acid on copper

26.____

27. An unknown gas dissolves readily in water. The water solution turns red litmus blue. The gas reacts with hydrogen chloride gas, forming white fumes.
The unknown gas is PROBABLY

    A. nitric oxide
    C. sulfur dioxide
    B. ammonia
    D. hydrogen sulfide

27.____

28. Of the following, the one whose water solution will be basic in reaction is 0.1 molar

    A. HCl
    B. $NaC_2H_3O_2$
    C. NaCl
    D. $HC_2H_3O_2$

28.____

29. An apple green flame test indicates the presence of

    A. chromium
    B. sodium
    C. strontium
    D. barium

29.____

30. In the balanced chemical equation for the reaction between copper and dilute nitric acid, the coefficient before the nitric acid is

    A. 1
    B. 3
    C. 4
    D. 8

30.____

31. The molecular weight of sodium hydroxide is 40.
To prepare 100 cc. of a 0.1 N solution would require a weight of sodium hydroxide, in grams, of

    A. 0.4
    B. 2
    C. 4
    D. 400

31.____

32. Concentrated solutions of potassium hydroxide should be stored in bottles with stoppers made of

    A. glass
    B. rubber
    C. cork
    D. aluminum

32.____

33. White phosphorus should be stored under

    A. carbon disulfide
    C. oil
    B. carbon tetrachloride
    D. water

33.____

34. It is dangerous to add concentrated sulfuric acid to

    A. calcium sulfate
    C. potassium permanganate
    B. sodium bisulfate
    D. clay

34.____

35. You should instruct students to carry concentrated sulfuric acid   35.____

    A. very carefully   B. in a covered metal can
    C. under no circumstances   D. in a cart

36. The formula for chloroform is   36.____

    A. CH_2Cl_2 B. $CHCl_3$ C. CH_3Cl D. $C_2H_4Cl_2$

37. *Wood* alcohol is the common name for   37.____

    A. ethyl alcohol   B. propyl alcohol
    C. glycerol   D. methyl alcohol

38. The FIRST thing to do if concentrated acid comes into contact with the skin is to   38.____

    A. wash with ammonia
    B. call a doctor
    C. pour sodium hydroxide over it
    D. wash with cold water for a long time

39. Hydrofluoric acid is GENERALLY stored in   39.____

    A. polyethylene bottles   B. glass bottles
    C. copper jars   D. platinum bottles

40. A liter is APPROXIMATELY equivalent to a(n)   40.____

    A. quart   B. pint   C. gallon   D. gill

41. The FIRST scientist to effect a nuclear reaction was   41.____

    A. Rutherford   B. J.J. Thomson
    C. Chadwick   D. Fermi

42. The chemical behavior of the atom is LARGELY determined by the   42.____

    A. atomic weight
    B. number of neutrons
    C. kind of charge in the nucleus
    D. electrons

43. Radioactive substances   43.____

    A. easily lose their orbital electrons
    B. have unstable nuclei
    C. gain electrons easily
    D. lack mesons

44. In the reaction $_7N^{15} + {_1}H^2 \rightarrow X + {_1}H^1$, X is   44.____

    A. $_9F^{17}$ B. $_8O^{15}$ C. $_8C^{14}$ D. $_7N^{16}$

45. In the reaction $C + O_2 \rightarrow CO_2$, the weight of CO_2, in grams, produced by burning 100 grams of carbon with 100 grams of oxygen is about (At. Wgts.: C = 12, O = 16)   45.____

    A. 100   B. 137   C. 150   D. 200

46. When sodium combines with chlorine, the sodium is   46._____

    A. oxidized and the chlorine is reduced
    B. reduced and the chlorine is oxidized
    C. oxidized and the chlorine remains unchanged
    D. unchanged while the chlorine is oxidized

47. An electric spark is passed through a mixture containing 3.2 grams of oxygen gas and   47._____
    0.6 grams of hydrogen gas. After the explosion and subsequent cooling to room temper-
    ature, there are in the container

    A. 3.2 grams of water and 0.6 grams of hydrogen
    B. 3.6 grams of water and 0.2 grams of hydrogen
    C. 3.8 grams of water and 0 grams of hydrogen
    D. 0.9 grams of water and 2.9 grams of oxygen

48. The columns of the modern periodic table contain elements which resemble each other   48._____
    in

    A. the number of neutrons   B. valence
    C. density   D. appearance

49. Carbon forms a large number of compounds because   49._____

    A. of the ability of carbon atoms to form covalent linkages with each other
    B. of its small ionic radius
    C. it forms triple bonds
    D. it is very active

50. The SIMPLEST way to recover silver from a solution of one of its compounds is to   50._____

    A. distill the solution   B. use the thermit process
    C. add powdered zinc   D. decompose the solution

KEY (CORRECT ANSWERS)

1. D	11. B	21. C	31. A	41. A
2. C	12. A	22. B	32. B	42. D
3. B	13. C	23. B	33. D	43. B
4. C	14. B	24. D	34. C	44. D
5. A	15. D	25. A	35. C	45. B
6. B	16. A	26. B	36. B	46. A
7. D	17. A	27. B	37. D	47. B
8. D	18. C	28. B	38. D	48. B
9. C	19. A	29. D	39. A	49. A
10. D	20. A	30. D	40. A	50. C

TEST 3

DIRECTIONS: Each question or incomplete statement is followed by several suggested answers or completions. Select the one that BEST answers the question or completes the statement. *PRINT THE LETTER OF THE CORRECT ANSWER IN THE SPACE AT THE RIGHT.*

1. In a chemical reaction, the valence of the element arsenic was changed from +5 to 0. All of the following statements are true EXCEPT the one stating that arsenic

    A. oxidized something else   B. was reduced
    C. gained electrons   D. lost protons

1.____

2. The neutralization of a base by an acid ALWAYS produces

    A. soluble products   B. water
    C. gas   D. sodium chloride

2.____

3. The pH of an acid solution could be

    A. 5   B. 7   C. 9   D. 13

3.____

4. The CORRECT formula of the hydronium ion is

    A. OH^- B. H_3O^+ C. H_4O^+ D. $H+$

4.____

5. When $CaCO_3$ reacts with CHI, the products are

    A. CaO, H_2O and CO_2 B. $CaCl_2$, H_2O and CO_2
    C. $CaOCl$, H_2O and CO_2 D. $CaCl_2$, Cl_2, CO_2 and H_2O

5.____

6. A solution of a non-volatile solute in water

    A. boils at 100° C
    B. freezes below 0° C
    C. has a higher vapor pressure than water at the same temperature
    D. always has a volume equal to the combined volumes of solute and solvent

6.____

7. An unknown gas has a density of 1.5 grams per liter under standard conditions. Its molecular weight is about

    A. 33.6   B. 22.4   C. 11.2   D. 67.2

7.____

8. Of the following sequences, the one that CORRECTLY represents the non-metals in the order of their increasing activity as non-metals is

    A. F, Cl, Br, I   B. F, I, Cl, Br
    C. I, Cl, Br, F   D. I, Br, Cl, F

8.____

9. Carbon will NOT reduce the oxide of

    A. sodium   B. iron   C. zinc   D. copper

9.____

10. The valence of the metal in the compound $Ca_3(PO_4)_2$ is plus

    A. 1   B. 2   C. 3   D. 6

10.____

11. Covalent bonds are MOST commonly found in   11.___

    A. salts   B. bases
    C. inorganic solids   D. organic compounds

12. Al_2O_3 and CBr_4, are the correct formulae of the oxide of aluminum and the bromide of carbon.   12.___
The formula of the compound aluminum carbide is

    A. AlC   B. Al_4C_3 C. Al_3C_4 D. Al_4C_2

13. A chalk and salt mixture could be separated into its components by   13.___

    A. subliming the salt out of the mixture
    B. adding water and distilling
    C. adding water, boiling, and filtering
    D. adding water, boiling, and cooling

14. The electrolysis of brine is used commercially to produce all of the following substances EXCEPT   14.___

    A. sodium hydroxide   B. hydrogen
    C. chlorine   D. sodium chloride

15. In the Hall process, cryolite is used as a   15.___

    A. source of aluminum   B. solvent
    C. source of fluorine   D. solute

16. All of the following are present in pig iron as impurities EXCEPT   16.___

    A. silicon   B. phosphorus   C. molybdenum   D. sulfur

17. The compound MOST generally found in petroleum is   17.___

    A. $CHCl_3$ B. C_8H_{18} C. CH_5N D. $C_7H_{15}OH$

18. When a non-metallic oxide such as N_2O_5 is dissolved in water,   18.___

    A. the solution is acidic
    B. the solution is basic
    C. the solution may be either acidic or basic
    D. no chemical change occurs

19. In developing a photographic plate,   19.___

    A. sodium thiosulfate is used as a reducing agent
    B. it is left in the developer until all of the silver bromide has been developed
    C. no visible change takes place
    D. the exposed plate is reduced most rapidly where most light has been absorbed

20. The plastic lucite is a polymer of   20.___

    A. methyl methacrylate   B. styrene
    C. butadiene   D. acrylonitrile

21. MOST animal fats are classed as   21._____

    A. alcohols   B. esters   C. aldehydes   D. acids

22. Hydrogen should be prepared in the classroom by combining   22._____

    A. sodium and hydrochloric acid
    B. zinc and sulfuric acid
    C. potassium chlorate and hydrochloric acid
    D. iron oxide and steam

23. The formula for baking soda is   23._____

    A. Na_2CO_3 B. NaOH   C. $NaHCO_3$ D. Na_2SO_4

24. The chemist GENERALLY credited with discovering deuterium is   24._____

    A. Hall   B. Urey
    C. Fermi   D. Oppenheimer

25. Thermit mixture is composed of   25._____

    A. magnesium and iron oxide
    B. iron and aluminum oxide
    C. aluminum and iron oxide
    D. magnesium and barium peroxide

26. The statement, *It is easier to raise a load with pulleys,* means that for the given load,   26._____
there is a reduction in the required

    A. force   B. work   C. distance   D. power

27. If, when three forces are applied to a body, the body is at rest, the resultant of these   27._____
forces is

    A. the weight of the object
    B. more than the largest force
    C. zero
    D. the equilibrant of the object

28. Reducing friction has no effect on the   28._____

    A. actual mechanical advantage
    B. efficiency
    C. ideal mechanical advantage
    D. work input

29. Machines can multiply   29._____

    A. work   B. energy   C. force   D. efficiency

30. Weights of 3 lb. and 7 lb. hang from a bar which is supported by a spring scale.   30._____
Neglecting the weight of the bar, the weight, in pounds, registered by the scale is

    A. 2.5   B. 4   C. 10   D. 21

31. A body starts from rest and falls freely for four seconds. The distance, in feet, the body will fall (neglecting air resistance) is
    31._____

    A. 64   B. 96   C. 256   D. 512

32. The width of the film, in inches, used in a 35 mm camera is
    32._____

    A. 1   B. 1.4   C. 2.5   D. 3.5

33. The pressure cooker cooks food more rapidly because the
    33._____

    A. water boils more rapidly
    B. water boils at a higher temperature
    C. less water is used
    D. pressure is reduced below normal

34. Any two objects of equal weight are necessarily at the same temperature if
    34._____

    A. they contain equal amounts of heat
    B. they lose heat at equal rates
    C. neither loses heat to the other when they are in contact
    D. their molecules have equal average speeds

35. Heat may be measured by
    35._____

    A. temperature change in a known quantity of water
    B. the expansion of mercury
    C. the bending of a bimetallic strip
    D. the expansion of hydrogen

36. The quantity of heat, in calories, required to change 10 grams of ice at 0° C to water at 20° C is
    36._____

    A. 100   B. 200   C. 1000   D. 5600

37. To double the pressure in a fixed volume of a gas at 0° C, its temperature, in $^\circ$ C, must be raised to
    37._____

    A. 100   B. 273   C. 373   D. 546

38. An object is placed 8 inches from a convex lens of 4 inch focal length. The image formed will be
    38._____

    A. larger than the object
    B. smaller than the object
    C. the same size as the object
    D. virtual

39. When light strikes the prisms in binoculars, it will be
    39._____

    A. reflected   B. refracted
    C. dispersed   D. absorbed

40. Evidence that light is a transverse wave phenomenon is obtained from
    40._____

    A. beats   B. polarization
    C. photoelectric effect   D. interference

41. The failure of a lens to focus, at a point, light of different colors is called   41.____

    A. interference   B. spherical aberration
    C. polarization   D. chromatic aberration

42. Two sounds of the same wavelength MUST have the same   42.____

    A. amplitude   B. frequency   C. intensity   D. quality

43. The human ear cannot distinguish tones that differ in   43.____

    A. phase   B. quality   C. intensity   D. pitch

44. Of the following, the one that is at MAXIMUM when resonance occurs in an electrical cir-   44.____
    cuit is

    A. impedance   B. resistance   C. reactance   D. current

45. Electromagnetic waves radiated into space are called _____ waves.   45.____

    A. rectified   B. carrier
    C. stationary   D. polarized

46. A TV broadcasting station transmits the picture (video signal) by means of _____ mod-   46.____
    ulation of _____ frequency waves.

    A. frequency; high   B. amplitude; high
    C. frequency; low   D. amplitude; low

47. The emission of electrons from certain metals when they are exposed to light is known   47.____
    as the _____ effect.

    A. thermionic   B. Edison
    C. photoelectric   D. thermoelectric

48. The process of varying the amplitude of a carrier wave is called   48.____

    A. modulation   B. regeneration
    C. oscillation   D. rectification

49. A transformer may be used to increase   49.____

    A. energy   B. power   C. voltage   D. wattage

50. An induction coil   50.____

    A. produces a large current
    B. changes AC to DC
    C. produces a high voltage
    D. steps down high voltages

247

KEY (CORRECT ANSWERS)

1.	D	11.	D	21.	B	31.	C	41.	D
2.	B	12.	B	22.	B	32.	B	42.	B
3.	A	13.	C	23.	C	33.	B	43.	A
4.	B	14.	D	24.	B	34.	C	44.	C
5.	B	15.	B	25.	C	35.	A	45.	B
6.	B	16.	C	26.	A	36.	C	46.	B
7.	A	17.	B	27.	C	37.	B	47.	C
8.	D	18.	A	28.	C	38.	C	48.	A
9.	A	19.	D	29.	C	39.	A	49.	C
10.	B	20.	A	30.	C	40.	B	50.	C

———

TEST 4

DIRECTIONS: Each question or incomplete statement is followed by several suggested answers or completions. Select the one that BEST answers the question or completes the statement. *PRINT THE LETTER OF THE CORRECT ANSWER IN THE SPACE AT THE RIGHT.*

1. The part NOT found in an AC generator is a(n)

   A. field magnet
   C. brush(es)
   B. armature
   D. commutator

   1.____

2. To protect a delicate watch from a magnetic field, its case should be made of

   A. cobalt
   C. soft iron
   B. aluminum
   D. steel

   2.____

3. The electrical device MOST similar to a galvanometer in operation is the

   A. bell
   C. motor
   B. electromagnet
   D. fuse

   3.____

4. A hand generator is easier to turn when the external circuit is open. This is BEST explained by a principle stated by

   A. Oersted   B. Ampere   C. Ohm   D. Lenz

   4.____

5. *60 cycle* current refers to

   A. wavelength
   C. frequency
   B. amplitude
   D. velocity

   5.____

6. One end of a metal rod is brought near the north pole of a magnet, and it is noted that they attract.
   This indicates that the metal rod is

   A. a permanent magnet
   C. a magnetic substance
   B. not a magnet
   D. made of iron

   6.____

7. One coulomb per second defines one

   A. volt   B. watt   C. ampere   D. ohm

   7.____

8. Electricity is stored in a

   A. dry cell
   C. storage battery
   B. condenser
   D. generator

   8.____

9. Increasing the distance between the plates of a charged capacitor

   A. *increases* the potential difference
   B. *decreases* the potential difference
   C. *decreases* the amount of charge
   D. *increases* the amount of charge

   9.____

10. A radioactive emission not bent by a magnetic field is a(n)

   A. proton
   C. beta particle
   B. gamma ray
   D. alpha particle

   10.____

11. $_4Be^9$ means that the number of protons in a beryllium nucleus is 11.____

    A. 4   B. 5   C. 9   D. 13

12. *Isotopes* is the name given to elements that have 12.____

    A. the same atomic number but different atomic mass
    B. the same atomic mass but different atomic number
    C. the same atomic mass and the same atomic number but different chemical properties
    D. similar chemical properties although they differ in both atomic mass and atomic number

13. Ionization is the basis for the 13.____

    A. Geiger counter and scintillation counter
    B. Geiger counter and cloud chamber
    C. cloud chamber and scintillation counter
    D. Geiger counter, cloud chamber, and scintillation counter

14. Atomic mass is determined by 14.____

    A. protons   B. neutrons
    C. protons plus neutrons   D. protons minus neutrons

15. The mass of a nucleus, as compared with the sum of the masses of the particles which compose it, is 15.____

    A. slightly greater   B. much greater
    C. equal   D. slightly less

16. To an observer on Earth, the BRIGHTEST planet is 16.____

    A. Jupiter   B. Saturn   C. Mars   D. Venus

17. The Russian Lunik revolves around the 17.____

    A. sun outside the earth's orbit
    B. sun inside the earth's orbit
    C. moon
    D. earth

18. The Northern Cross lies in the constellation 18.____

    A. Cygnus   B. Bootes   C. Lyra   D. Pegasus

19. A galaxy visible to the unaided eye lies in the constellation 19.____

    A. Andromeda   B. Ursa Minor
    C. Auriga   D. Canis Major

20. A rock composed of angular fragments cemented together into a coherent mass is a 20.____

    A. breccia   B. tufa   C. conglomerate   D. dacite

21. In Moh's scale of mineral hardness, quartz is number 21.____

    A. 5   B. 6   C. 7   D. 8

22. A rock which shows foliated structure is   22.____

    A. marble   B. serpentine   C. schist   D. quartzite

23. A river is classified as mature when it includes a   23.____

    A. chain of lakes in its course
    B. gorge
    C. series of meanders
    D. series of rapids

24. On a Mercator projection, a straight line joining New York City and Liverpool   24.____

    A. has constant direction
    B. has constant scale
    C. is the arc of a great circle
    D. has a larger scale near Liverpool than near New York

25. An esker is a   25.____

    A. winding, roughly stratified glacial ridge
    B. linear, unstratified glacial ridge
    C. roughly circular glacial mound
    D. series of glacial elevations and depressions

26. An example of an active volcano of the *quiet* type is   26.____

    A. Krakatoa   B. Mauna Loa
    C. Mt. Lassen   D. Mt. Vesuvius

27. Stone Mt., Georgia is classified as a   27.____

    A. butte   B. mesa
    C. monadnock   D. volcanic neck

28. The velocity of escape of a projectile from the Earth, in number of miles per hour, is about   28.____

    A. 7,000   B. 18,000   C. 25,000   D. 35,000

29. An outstanding example of a glacial trough is the   29.____

    A. Grand Canyon of the Colorado
    B. Yellowstone Canyon in Yellowstone National Park
    C. Yosemite Valley in Yosemite National Park
    D. Zion Canyon in Zion National Park

30. The Keewatin Glacier of the Pleistocene ice age was centered in   30.____

    A. north central Canada   B. Labrador
    C. Alaska   D. Greenland

31. Lost rivers or underground streams are MOST likely to occur in regions whose bedrock is   31.____

    A. limestone   B. slate
    C. granite   D. conglomerate

32. The Royal Gorge of the Arkansas River represents a river valley which is   32.____

    A. young   B. mature   C. old   D. subdued

33. Sink holes are the result of the work of   33.____

    A. earthquakes   B. underground water
    C. streams   D. glaciers

34. The mineral which is LEAST susceptible to chemical weathering is   34.____

    A. feldspar   B. hornblends
    C. augite   D. quartz

35. Of the following, the mountains of GREATEST geologic age are the   35.____

    A. Appalachians   B. Rockies
    C. Sierra Nevadas   D. Cascades

36. Laccoliths are found in   36.____

    A. domed mountains   B. block mountains
    C. folded mountains   D. volcanoes

37. The normal percentage of dissolved mineral matter in sea water (by weight) is APPROX-   37.____
IMATELY

    A. 1.5   B. 2.5   C. 3.5   D. 4.5

38. A shoreline formed as a result of submergence is a _____ shoreline.   38.____

    A. coastal plain   B. delta
    C. fiord   D. volcano

39. Spring tides occur at   39.____

    A. full moon *only*
    B. new moon *only*
    C. both full and new moon
    D. first and last quarter phases

40. An annular eclipse of the sun takes place at the phase of the moon called   40.____

    A. new moon   B. new gibbous
    C. new crescent   D. full moon

41. When it is noon, Eastern Standard Time, in New York City, the standard time at the 120W   41.____
meridian is

    A. 9 A.M.   B. 10 A.M.   C. 2 P.M.   D. 3 P.M.

42. On June 21, in New York City, the sun   42.____

    A. rises in the northeast
    B. sets in the southwest
    C. reaches the zenith at local noon
    D. is north of the zenith at local noon

43. The Palisades of New Jersey originated as an igneous intrusion during the period known as   43._____

    A. Eocene   B. Cretaceous
    C. Permian   D. Triassic

44. A region whose warmest monthly temperature average is 80° F, while its coldest monthly temperature average is 77° F, MUST have a climate typified as   44._____

    A. marine west coast   B. Mediterranean
    C. tropical desert   D. tropical rainforest

45. A necessary condition for the formation of sleet is a   45._____

    A. cold front   B. strong pressure gradient
    C. steep lapse rate   D. temperature inversion

46. The dry adiabetic lapse rate per 1000 feet is   46._____

    A. 2.5° F   B. 3.5° F   C. 4.5° F   D. 5.5° F

47. The prevailing wind at 40S latitude is   47._____

    A. northwesterly   B. northeasterly
    C. southwesterly   D. southeasterly

48. The European equivalent of the American Chinook wind is known as the   48._____

    A. bora   B. buran   C. foehn   D. mistral

49. Cumulonimbus clouds are MOST likely to occur in connection with a(n) _____ air mass.   49._____

    A. mTk   B. mTw   C. cPk   D. cPw

50. At perigee, our moon's distance, expressed in miles, from the earth is about   50._____

    A. 205,000   B. 220,000   C. 235,000   D. 245,000

KEY (CORRECT ANSWERS)

1. D	11. A	21. C	31. A	41. A
2. C	12. A	22. C	32. A	42. A
3. C	13. B	23. D	33. B	43. D
4. D	14. C	24. A	34. D	44. D
5. C	15. D	25. A	35. A	45. D
6. C	16. D	26. B	36. A	46. D
7. C	17. A	27. C	37. C	47. A
8. B	18. A	28. C	38. C	48. C
9. A	19. A	29. C	39. C	49. A
10. B	20. A	30. A	40. A	50. B

EXAMINATION SECTION

TEST 1

DIRECTIONS: Each question or incomplete statement is followed by several suggested answers or completions. Select the one that BEST answers the question or completes the statement. *PRINT THE LETTER OF THE CORRECT ANSWER IN THE SPACE AT THE RIGHT.*

1. While a senior in high school, I was absent
    A. never
    B. seldom
    C. frequently
    D. more than 10 days
    E. only when I felt bored

1._____

2. While in high school, I failed classes
    A. never
    B. once
    C. twice
    D. more than twice
    E. at least four times

2._____

3. During class discussions in my high school classes, I usually
    A. listened without participating
    B. participated as much as possible
    C. listened until I had something to add to the discussion
    D. disagreed with others simply for the sake of argument
    E. laughed at stupid ideas

3._____

4. My high school grade point average (on a 4.0 scale) was
    A. 2.0 or lower
    B. 2.1 to 2.5
    C. 2.6 to 3.0
    D. 3.1 to 3.5
    E. 3.6 to 4.0

4._____

5. As a high school student, I completed my assignments
    A. as close to the due date as I could manage
    B. whenever the teacher gave me an extension
    C. frequently
    D. on time
    E. when they were interesting

5._____

6. While in high school, I participated in
    A. athletic and non-athletic extracurricular activities
    B. athletic extracurricular activities
    C. non-athletic extracurricular activities
    D. no extracurricular activities
    E. mandatory afterschool programs

6._____

7. In high school, I made the honor roll   7._____
   - A. several times
   - B. once
   - C. more than once
   - D. twice
   - E. I cannot remember

8. Upon graduation from high school, I received _____ honors.   8._____
   - A. academic and non-academic
   - B. academic
   - C. non-academic
   - D. no
   - E. I cannot remember

9. While attending high school, I worked at a paid job or as a volunteer 9._____
   - A. never
   - B. every so often
   - C. 5 to 10 hours a month
   - D. more than 10 hours a month
   - E. more than 15 hours a month

10. During my senior year of high school, I skipped school   10._____
    - A. whenever I could
    - B. once a week
    - C. several times a week
    - D. not at all
    - E. when I got bored

11. I was suspended from high school   11._____
    - A. not at all
    - B. once or twice
    - C. once or twice, for fighting
    - D. several times
    - E. more times than I can remember

12. During high school, my fellow students and teachers considered me 12._____
    - A. above average
    - B. below average
    - C. average
    - D. underachieving
    - E. underachieving and prone to fighting

13. An effective leader is someone who   13._____
    - A. inspires confidence in his/her followers
    - B. inspires fear in his/her followers
    - C. tells subordinates exactly what they should do
    - D. creates an environment in which subordinates feel insecure about their job security and performance
    - E. makes as few decisions as possible

14. While a student, I spent my summers and holiday breaks   14._____
    A. in summer or remedial classes
    B. traveling
    C. working
    D. relaxing
    E. spending time with my friends

15. As a high school student, I cut classes   15._____
    A. frequently
    B. when I didn't like them
    C. sometimes
    D. rarely
    E. when I needed the sleep

16. In high school, I received academic honors   16._____
    A. not at all
    B. once
    C. twice
    D. several times
    E. I cannot remember

17. As a student, I failed _____ classes.   17._____
    A. no
    B. two
    C. three
    D. four
    E. more than four

18. Friends describe me as   18._____
    A. introverted
    B. hot-tempered
    C. unpredictable
    D. quiet
    E. easygoing

19. During my high school classes, I preferred to   19._____
    A. remain silent during discussions
    B. do other homework during discussions
    C. participate frequently in discussions
    D. argue with others as much as possible
    E. laugh at the stupid opinions of others

20. As a high school student, I was placed on academic probation   20._____
    A. not at all
    B. once
    C. twice
    D. three times
    E. more than three times

21. At work, being a team player means to   21._____
    A. compromise your ideals and beliefs
    B. compensate for the incompetence of others
    C. count on others to compensate for your inexperience
    D. cooperate with others to get a project finished
    E. rely on others to get the job done

22. My friends from school remember me primarily as a(n)   22._____
    A. person who loved to party
    B. ambitious student
    C. athlete
    D. joker
    E. fighter

23. My school experience is memorable primarily because of   23._____
    A. the friends I made
    B. the sorority/fraternity I was able to join
    C. the social activities I participated in
    D. my academic achievements
    E. the money I spent

24. A friend who is applying for a job asks you to help him pass the   24._____
mandatory drug test by substituting your urine sample for his. You should
    A. help him by supplying the sample
    B. supply the sample and insist he seek drug counseling
    C. supply the sample, but tell him that this is the only time you'll help
        in this way
    D. call the police
    E. refuse

25. As a student, I handed in my assignments when   25._____
    A. they were due
    B. I could get an extension
    C. they were interesting
    D. my friends reminded me to
    E. I was able to

KEY (CORRECT ANSWERS)

1. A	11. A	21. D
2. A	12. A	22. B
3. C	13. A	23. D
4. E	14. C	24. E
5. D	15. D	25. A
6. A	16. D	
7. A	17. A	
8. A	18. E	
9. E	19. C	
10. D	20. A	

TEST 2

DIRECTIONS: Each question or incomplete statement is followed by several suggested answers or completions. Select the one that BEST answers the question or completes the statement. *PRINT THE LETTER OF THE CORRECT ANSWER IN THE SPACE AT THE RIGHT.*

1. At work you are accused of a minor infraction which you did not commit. Your first reaction is to
    A. call a lawyer
    B. speak to your supervisor about the mistake
    C. call the police
    D. yell at the person who did commit the infraction
    E. accept the consequences regardless of your guilt or innocence

1._____

2. As a student, I began to prepare for final exams
    A. the night before taking them
    B. when the professor handed out the review sheets
    C. several weeks before taking them
    D. when my friends began to prepare for their exams
    E. the morning of the exam

2._____

3. At work, I am known as
    A. popular
    B. quiet
    C. intense
    D. easygoing
    E. dedicated

3._____

4. The most important quality in a coworker is
    A. friendliness
    B. cleanliness
    C. good sense of humor
    D. dependability
    E. good listening skills

4._____

5. In the past year, I have stayed home from work
    A. frequently
    B. only when I felt depressed
    C. rarely
    D. only when I felt overwhelmed
    E. only to run important errands

5._____

6. For me, the best thing about school was the
    A. chance to strengthen my friendships and develop new ones
    B. chance to test my abilities and develop new ones
    C. number of extracurricular activities and clubs
    D. chance to socialize
    E. chance to try several different majors

6._____

7. As an employee, my weakest skill is   7._____
    A. controlling my temper
    B. organizational ability
    C. ability to effectively understand directions
    D. ability to effectively manage others
    E. ability to communicate my thoughts in writing

8. As an employee, my greatest strength would be   8._____
    A. my sense of loyalty
    B. organizational ability
    C. punctuality
    D. dedication
    E. ability to intimidate others

9. If asked by my company to learn a new job-related skill, my reaction   9._____
    would be to
    A. ask for a raise
    B. ask for overtime pay
    C. question the necessity of the skill
    D. cooperate with some reluctance
    E. cooperate with enthusiasm

10. When I disagree with others, I tend to   10._____
    A. listen quietly despite my disagreement
    B. laugh openly at the person I disagree with
    C. ask the person to explain their views before I respond
    D. leave the conversation before my anger gets the best of me
    E. point out exactly why the person is wrong

11. When I find myself in a situation which is confusing or unclear, my   11._____
    reaction is to
    A. pretend I am not confused
    B. remain calm and, if necessary, ask someone else for clarification
    C. grow frustrated and angry
    D. walk away from the situation
    E. immediately insist that someone explain things to me

12. If you were placed in a supervisory position, which of the following   12._____
    abilities would you consider to be most important to your job
    performance?
    A. Stubbornness
    B. The ability to hear all sides of a story before making a decision
    C. Kindness
    D. The ability to make and stick to a decision
    E. Patience

13. What is your highest level of education?   13._____
    A. Less than a high school diploma
    B. High school diploma or equivalency
    C. Graduate of community college
    D. Graduate of a four-year accredited college
    E. Degree from graduate school

14. When asked to supervise other workers, your approach should be to   14._____
    A. ask for management wages since you're doing management work
    B. give the workers direction and supervise every aspect of the process
    C. give the workers direction and then allow them to do the job
    D. hand the workers their job specifications
    E. do the work yourself, since you're uncomfortable supervising others

15. Which of the following best describes you?   15._____
    A. Need little or no supervision
    B. Resent too much supervision
    C. Require as much supervision as my peers
    D. Require slightly more supervision than my peers
    E. Require close supervision

16. You accept a job which requires an ability to perform several tasks at once. What is the best way to handle such a position?   16._____
    A. With strong organizational skills and close attention to detail
    B. By delegating the work to someone with strong organizational skills
    C. Staying focused on one task at a time, no matter what happens
    D. Working on one task at a time until each task is successfully completed
    E. Asking your supervisor to help you

17. Which of the following best describes your behavior when you disagree with someone? You   17._____
    A. state your own point of view as quickly and loudly as you can
    B. listen quietly and keep your opinions to yourself
    C. listen to the other person's perspective and then carefully point out all the flaws in their logic
    D. list all of the ignorant people who agree with the opposing point of view
    E. listen to the other person's perspective and then explain your own perspective

18. As a new employee, you make several mistakes during your first week of work. You react by   18._____
    A. learning from your mistakes and moving on
    B. resigning
    C. blaming it on your supervisor
    D. refusing to talk about it
    E. blaming yourself

19. My ability to communicate effectively with others is   19._____
    A. below average
    B. average
    C. above average
    D. far above average
    E. far below average

20. In which of the following areas are you most highly skilled?   20._____
    A. Written communication
    B. Oral communication
    C. Ability to think quickly in difficult situations
    D. Ability to work with a broad diversity of people and personalities
    E. Organizational skills

21. As a worker, you are assigned to work with a partner whom you dislike.   21._____
    You should
    A. immediately report the problem to your supervisor
    B. ask your partner not to speak to you during working hours
    C. tell your colleagues about your differences
    D. tell your partner why you dislike him/her
    E. work with your partner regardless of your personal feelings

22. During high school, what was your most common afterschool activity?   22._____
    A. Remaining after school to participate in various clubs and
       organizations (band, sports, etc.)
    B. Making up for missed classes
    C. Punishment or detention
    D. Going straight to an afterschool job
    E. Spending the afternoon at home or with friends

23. During high school, in which of the following subjects did you receive the   23._____
    highest grades?
    A. English, history, social studies
    B. Math, science
    C. Vocational classes
    D. My grades were consistent in all subjects
    E. Classes I liked

24. When faced with an overwhelming number of duties at work, your   24._____
    reaction is to
    A. do all of the work yourself, no matter what the cost
    B. delegate some responsibilities to capable colleagues
    C. immediately ask your supervisor for help
    D. put off as much work as possible until you can get to it
    E. take some time off to relax and clear your mind

25. Which of the following best describes your desk at your current or most   25._____
    recent job?
    A. Messy and disorganized
    B. Neat and organized
    C. Messy but organized
    D. Neat but disorganized
    E. Messy

KEY (CORRECT ANSWERS)

1. B	11. B	21. E
2. C	12. D	22. A
3. E	13. E	23. D
4. D	14. C	24. B
5. C	15. A	25. B
6. B	16. A	
7. E	17. E	
8. D	18. A	
9. E	19. C	
10. C	20. C	

TEST 3

DIRECTIONS: Each question or incomplete statement is followed by several suggested answers or completions. Select the one that BEST answers the question or completes the statement. *PRINT THE LETTER OF THE CORRECT ANSWER IN THE SPACE AT THE RIGHT.*

1. When asked to take on extra responsibility at work, in order to help out a coworker who is overwhelmed, your response is to
   A. ask for overtime pay
   B. complain to your supervisor that you are being taken advantage of
   C. help the coworker to the best of your ability
   D. ask the coworker to come back some other time
   E. give the coworker some advice on how to get his/her job done

   1._____

2. At my last job, I was promoted
   A. not at all
   B. once
   C. twice
   D. three times
   E. more than three times

   2._____

3. You are faced with an overwhelming deadline at work. Your reaction is to
   A. procrastinate until the last minute
   B. procrastinate until someone notices that you need some help
   C. notify your supervisor that you cannot complete the work on your own
   D. work in silence without asking any questions
   E. arrange your schedule so that you can get the work done before the deadline

   3._____

4. When you feel yourself under deadline pressure at work, your response is
   A. make sure you keep to a schedule which allows you to complete the work on time
   B. wait until just before the deadline to complete the work
   C. ask someone else to do the work
   D. grow so obsessive about the work that your coworkers feel compelled to help you
   E. ask your supervisor immediately for help

   4._____

5. Which of the following best describes your appearance at your current or most recent position?
   A. Well-groomed, neat and clean
   B. Unkempt, but dressed neatly
   C. Messy and dirty clothing
   D. Unshaven and untidy
   E. Clean-shaven, but sloppily dressed

   5._____

6. Which of the following best describes the way you react to making a difficult decision?   6._____
    A. Consult with the people you're closest to before making the decision
    B. Make the decision entirely on your own
    C. Consult only with those people whom your decision will affect
    D. Consult with everyone you know, in an effort to make a decision that will please everyone
    E. Forget about the decision until you have to make it

7. If placed in a supervisory role, which of the following characteristics would you rely on most heavily when dealing with the employees you supervise?   7._____
    A. Kindness
    B. Cheeriness
    C. Honesty
    D. Hostility
    E. Aloofness

8. When confronted with gossip at work, your typical reaction is to   8._____
    A. participate
    B. listen without participating
    C. notify your supervisor
    D. excuse yourself from the discussion
    E. confront your coworkers about their problem

9. In the past two years, how many jobs have you held?   9._____
    A. None
    B. One
    C. Two
    D. Three
    E. More than three

10. In your current or most recent job, your favorite part of the job is the part which involves   10._____
    A. telling other people what they're doing wrong
    B. supervising others
    C. working without supervision to finish a project
    D. written communication
    E. oral communication

11. Your supervisor asks you about a colleague who is applying for a position which you also want. You react by   11._____
    A. commenting honestly on the colleague's work performance
    B. enhancing the person's negative traits
    C. informing your supervisor about your colleague's personal problems
    D. telling your supervisor that you would be better in the position
    E. refusing to comment

12. Which of these best describes your responsibilities in your last job?　12._____
    A. Entirely supervisory
    B. Much supervisory responsibility
    C. Equal amounts of supervisory and non-supervisory responsibility
    D. Some supervisory responsibilities
    E. No supervisory responsibilities

13. How much written communication did your previous or most recent job　13._____
require of you?
    A. A great deal
    B. Some
    C. I don't remember
    D. A small amount
    E. None

14. In the past two years, how many times have you been fired from a job?　14._____
    A. None
    B. Once
    C. Twice
    D. Three times
    E. More than three times

15. How many hours per week have you spent working for volunteer　15._____
organizations in the past year?
    A. 10 to 20
    B. 5 to 10
    C. 3 to 5
    D. 1 to 3
    E. None

16. Your efforts at volunteer work usually revolve around which of the　16._____
following types of organizations?
    A. Religious
    B. Community-based organization working to improve the community
    C. Charity on behalf of the poor
    D. Charity on behalf of the infirm or handicapped
    E. Other

17. Which of the following best describes your professional history?　17._____
Promoted at _____ coworkers.
    A. a much faster rate than
    B. a slightly faster rate than
    C. the same rate as
    D. a slightly slower rate than
    E. a much slower rate than

18. Which of the following qualities do you most appreciate in a coworker?　18._____
    A. Friendliness
    B. Dependability
    C. Good looks
    D. Silence
    E. Forgiveness

19. When you disagree with a supervisor's instructions or opinion about how to complete a project, your reaction is to   19._____
- A. inform your supervisor that you refuse to complete the project according to his or her instructions
- B. inform your colleagues of your supervisor's incompetence
- C. accept your supervisor's instructions in silence
- D. voice your concerns and then complete the project according to your own instincts
- E. voice your concerns and then complete the project according to your supervisor's instructions

20. Which of the following best describes your reaction to close supervision and specific direction from your supervisors? You   20._____
- A. listen carefully to the direction, then figure out a way to do the job more effectively
- B. complete the job according to the given specifications
- C. show some initiative by doing the job your way
- D. ask someone else to do the job for you
- E. listen carefully to the directions, and then figure out a better way to do the job which will save more money

21. At work, you are faced with a difficult decision. You react by   21._____
- A. seeking advice from your colleagues
- B. following your own path regardless of the consequences
- C. asking your supervisor what you should do
- D. keeping the difficulties to yourself
- E. working for a solution which will please everyone

22. If asked to work with a person whom you dislike, your response would be   22._____
- A. to ask your supervisor to allow you to work with someone else
- B. to ask your coworker to transfer to another department or project
- C. talk to your coworker about the proper way to behave at work
- D. pretend the coworker is your best friend for the sake of your job
- E. set aside your personal differences in order to complete the job

23. As a supervisor, which of the following incentives would you use to motivate your employees?   23._____
- A. Fear of losing their jobs
- B. Fear of their supervisors
- C. Allowing employees to provide their input on a number of policies
- D. Encouraging employees to file secret reports regarding colleagues' transgressions
- E. All of the above

24. A fellow worker, with whom you enjoy a close friendship, has a substance abuse problem which has gone undetected. You suspect the problem may be affecting his job. You would

    A. ask the worker if the problem is affecting his job performance
    B. warn the worker that he must seek counseling or you will report him
    C. wait a few weeks to see whether the worker's problem really is affecting his job
    D. discuss it with your supervisor
    E. wait for the supervisor to discover the problem

24._____

25. In the past two months, you have missed work

    A. never
    B. once
    C. twice
    D. three times
    E. more than three times

25._____

KEY (CORRECT ANSWERS)

1. C	11. A	21. A
2. C	12. D	22. E
3. E	13. B	23. C
4. A	14. A	24. D
5. A	15. C	25. A
6. A	16. B	
7. C	17. A	
8. D	18. B	
9. B	19. E	
10. C	20. B	

EXAMINATION SECTION
TEST 1

For each of the following items, circle the answer that best reflects the accuracy of the given statement, according to your own values, opinions, and experience.

1. In most situations, I value cooperation over competition.

   A. Very Accurate   B. Moderately Accurate
   C. Neither Accurate nor Inaccurate   D. Moderately Inaccurate
   E. Very Inaccurate

2. In work or in school, I've tried to do more than what's expected of me.

   A. Very Accurate   B. Moderately Accurate
   C. Neither Accurate nor Inaccurate   D. Moderately Inaccurate
   E. Very Inaccurate

3. Most of my problems are caused by other people.

   A. Very Accurate   B. Moderately Accurate
   C. Neither Accurate nor Inaccurate   D. Moderately Inaccurate
   E. Very Inaccurate

4. It's reasonable to say that a person's race is in some way related to the likelihood that he or she will commit a crime.

   A. Very Accurate   B. Moderately Accurate
   C. Neither Accurate nor Inaccurate   D. Moderately Inaccurate
   E. Very Inaccurate

5. My respect for a person's authority relies entirely on my respect for them as an individual, and has nothing to do with his or her official position.

   A. Very Accurate   B. Moderately Accurate
   C. Neither Accurate nor Inaccurate   D. Moderately Inaccurate
   E. Very Inaccurate

6. When I was in school, I never cheated on a test or assignment.

   A. Very Accurate   B. Moderately Accurate
   C. Neither Accurate nor Inaccurate   D. Moderately Inaccurate
   E. Very Inaccurate

7. I feel comfortable around most people, even if they're strangers.

   A. Very Accurate   B. Moderately Accurate
   C. Neither Accurate nor Inaccurate   D. Moderately Inaccurate
   E. Very Inaccurate

8. It's acceptable for an employee to borrow property from the workplace if the person who takes it intends to return it when he or she is finished with it.

   A. Very Accurate   B. Moderately Accurate
   C. Neither Accurate nor Inaccurate   D. Moderately Inaccurate
   E. Very Inaccurate

9. If it's clear that a person is not likely to receive adequate punishment for a crime or infraction, it's only fair to inflict some form of discipline on that person to make up for any likely lapses injustice.

    A. Very Accurate   B. Moderately Accurate
    C. Neither Accurate nor Inaccurate   D. Moderately Inaccurate
    E. Very Inaccurate

10. In previous work experience, I have been reluctant or unable to take on extra work or overtime on short notice.

    A. Very Accurate   B. Moderately Accurate
    C. Neither Accurate nor Inaccurate   D. Moderately Inaccurate
    E. Very Inaccurate

11. The casual use of illegal substances, if it's done only recreationally and on weekends, has no effect on a person's performance on the job during the work week.

    A. Very Accurate   B. Moderately Accurate
    C. Neither Accurate nor Inaccurate   D. Moderately Inaccurate
    E. Very Inaccurate

12. I am sometimes overwhelmed by events.

    A. Very Accurate   B. Moderately Accurate
    C. Neither Accurate nor Inaccurate   D. Moderately Inaccurate
    E. Very Inaccurate

13. If I don't agree with a certain rule, I see nothing wrong with breaking it, as long as it doesn't hurt anyone else.

    A. Very Accurate   B. Moderately Accurate
    C. Neither Accurate nor Inaccurate   D. Moderately Inaccurate
    E. Very Inaccurate

14. I get angry easily.

    A. Very Accurate   B. Moderately Accurate
    C. Neither Accurate nor Inaccurate   D. Moderately Inaccurate
    E. Very Inaccurate

15. As long as an employee finishes all his work on time at the end of the day, there's nothing wrong with coming back from lunch late.

    A. Very Accurate   B. Moderately Accurate
    C. Neither Accurate nor Inaccurate   D. Moderately Inaccurate
    E. Very Inaccurate

16. I enjoy beginning new things.

    A. Very Accurate   B. Moderately Accurate
    C. Neither Accurate nor Inaccurate   D. Moderately Inaccurate
    E. Very Inaccurate

17. When I have a number of tasks to be done, I prioritize them and tackle them immediately in order of importance.

    A. Very Accurate
    C. Neither Accurate nor Inaccurate
    E. Very Inaccurate
    B. Moderately Accurate
    D. Moderately Inaccurate

18. I would have no reservations about working for a supervisor who is of a different race or gender than I am.

    A. Very Accurate
    C. Neither Accurate nor Inaccurate
    E. Very Inaccurate
    B. Moderately Accurate
    D. Moderately Inaccurate

19. I'd rather help other people to do better than punish them for doing wrong.

    A. Very Accurate
    C. Neither Accurate nor Inaccurate
    E. Very Inaccurate
    B. Moderately Accurate
    D. Moderately Inaccurate

20. In the past, I've had personality clashes with fellow students or co-workers whom I disliked or with whom I disagreed.

    A. Very Accurate
    C. Neither Accurate nor Inaccurate
    E. Very Inaccurate
    B. Moderately Accurate
    D. Moderately Inaccurate

21. Confrontations are usually unpleasant, but sometimes necessary.

    A. Very Accurate
    C. Neither Accurate nor Inaccurate
    E. Very Inaccurate
    B. Moderately Accurate
    D. Moderately Inaccurate

22. I generally believe that other people have good intentions.

    A. Very Accurate
    C. Neither Accurate nor Inaccurate
    E. Very Inaccurate
    B. Moderately Accurate
    D. Moderately Inaccurate

23. When I have a lot of information to sort through, I have difficulty making up my mind.

    A. Very Accurate
    C. Neither Accurate nor Inaccurate
    E. Very Inaccurate
    B. Moderately Accurate
    D. Moderately Inaccurate

24. In tense situations, I choose my words with care.

    A. Very Accurate
    C. Neither Accurate nor Inaccurate
    E. Very Inaccurate
    B. Moderately Accurate
    D. Moderately Inaccurate

25. A person who works through his or her lunch break should automatically be able to go home early.

    A. Very Accurate   B. Moderately Accurate
    C. Neither Accurate nor Inaccurate   D. Moderately Inaccurate
    E. Very Inaccurate

Experiences and Traits

For each of the 25 items, score your response according to the list below. Then add the scores of all 25 items to arrive at a single number.

1. A=4;B=3;C=2;D=1;E=0
2. A=4;B=3;C=2;D=1;E=0
3. A=0;B=1;C=2;D=3;E=4
4. A=0;B=1;C=2;D=3;E=4
5. A=0;B=1;C=2;D=3;E=4

6. A=4;B=3;C=2;D=1;E=0
7. A=4;B=3;C=2;D=1;E=0
8. A=0;B=1;C=2;D=3;E=4
9. A=0;B=1;C=2;D=3;E=4
10. A=0;B=1;C=2;D=3;E=4

11. A=0;B=1;C=2;D=3;E=4
12. A=0;B=1;C=2;D=3;E=4
13. A=0;B=1;C=2;D=3;E=4
14. A=0;B=1;C=2;D=3;E=4
15. A=0;B=1;C=2;D=3;E=4

16. A=4;B=3;C=2;D=1;E=0
17. A=4;B=3;C=2;D=1;E=0
18. A=4;B=3;C=2;D=1;E=0
19. A=4;B=3;C=2;D=1;E=0
20. A=0;B=1;C=2;D=3;E=4

21. A=4;B=3;C=2;D=1;E=0
22. A=4;B=3;C=2;D=1;E=0
23. A=0;B=1;C=2;D=3;E=4
24. A=4;B=3;C=2;D=1;E=0
25. A=0;B=1;C=2;D=3;E=4

The following scores serve as an approximate guide to your compatibility with a career in law enforcement but should not be taken as the final word.

    85-100 points   Most compatible
    70-84 points   Compatible
    50-69 points   Somewhat compatible
    0-49 points   Incompatible

—

TEST 2

For each of the following items, circle the answer that best reflects the accuracy of the given statement, according to your own values, opinions, and experience.

1. I find it difficult to approach people I don't know well.

   A. Very Accurate
   B. Moderately Accurate
   C. Neither Accurate nor Inaccurate
   D. Moderately Inaccurate
   E. Very Inaccurate

2. I'm not really interested in hearing about other people's problems.

   A. Very Accurate
   B. Moderately Accurate
   C. Neither Accurate nor Inaccurate
   D. Moderately Inaccurate
   E. Very Inaccurate

3. Sometimes I don't know why I do the things I do.

   A. Very Accurate
   B. Moderately Accurate
   C. Neither Accurate nor Inaccurate
   D. Moderately Inaccurate
   E. Very Inaccurate

4. I am hesitant to take charge of a group that has no clear leadership.

   A. Very Accurate
   B. Moderately Accurate
   C. Neither Accurate nor Inaccurate
   D. Moderately Inaccurate
   E. Very Inaccurate

5. I enjoy examining myself and the direction my life is taking.

   A. Very Accurate
   B. Moderately Accurate
   C. Neither Accurate nor Inaccurate
   D. Moderately Inaccurate
   E. Very Inaccurate

6. I believe there is no absolute right or wrong.

   A. Very Accurate
   B. Moderately Accurate
   C. Neither Accurate nor Inaccurate
   D. Moderately Inaccurate
   E. Very Inaccurate

7. I always pay my bills on time.

   A. Very Accurate
   B. Moderately Accurate
   C. Neither Accurate nor Inaccurate
   D. Moderately Inaccurate
   E. Very Inaccurate

8. In this world it's difficult to be both honest and successful.

   A. Very Accurate
   B. Moderately Accurate
   C. Neither Accurate nor Inaccurate
   D. Moderately Inaccurate
   E. Very Inaccurate

9. I am intimidated by strong personalities.

   A. Very Accurate   B. Moderately Accurate
   C. Neither Accurate nor Inaccurate   D. Moderately Inaccurate
   E. Very Inaccurate

10. In past work experience, I was unable to find value in work that wasn't personally rewarding to me.

    A. Very Accurate   B. Moderately Accurate
    C. Neither Accurate nor Inaccurate   D. Moderately Inaccurate
    E. Very Inaccurate

11. I often do things I later regret.

    A. Very Accurate   B. Moderately Accurate
    C. Neither Accurate nor Inaccurate   D. Moderately Inaccurate
    E. Very Inaccurate

12. I feel sympathy for those who are worse off than I am.

    A. Very Accurate   B. Moderately Accurate
    C. Neither Accurate nor Inaccurate   D. Moderately Inaccurate
    E. Very Inaccurate

13. If a rule gets in the way of my doing my job well, I'll look for ways around it.

    A. Very Accurate   B. Moderately Accurate
    C. Neither Accurate nor Inaccurate   D. Moderately Inaccurate
    E. Very Inaccurate

14. I think a person's dress and appearance are important in the work environment.

    A. Very Accurate   B. Moderately Accurate
    C. Neither Accurate nor Inaccurate   D. Moderately Inaccurate
    E. Very Inaccurate

15. There have been times when my own personal use of drugs or alcohol has adversely affected my job performance.

    A. Very Accurate   B. Moderately Accurate
    C. Neither Accurate nor Inaccurate   D. Moderately Inaccurate
    E. Very Inaccurate

16. In past work or school experience, I have never been in a position to supervise the work of others.

    A. Very Accurate   B. Moderately Accurate
    C. Neither Accurate nor Inaccurate   D. Moderately Inaccurate
    E. Very Inaccurate

17. If I need to, I can talk other people into doing what I think is necessary.

   A. Very Accurate   B. Moderately Accurate
   C. Neither Accurate nor Inaccurate   D. Moderately Inaccurate
   E. Very Inaccurate

18. I usually prefer order to chaos.

   A. Very Accurate   B. Moderately Accurate
   C. Neither Accurate nor Inaccurate   D. Moderately Inaccurate
   E. Very Inaccurate

19. When I'm faced with an ethical dilemma, I listen to my conscience.

   A. Very Accurate   B. Moderately Accurate
   C. Neither Accurate nor Inaccurate   D. Moderately Inaccurate
   E. Very Inaccurate

20. When I communicate with other people, I can easily sense their emotional state.

   A. Very Accurate   B. Moderately Accurate
   C. Neither Accurate nor Inaccurate   D. Moderately Inaccurate
   E. Very Inaccurate

21. I set high standards for myself and others.

   A. Very Accurate   B. Moderately Accurate
   C. Neither Accurate nor Inaccurate   D. Moderately Inaccurate
   E. Very Inaccurate

22. In school or at work, I am never late.

   A. Very Accurate   B. Moderately Accurate
   C. Neither Accurate nor Inaccurate   D. Moderately Inaccurate
   E. Very Inaccurate

23. I sometimes make assumptions about people based on their racial or ethnic backgrounds.

   A. Very Accurate   B. Moderately Accurate
   C. Neither Accurate nor Inaccurate   D. Moderately Inaccurate
   E. Very Inaccurate

24. I tend to focus on the positive aspects of a complex situation, rather than the negatives.

   A. Very Accurate   B. Moderately Accurate
   C. Neither Accurate nor Inaccurate   D. Moderately Inaccurate
   E. Very Inaccurate

25. I can manage several tasks at the same time.

   A. Very Accurate   B. Moderately Accurate
   C. Neither Accurate nor Inaccurate   D. Moderately Inaccurate
   E. Very Inaccurate

Experiences and Traits

For each of the 25 items, score your response according to the list below. Then add the scores of all 25 items to arrive at a single number.

1. A=0;B=1;C=2;D=3;E=4
2. A=0;B=1;C=2;D=3;E=4
3. A=0;B=1;C=2;D=3;E=4
4. A=0;B=1;C=2;D=3;E=4
5. A=4;B=3;C=2;D=1;E=0

6. A=0;B=1;C=2;D=3;E=4
7. A=4;B=3;C=2;D=1;E=0
8. A=0;B=1;C=2;D=3;E=4
9. A=0;B=1;C=2;D=3;E=4
10. A=0;B=1;C=2;D=3;E=4

11. A=0;B=1;C=2;D=3;E=4
12. A=4;B=3;C=2;D=1;E=0
13. A=0;B=1;C=2;D=3;E=4
14. A=4;B=3;C=2;D=1;E=0
15. A=0;B=1;C=2;D=3;E=4

16. A=0;B=1;C=2;D=3;E=4
17. A=4;B=3;C=2;D=1;E=0
18. A=4;B=3;C=2;D=1;E=0
19. A=4;B=3;C=2;D=1;E=0
20. A=4;B=3;C=2;D=1;E=0

21. A=4;B=3;C=2;D=1;E=0
22. A=4;B=3;C=2;D=1;E=0
23. A=0;B=1;C=2;D=3;E=4
24. A=4;B=3;C=2;D=1;E=0
25. A=4;B=3;C=2;D=1;E=0

The following scores serve as an approximate guide to your compatibility with a career in law enforcementbut should not be taken as the final word.

85-100 points	Most compatible
70-84 points	Compatible
50-69 points	Somewhat compatible
0-49 points	Incompatible